THE INSIDER'S GUIDE TO

NEPAL

by Brian Tetley
Photographed by Mohamed Amin and
Duncan Willetts

MPC

Contents

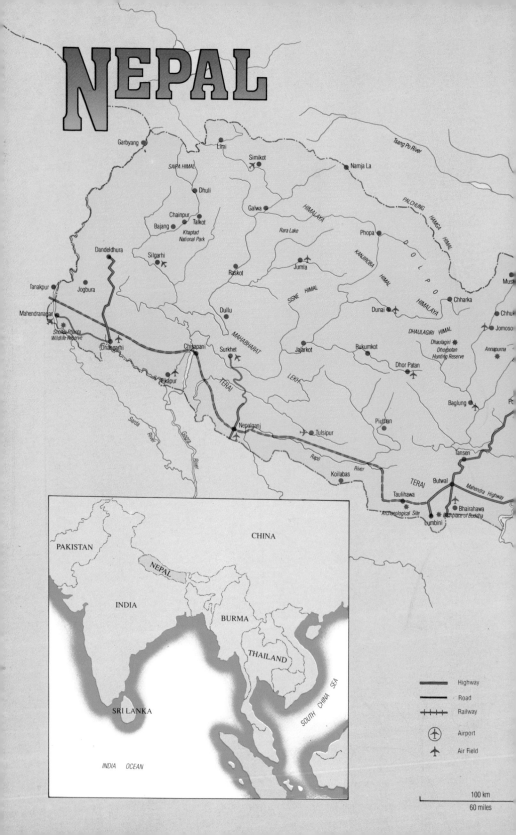

NEPAL

Garbyang
Limi
Simikot
SAIPA HIMAL
Namja La
Tsang Po River
Dhuli
PALCHUNG HAMGA HIMAL
Chainpur
Galwa
Bajang Talkot
HIMALAYA
Khaptad National Park
Phopa
D O L P O
Dandeldhura
Rara Lake
KANJIROBA HIMAL
Silgarhi
Raskot
Jumla
SIGNE HIMAL
Chharka
Tanakpur
Jogbura
Mus
HIMALAYA
Mahendranagar
Dullu
Dunai
Chhu
Jomoso
Shukla Phanta Wildlife Reserve
MAHABHARAT
DHAULAGIRI HIMAL
Dhaulagiri Dhorpotan Hunting Reserve
Annapurna
Dhangarhi
Chisapani
Surkhet
Jajarkot
Bukumkot
Dhor Patan
Tikapur
TERAI
LEKH
Baglung
Po
Sarda River
Nepalganj
Piuthan
Rapti
Surve
Karnali River
Tulsipur
River
Tansen
Koilabas
Rapti River
TERAI
Butwal
Taulihawa
Mahendra Highway
Archaeological Site
Bhairahawa
Birthplace of Buddha
Lumbini

PAKISTAN
CHINA
NEPAL
INDIA
BURMA
THAILAND
SRI LANKA
SOUTH CHINA SEA
INDIA OCEAN

——— Highway
——— Road
+++++ Railway
✈ Airport
✈ Air Field

100 km
60 miles

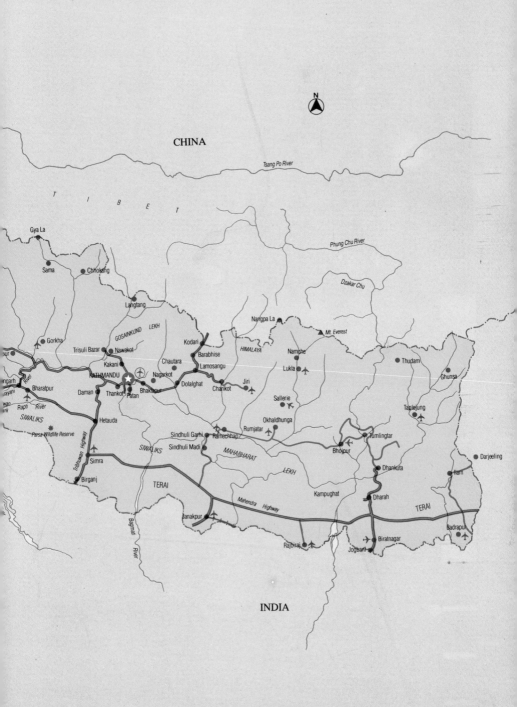

Vertical
Perspec-
tives

IMAGINE a land where the loudest noise is the wind flowing through the mountain passes far above, or the distant rumble of a river crashing through its canyon far below, or the musical plunk of a rice mill somewhere on a verdant hillside, of goats or roosters calling from the next valley, or the chatter of children from a walled schoolyard. Imagine a panorama of green steep hills rising to rolling crests of glissading stone, then far above them soaring peaks of sheer white ice, and above these, towering over the earth and blocking off the sky, great bastions of razor-sharp glacier and jagged black rock — these are the Himalayas, the Roof of the World, and this is Nepal, the hidden, mystical kingdom of peace, beauty, and serenity.

Once the province only of its hearty, strong, and friendly people, then of a few intrepid climbers who came to conquer and die on its fierce mountains, Nepal is now accessible to anyone with a reasonably good constitution and a love for the beauty and mystery of the world. From its fascinating, ancient capital of Kathmandu to its most remote trails and villages, from its flat Terai forests to its precipitous mountain torrents and wind-swept vistas, from its Hindi-speaking lowlanders to the proud and kindly Sherpas and Tibetans of its higher climes, Nepal is fascinating, complex, compelling, and unforgettable. Few people visit Nepal just once, for to go to Nepal is to promise to return.

And many a tourist who comes to Nepal is content for hours, even days, to sit on a hotel balcony or on a quiet hillside and contemplate the peaks, for nowhere else on earth is there exposed a more astounding range of great mountains seeming to leap straight up from the body of the earth itself, nowhere else do so many colors bloom together: the red and purple of rhododendrons, the terra-cotta earth, the greens of forest, fields, and paddies, the blacks of stone and cliff and hardened ice, the varied whites and crystalline purity of snow, snow-cloud, clouds, and wind.

But there's no need to sit still in Nepal. Kathmandu has sights and sounds for every eye and ear, variations for every mind and culture. Centuries lurk in its alleys and carved façades, its emblazoned temples and sharp rooflines; strange odors recall past lives and

other ways — to come to Kathmandu is to reach back into oneself. There are days, weeks, one could spend wandering this city and the paths the spread out from it across the nearby hills, but there's more wandering than this to be done: there's hikes to take in every conceivable direction — up and down, to all the cardinal points and far beyond.

And if Kathmandu is a unique experience, rural Nepal is totally another: a quick trip back ten centuries or more, back to the time when anywhere you wanted to go you went on foot, at the human body's pace, when the sounds are all ancient and easily recognized, do not disturb the soul. Hiking rural Nepal is to rediscover what's been lost in the twentieth century, and to hike with the vision of the peaks around and above is to remember, as Keats said, that some things are truly beautiful and that in beauty there is truth.

The beauty of Nepal above all is in its vertical perspectives — for it contains eight of the world's 10 highest peaks, all of them above 8,000 m (26,250 ft). And although Nepal is the highest nation in the world, it is also one of the smallest, little bigger than the state of Florida, or than England and Wales combined. Yet it is surrounded by the world's two world's most populous countries, India and China, and within its 141,414 sq km (54,586 sq miles) are more contrasts of cultures and landscapes than in countries many times its size.

Isolated from the rest of the world for most of human history, Nepal is a feudal kingdom whose life and customs are still rooted firmly in the Middle Ages, with the charm and peace which come from an ancient, largely undisturbed way of life. The lack of modern infrastructure — roads, vehicles, telephones, television and many of the other miseries of contemporary "civilization" — has spared Nepal much of the ugliness and tension of Western life. Gifted with by far the most magnificent mountain scenery in the world, and a variety of climates from tropical to alpine, this small nation is totally unique on earth. It is a rare traveler who returns from Nepal without having experienced a rare sense of beauty and peace,

OPPOSITE the divine "fish-tail" peaks of Nepal's most sacred mountain, Machhapuchhare, which rises 6,993 m (22,940 ft) north-west of Pokhara.

without having changed in a manner that the Nepalis would only term spiritual.

Nepal's location in the sub-tropics, and its wide altitude range — from 60 to 8,848 m (200 to 29,028 ft) — provide conditions under which most types of vegetation, from rain forest to arctic montane, can grow. Thus in Nepal one finds an incredible variety of animals, birds, reptiles, insects, and plants. And although population growth and increasing competition for scarce natural resources has exterminated many species and reduced others, Nepal is still the Shangri-La described in *Lost Horizons*, the place so far away the visitor is surprised to find himself.

Perhaps it is the mystery, the scenery, the history and the sense of peace that have led to an increase in Nepal's tourists from a few thousand a year at the start of the 1960's to more than 250,000 today, with tourism revenue in 1990 estimated at over $75 million. But Nepal is still a land unknown, and if you wish you can travel for days without seeing anyone but local villagers; in many parts of Nepal, Westerners are still rare.

WITHIN THE FROZEN EMBRACE

The Himalayas, which curve like a scimitar more than 3,000 km (1,800 miles) across the subcontinent from northern Pakistan in the west to Burma in the east, form the backbone of Nepal. The average height of northern Nepal is well above 6,000 m (19,686 ft), yet all this was once a sea. The peak of Everest, Sagamartha ("Goddess of the Universe"), at 8,848 m (29,028 ft), is marine rock of the Cretaceous age. Eighty to 60 million years ago, it formed the bed of the Tethys Sea, separating Asia and India. Then, at the end of the Mesozoic era, the Asian continent collided with the island of India. The tremendous pressure forced up the bed of the Tethys Sea, forming the Tibetan Marginal Range on the Nepal-Tibet border.

Later, in the Miocene era, some 10 to 15 million years ago, the movement of the earth's tectonic plates again forced India against Asia, uplifting the main Himalaya chain.

Distant view of the highest point on earth, 8,848 m (29,028 ft) Everest, surrounded by its equally majestic cohorts of Nuptse and Lhotse.

These higher mountains cut off the more humid air approaching from oceans to the south, causing increased precipitation on these newly formed, steep southern slopes. This greater rainfall gave the rivers such volume and thus force that they cut through the mountains almost as quickly as they were being raised.

It was not until the Pleistocene period, 600,000 years ago, that the Himalayas gave rise to the lofty peaks we know today. A final collision of Asia and India forced the mountains even higher so their rivers could no

longer erode them. The Mahabharat Range and Siwalik Hills in southern Nepal were also formed, and the Mahabharat Range dammed some of the rivers flowing south, forming a large prehistoric lake in the Kathmandu valley. The lake dried up approximately 200,000 years ago.

The Himalayas run along Nepal's entire 885-km (550-mile) northern border with Tibet. They are considered the youngest mountains in the world; many geologists believe they are still undergoing change. When seen from the air, their panorama stretches farther than the human eye can see, and it seems impossible that anyone, or anything, can live within their frozen embrace. Yet locked in thousands of secret valleys are Nepal's mountain towns, accessible only by narrow footpaths carved or worn into the rock.

In most of Nepal, travel is by trail, footpath, and suspension bridge over some of the toughest terrain in the world. In 1955, the country had only 624 km (387 miles) of road. By 1990, it had at least 7,500 km (4,660 miles). The network of roads built since the

1970's links the major midland towns, resort areas, and the south-north borders of Nepal. Yet in the 1990's no road traverses the country from east to west.

Although traditional Nepali society is changing with the country's modernization drive, anyone wishing to avoid roads has no trouble getting into the back country.

All length and little breadth, Nepal measures only 240 km (150 miles) at its widest point, and 150 km (93 miles) at its narrowest. From the narrow strip of flat, fertile, checkerboard plain which lies 67 m (220 ft) above sea level along the Indian border it climbs to more than 8,848 m (29,028 ft).

Within a span of 12 hours you can fly with the rising sun along the daunting barrier of the Himalayas, from Annapurna to Kanchenjunga and back to Kathmandu then drive along a road cut into the side of a deep Himalayan river gorge and down the precipitous flanks of the Mahabharat range to the emerald plains of the Terai, and there ride an elephant among a herd of rhino as the sun sets. Similarly, the south-north land journey by car from the sea-level border to the mountains is a swift and stunning transformation of environment. In a day, one can leave the Indian border in early morning and in late afternoon reach the Tibetan border, and then return to Kathmandu by nightfall. The east-west traverse, however, takes many weeks and is only possible on foot. It can be one of the world's toughest, most difficult treks.

No more than 160 km (100 miles) separates Everest from the tropical plains where its melting snows swell the floodwaters of some of the major tributaries of the sacred Ganges. Nepal's rivers begin as a trickle of ice melt, and become raging waters as they are joined and swollen by countless tributaries. Over millennia they have cut some of the deepest gorges in the world, plunging from 5,180 m (17,000 ft) to just above sea level. At full flood, these waters take just 12 hours to complete a journey from Arctic ice to tropical jungle.

Among Nepal's plains, mountains, and rivers is a tapestry of vivid cultural contrasts, 35 ethnic cultures including those of the Gurkha and the Sherpa.

But with an average per capita income of less than $160 a year, Nepal's people live, many of them, on the edge of or in poverty. The majority of farmers scratch a frugal living from their rice paddies and grain fields in the hills, mountains, or the overcrowded Terai plains of the south. In the towns and cities there is also much poverty, particularly among the Tibetan refugees chased out of their own mountain kingdom by conquering, ravaging Chinese armies in recent years.

Yet whatever faith the people of Nepal follow, be it Hinduism, Buddhism, animism, or cheery pagan atheism, they tend to celebrate each other's feasts notwithstanding, and within a poverty of means commemorate life and faith year round with festivals saluting incarnate and reincarnate deities alike.

Kathmandu, the capital and seat of the royal family, lies at the center of the country, 1,331 m (4,368 ft) above sea level, on roughly the same latitude as Florida. Neither too hot in summer nor too cold in winter, Kathmandu, like most of midland Nepal, is favored with one of the world's more agreeable climates. Summer temperatures reach around 30°C (86°F) and the mean winter temperature is 10°C (50°F). The Nepalis attribute the pleasant climate to the generosity of the gods, and justifiably celebrate their divine fortune by reaping at least three harvests a year.

The tree-clad slopes of the Kathmandu valley, verdant with stands of oak, alder, rhododendron, and jacaranda, climb to 1,980 to 2,133 m (6,500 to 7,000 ft). Their ridges provide unsurpassed views of the Himalayas, particularly during the winter months from October to May, the best time to visit Nepal, when the skies are cloudless almost every day. Most of Kathmandu's citizens are Newaris, one of Nepal's many ethnic groups. Farming in the mountains above these temperate valleys is less productive, but in many valleys potatoes are cultivated to altitudes of 4,000 m (13,000 ft), and barley even higher.

GEOGRAPHY FROM BOTTOM TO TOP

Nepal is divided into five geographical regions: the Terai, Siwalik, Mahabharat, midlands or Pahar, and Himalayas. The government has separated the country into 14 administrative zones subdivided into 75 development districts of varying importance.

The Terai, part of the great Ganges Plain, accounts for just over 20 percent of Nepal's land area, extending north from the southern border with India to the first foothills. Never wider than 32 km (20 miles), it is hot and humid most of the year. Until recently it was covered by dense forests filled with wildlife, from rare butterflies to Bengal

tigers, but in the last two or three decades these forests had been cut and the wildlife exterminated. Since then there has been a large influx of settlers and now the Terai is where the majority of the Nepalis live.

This human settlement has ravaged the Terai. Where British hunter and explorer Jim Corbett in the 1930's stalked man-eating tigers and fished for huge fighting bream in the shade of ancient forests, there are now only eroded river valleys up to a mile wide

OPPOSITE: All Kathmandu valley turns out to join the eight-day Indra Jatra Festival, the annual celebration of the monsoon rains and the conquest of the area by the ruling dynasty in the eighteenth century. ABOVE: Sherpa porter climbs a high pass in the Everest region.

and a patchwork of forest and cultivated areas. For much of the year river beds are dry; during the summer they are flooded from bank to bank with silted torrents changing course from year to year. Many houses stand on stilts. Like so many places on the planet, the Terai has become proof of the instantaneous and irreversible damage of population growth.

The Siwalik zone, with the Churia Range, rises from the Terai to 1,200 m (4,000 ft). Its steep slopes and dry climate have left it relatively uninhabited. To the north are wide valleys, such as Rapti Dun, which in places separate the Siwalik from the Mahabharat.

The Mahabharat forms a barrier between the plains and the fertile midlands. It too is sparsely populated, but covered with terraced slopes. Most of Nepal's water passes through this region which until very recently had lush deciduous forests that have nearly all been cut for fuelwood. Somewhat off the beaten track, it has mountain passes as low as 210 m (700 ft) and peaks over 2,700 m (9,000 ft).

More than 40 percent of the population occupies the temperate valleys of Kathmandu and Pokhara that dominate the Pahar zone or midlands. Here the soil is largely alluvial and fertile; crops of nearly every kind can be grown at altitudes between 600 and 2,100 m (2,000 and 7,000 ft).

Higher in the Himalayas, human habitation is more isolated in remote valleys or sheltered where possible on the elevated plateaus. Here people live much as they did a thousand years ago, some still rooted in the Stone Age. Most of the high country is above treeline, for much of the year its rocky slopes covered by snow.

Nepal has one of the world's highest birthrates, with its population growing so fast the country may soon find itself hard-pressed for food. Over-cultivation of the precipitous valley slopes above the river gorges has already turned the landscape into a textbook case of deforestation and soil erosion. With its steep farmlands

unprotected by the deep root systems and sheltering foliage of perennial vegetation, the fierce monsoon rains wash away the fragile topsoil and can bring thousands of tons of mountainside landsliding down the slopes. Yet the beauty of Nepal's landscape remains virtually indestructible. The sheer scale and form, even of the eroded walls of the valleys, are still magnificent enough to take the breath away.

It is these same mountain walls that have kept Nepal remote from the world until this century.

MONSOON CLIMATE

The country's climate is dominated by the monsoons of southern Asia. Usually for four months each year (June to September), it rains throughout most of the country, up to 25 cm (100 inches). Drought conditions prevail generally for the remainder of the year, with only occasional thunderstorms or snows in the mountains.

October and November are probably the best months to visit Nepal, as the countryside is still lush from the monsoon rains and usually not too hot in the lowlands nor too cold in the mountains. December can be too cold to enjoy trekking in the mountains, and in January and March the snow will be too deep. In March and April the countryside is generally very dry, but the rhododendrons are in bloom on the hillsides and multicolored butterflies and summer birds are omnipresent. May is a fickle month — some years it is dry and pleasant, other wet and gray.

While the Terai can be unbearably hot and the Himalaya subzero, Kathmandu has an almost ideal climate, with frost virtually unknown. The Kathmandu valley does however get very dusty in March and April and can often be shrouded in haze.

Although the monsoon cycle is relatively predictable, it is good to remember always that the weather, like the hiking trails, is unpredictable. The following note appears on many trekking maps and should be kept in mind:

"In Nepal all paths and bridges are liable to disappear or change at no notice due to monsoons, acts of Gods, etc."

OPPOSITE TOP: Tethering yaks at Nar Valley. BOTTOM: Phortse village clings to a barren mountainside near Solu Khumbu.

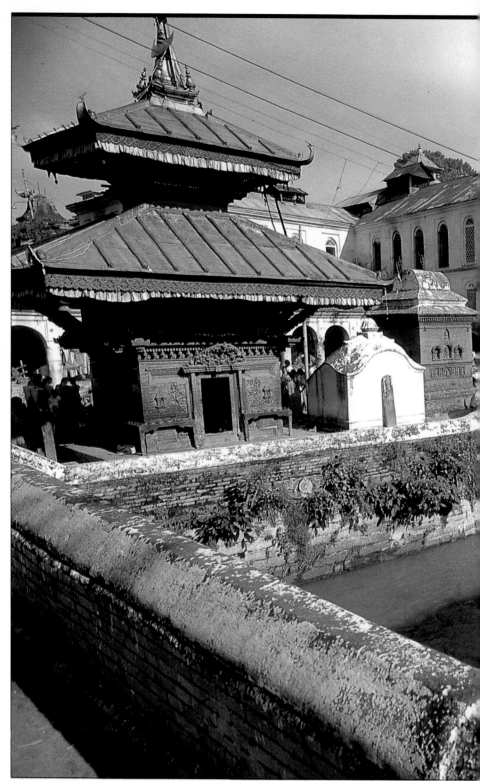

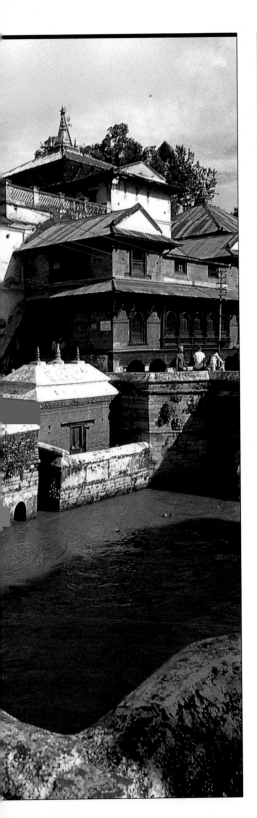

Emerging from Antiquity

AS A modern country Nepal has existed for less than two hundred years, but its history extends back to the very beginnings of humankind. Virtually unknown to the rest of the world until 1950, the prehistory and history of the region has only in the past 20 years been discovered and translated. Much is shrouded in legends.

PREHISTORY

Some archaeologists believe that even before the Himalayas reached their present grandeur, *Orepithecus,* one of our early ancestors, inhabited the region. About a million years ago primitive humans had formed tribes in the hills and were making and using primitive tools. As the Himalayas grew so did the population. Little is known about these early inhabitants, but both Hindu and Buddhist legends confirm that humans were here during the time a lake filled the Kathmandu valley, and that there were relatively developed societies with oral traditions and an animistic religion.

THE KIRANTI INVADERS AND THE BIRTH OF BUDDHA

Somewhere around 700 BC Kiranti invaders arrived from India. Their militaristic exploits are described in ancient Indian texts, *Mahabharata* and *Ramayana,* but their influence probably only extended over a portion of the Terai and the midlands, where they established Patan as their stronghold. They assimilated the pre-existing cultures, and, for at least seven centuries, controlled north-south trade and travel.

It was during this epoch that Buddha was born, that is to say, took on the form of man, in 563 BC at Lumbini. Buddha himself preached in the Kathmandu valley as well as northern India, and his teachings spread throughout Asia.

In 250 BC the most ruthless of the Indian Emperors, Ashoka, visited Nepal in peace. Nicknamed the "Sorrowless One", Ashoka had converted to Buddhism after a bloody battle in southern India, the carnage of which haunted him the rest of his life. He renounced

violence and became one of Buddha's most ardent disciples. His trip to Nepal was one of rebirth. With his daughter Carumati, he visited Buddha's birthplace and constructed a memorial pillar.

From Lumbini, the emperor Ashoka went to the Kathmandu valley to bathe in the Bagmati river. Carumati was married to a Kiranti prince and remained in Patan. Memorials to the marriage and his visit were erected in the city; the Ashoka Stupa still remains from this era. Ashoka sponsored Buddhist missionaries throughout Nepal and the rest of Asia as well. His own son became a monk and took the Buddhist gospel to Ceylon.

In his own empire, Ashoka supported religious tolerance, which perhaps he had learned on his trip to the Kathmandu valley, where, even in the third century BC, it appears that Buddhism co-existed with Hinduism. Another theory argues that it was during Ashoka's reign the Hindus came from India to Nepal. In any case, the Hindu shrine, Pashupatinath, and the surrounding settlement date to this time, and Hindu legends predate it.

Over the next two centuries, until perhaps 50 BC, the Kiranti influence waned in the valley. Other groups migrated here and mingled with existing populations to become the people commonly referred to as Newaris. In the hills and mountains tribal societies and kingdoms also expanded and diversified.

After the Kiranti, the valley was ruled by the Somavashis who also originally came from India. Under the Somavashis, the Hindu religion flourished and a four-caste system was introduced. They renovated the holy shrine, Pashupatinath, and in the first century AD constructed a temple on the site. It was also during their rule that the roofs of the temples in Patan were gilded.

THE GOLDEN AGE

Eventually the Somavashis were conquered by the Licchavi, who ruled the valley from the fifth through seventh centuries. These Hindu rulers also come from India and are credited with bringing an age of enlightenment with them. They fostered the study of Sanskrit and the production of carvings, many with elaborate inscriptions and dedications.

One notable Licchavi ruler, Manadeva, built the Changu Narayan temple in 388 Saka Sambat (AD 467), so its inscriptions tell us. A stele there praises Manadeva's victories over the Malla tribes and the subjugation of the Thakuris.

Two centuries later the last Licchavi ruler, Shevadeva, gave his daughter in marriage to one of his strongest Thakuri vassals, Am-

(Bhrikuti), and White Tara (the Chinese princess).

In AD 643 and 647 the Chinese sent their first diplomatic missions to the Kathmandu valley. The records of Wang Huen Tse, the leader of the second mission, show that he had mixed feeling about Ni-Po-Lo and its inhabitants: "The kingdom of Ni-Po-Lo ... is situated in the middle of snowy mountains and indeed presents an uninterrupted series of hills and valleys. Its soil is suited to the cultivation of grain and abounds in flora and fruits.... . Coins of red copper are used

suvarman, who was well-educated and had written a Sanskrit grammar. As Shevadeva preferred the monastic life to his royal duties, Amsuvarman assumed many of his father-in-law's duties during the latter's lifetime.

On the death of Shevadeva in AD 605, Amsuvarman appointed himself king. He expanded his influence beyond the valley by marrying his daughter Bhrikuti to the Tibetan King Sron Tsan Gampo. Bhrikuti is credited with converting the Tibetan king and his other wife, a Chinese princess, to Buddhism, thus beginning the eventual transmission of the religion to Tibet and China. The two brides have been canonized in the Buddhist tradition and are worshiped as the goddesses of compassion — Green Tara

Emerging from Antiquity

for exchange. The climate is very cold. The national character is stamped with falseness and perfidy; the inhabitants are all of a hard and savage nature: to them neither good faith nor justice nor literature appear, but they are gifted with considerable skill in the art. Their bodies are ugly and their faces are mean. Among them are both true believers [Buddhists] and heretics [Hindus]. Buddhists convents and the temples of the Hindu gods touch each other. It is reckoned that there are about two thousand religious who study both the Greater and Lesser Vehicle. The number of Brahmans and the

ABOVE: Buddha's 540 BC birthplace at Lumbini on the Terai plains which border India.

nonconformists has never been ascertained exactly."

Other members of the missions were more impressed with the Nepali culture and art. Years later, Nepali architects were invited to China to build the first pagodas there.

This golden age of Nepal was followed by a dark ages during which tribes were at constant war with one and other. Gone was art, learning, and religious tolerance; few record or relics remain from this period. Some historians believe that during this era in the reign of a Thakuri king, Guakanadeva, around 950, the city of Kathmandu, then known as Kantipur, became the regional capital, and the towns of Bhadgaon and Kirtipur were established. Commerce with India and Tibet increased and Tantric rites and ideals were introduced and integrated into the religions.

THE MALLA DYNASTY

When in the eleventh century the Muslims took power in India and, under Muhammed Ghauri, extended their empire into the northern kingdoms, both Hindus and Buddhists fled north to Nepal and Tibet. It was from these refugees that rose the Malla dynasty that dominated the valley until the eighteenth century.

About the year 1200, Arideva emerged as a sufficiently strong leader to bring relative peace to the valley. He supposedly coined the name "Malla" for his descendants and thus the dynasty. According to popular legend, he was wrestling when the birth of his son was brought to him. The king gave him the title "Malla," meaning wrestler in Sanskrit.

There were peaceful periods under the Mallas, but these were interrupted by Muslim invasions from India. During a fourteenth century attack, the Muslims sacked many temples and shrines in the valley. Nonetheless arts, architecture, and learning advanced; there were three universities in the valley; religious tolerance was so complete that Buddhists and Hindus worshiped in the same temples and celebrated each other's religious festivals.

During the Malla rule, Christian monks came to the valley and were allowed to preach their religion. For many years there was a Catholic church near Kathmandu. But in their religious fervor, these Christian missionaries supposedly burned more than 3,000 "pagan" books and manuscripts as "works of the devil." For this they were expelled, taking only a handful of native converts with them.

Under the reign of Jaya Sthiti Malla, which began in 1382, a caste system was reintroduced after a Brahman priest convinced the king that the gods look with disfavor upon caste-less societies. The Brahman priests placed themselves at the top of the caste, with 64 professional groups below and shoemakers, butchers, blacksmiths, and sweepers at the bottom, the "untouchables." The second caste was the warriors, to which the royal families belonged. This caste was again subdivided into sub-castes, which led to suspicion and dissent among rulers and contributed substantially to the civil strife of the time.

The most aggressive of the Malla rulers, Jaksha Malla, extended the boundaries of his kingdom to include much of what is now modern Nepal. His territory extended north to Tibet and south to the Ganges river. He oversaw the construction of canals and water supply systems.

Unfortunately, shortly before his death he divided the valley amongst his children: Bhadgaon (also known as Bhaktapur), Banepa, and Kathmandu went to his three sons, Patan to his daughter. The heirs, not content with their inheritances, were soon warring with each other. Banepa became part of Bhadgaon and Patan eventually lost its independence to Kathmandu.

The valley remained divided during the next 200 years, but there were several rulers of note in Kathmandu, Patan, and Bhadgaon. Pratap Malla, king of Kathmandu from 1640 to 1674, was a man of letters, and demonstrated his knowledge of fifteen languages on a plaque in the Royal Palace. He also erected the statue of Hanuman, the monkey god, at the entry to the palace, which since then has been known as Hanuman Dhoka. He was also responsible for the construction the steps and gold thunderbolt at Swayambunath.

Under King Siddhi Narasimba Malla (1618–1661), Patan grew considerably.

Siddhi Narasimba oversaw a major construction effort that included 2,400 individual houses. He was a religious man, and one day left on a pilgrimage from which he never returned.

The life of King Bhupatendra Malla of Bhadgaon reads much like a fairy tale. The wicked witch was his father's second wife, who wanted her own son to inherit the throne. Bhupatendra was the son of the first wife and therefore first in line. The second wife decided to have the young prince killed. Her conspirators took the boy from the palace into the forest to murder him. However, they did not have the courage to carry out the stepmother's wish, and abandoned the child instead. The prince was found by a carpenter who raised him as his own son.

Years later, the carpenter took his son with him to work in the Royal Palace. The king, the boy's real father, recognized him and welcomed him back as the rightful heir.

Bhupatendra became king in 1696 when his father died, and his reign was marked by incessant construction. The best remaining structures from this period are the Palace of 55 Windows and the temple of Nayatapola. This was one of the most prosperous eras in the city.

THE UNIFICATION OF NEPAL

In spite of, or perhaps because of, the relative prosperity of the many divided kingdoms in the valley, they were at constant war with each other. Outside the valley, meanwhile, other principalities were flourishing. Little is documented about life in these outlying kingdoms, but from one, Gorkha, came the leader of modern Nepal, Prithvi Narayan Shah.

The following story is told of him as a young boy in the land of the Gurkhas and fortified towns: One day when he was six years old, Prithvi Narayan went to the temple where he met an unhappy old man. "I am hungry. Can you give me some curd?" begged the old man. Prithvi Narayan fetched some curd. The old man ate his fill but kept a little in his mouth.

"Hold out your hand!" ordered the old man. The boy obeyed and the old man spit what was left in his mouth into it. "Eat!" he commanded. Prithvi Narayan was not inclined to follow this order and dropped the curdled milk to the ground.

"If you had eaten my spittle from your hand," the old man said, "you would have been able conquer all the countries of your dreams. Since you have thrown it away, you will only be able to conquer those kingdoms into which you can walk." And the ancient one suddenly disappeared.

After becoming king of Gorkha in 1742, Prithvi Narayan spent 25 years expanding his territory and unifying a large part of Nepal. He was a great conqueror, but, as prophesied, he never did realize all his dreams.

Prithvi Narayan began his assault on the valley with careful planning and sound tactics. He first took over the fortifications of Nawakot in the Trisuli valley, through which passed much of the commerce with Tibet.

Sculptures of Buddhist and Hindu deities encircle ornamental pool where Patan's eighteenth-century royal families bathed. The pool is encircled by a protective symbol, a large stone snake known as Nagbandh.

The Malla kings united to send troops against Nawakot but were unsuccessful in breaking Prithvi Narayan's commercial blockage. Prithvi Narayan moved on to isolate the valley by cutting off the remaining trade routes and sent Brahman priests into the valley to stir up unrest.

The intrigues in the valley kingdoms aided Prithvi Narayan's plans. In Kathmandu, King Jaya Prakash had been exiled by his wife, whom he eventually killed. Jaya's brother, the King of Patan, was deposed by the Pradhans, a rival family, who spared his life but blinded him. Jaya came to his brother's aid, suppressed the Pradhan coup, forced them to beg in the streets, and paraded their wives as witches.

Prithvi Narayan's economic blockage was not as successful as he had anticipated. Apparently only Patan offered allegiance in return for the right of passage. Prithvi Narayan sent his brother to rule Patan, but he was deposed and killed after a short time. Changing his tactics, Prithvi Narayan decided to lay siege to the valley, and chose Kirtipur as he first point of attack. He offered amnesty in return for surrender and was flatly refused. He swore to raze the city to the ground and mark every inhabitant for life.

After a two-year siege, the starving city surrendered. Prithvi Narayan forced the men to tear down their own temples and palaces, after which they were led one by one to the executioner who cut off their noses and lips. Only those who played wind instruments were exempt. One account of the episode claims Prithvi Narayan weighed this flesh bounty — 86 pounds in all. For generations the Kirtipur was hence known as Naskatipur, The City of the Nose-less Ones.

Neither Patan nor Kathmandu offered much resistance to Prithvi Narayan and his Gurkha armies. He easily took Kathmandu on September 1768 during the festival of Indra Jatra, when most of the population was celebrating. Jaya Prakash took refuge in Bhadgaon, but within a year the Gurkhas had taken it also.

With control of the valley, Prithvi Narayan now held everything from Lamjung to Everest. He made Kathmandu his capital

and maintained a policy of exclusion of Europeans, particularly missionaries. "First the Bible, then trading stations, then the cannon," he said. He planned a campaign to conquer Tibet, but died in 1774 without realizing his goal.

Prithvi Narayan was succeeded by his son, Pratap Singh Shah, who made little progress on his father's grand empire because he died four year later, leaving his 2-year-old son, Rana Bahadur Shah, on the throne. Administration of the kingdom fell to a regent who also followed in the footsteps of Prithvi Narayan. He sent armies to Kashmir, Sikkim, and Tibet. The Gurkha invasion of Tibet in 1790 and sacking of the Grand Lama's palace at Tashi-Lhumpo brought China into the conflict. Afraid of

being overrun, Nepal requested military aid from the British East Indian Company. British troops, however, did not arrive until after a treaty had been signed in 1792 at Nawakot. Under the Nawakot treaty, Nepal agreed to honor the Tibetan boundaries and to pay an annual tribute to the Chinese emperor. A British representative remained in Nepal in a semiofficial capacity.

In 1795, at the age of 19, Rana Bahadur Shah assumed leadership of his country and had his regent imprisoned and killed. Bahadur Shah was an erratic if not insane ruler; his wife Tripura Sundavi and chief counselor Bhim Sen Thapa held the reigns of the kingdom. After Bahadur Shah was stabbed to death by his brother, Bhim Sen assumed the title of Prime Minister while serving as regent for the infant heir, Rajendra Bikram Shah. Bhim Sen directed Nepal for the next 30 years. He oversaw the army during a two-year border conflict (1814–1816) with the British East Indian Company. Against the well-equipped British and Indian armies, he led 12,000 men, some of whom were armed with bows and arrows. For heavier weapons they had only a few leather Tibetan cannons, made from yak hides tightly rolled together.

The Treaty of Segauly, signed in 1816, was a compromise, not a victory for either side. The Prime Minister ceded some territories along his southern border, agreed to the

Elegant medieval architecture in Kathmandu.

stationing of a permanent British Resident in Kathmandu, and permitted the enrollment of three Gurkha regiments into the British Army.

When Rajendra Bikram Shah came of age, he progressively reduced Bhim Sen's power and eventually removed him as Prime Minister. Later Bhim Sen was imprisoned and in 1839 committed suicide. Another short period of relative chaos and royal intrigue followed out of which came the Rana prime ministers who ruled Nepal until after World War II.

THE RANA RULE

Rajendra Bikram Shah's wife was a scheming, ambitious, and unfaithful queen. When one of her lovers was murdered, she decided to revenge herself, and enlisted the help of one Jang Bahadur Rana, an equally ambitious officer in the Royal Guard. Convinced that a member of the Royal Council was responsible, she asked Jang Bahadur to call a meeting of the Council at the Kot in the center of Durbar Square. Closing the gates to open courtyard, she demanded of the more than 500 noblemen that the person responsible for her lover's death be identified and punished

accordingly. One pointed to Jang Bahadur as the murderer; in the ensuing mayhem, all the leading nobles were massacred by three regiments under Jang Bahadur's command. The identity of the assassin is not certain. Some accounts of the Kot massacre claim the Rajendra Bikram Shah himself was responsible for his wife's lover's death.

Nonetheless Jang Bahadur Rana installed himself as "His Highness the Maharaja" and Prime Minister. He then forced the Rajendra Bikram Shah to abdicate in favor of his son, and exiled the king and queen to India. He gave the crown to the young prince, Sirendra Birkham Shah, and his eventual heirs, as it was believed that the spirit of Vishnu lived in the royal Shah line. However, Sirendra and his successors were in essence little but royal captives of Jang Bahadur and the other Ranas. Thereafter, only once a year did the Ranas permit the king to show himself before the general public which believed, as some Nepalis still do today, that they would receive forgiveness for all their sins merely by looking at him.

Thus the Prime Minister came to hold supreme command in Nepal; Jang Bahadur Rana decreed the position hereditary, passing from brother to younger brother, or brother to cousin. This first Rana Prime Minister was an adept statesman and politician. He sought the friendship of Europe but kept his country isolated from foreign influences. In 1850 he accepted an invitation from Queen Victoria and Napoleon III to visit Europe. He was royally received in London and Paris, as though he were the king.

His year long journey firmed international friendships but angered the local Brahmans who believed that anyone crossing the "black waters" of the ocean would return an untouchable. On his return, Jang Bahadur Rana purified himself in the Ganges and visited most of the major Hindu shrines in India and Nepal to prove he had not been contaminated by his trip.

The following Rana reign was notable for oppressive policies and favoritism based on its own set of castes within the family. There were A-, B-, and C-Ranas, a breakdown that greatly contributed to the demise of the dynasty. The top government position went to A-Ranas, who were the pure Ranas in the direct line descending from Jang Bahadur. The A-Ranas had the right to live in palaces of more than 100 rooms. B-Ranas, descendants of Rana men who had married below them, received important civilian and military posts but could not have more than 70 rooms in their palaces. C-Ranas, offsprings of harem girls, had large villas and high army posts, but could never rise to the rank of general.

In 1940 the Prime Minister arrested 100 men and executed four of their leaders for the crime of communicating with the king. Many of the royal supporters remained in prison for extended periods of time; others took refuge in India. Martyrs' Memorial in Kathmandu commemorates these independence fighters. Although there was not a revolution in the sense of widespread open warfare, during the last years of Rana domination persecution of the educated non-Rana Nepalis was commonplace with little or no interference from the British. As

Autocratic though they were, the Ranas did bring about some positive advances in the country. Slavery and *sati*, (suttee) the practice of the wife throwing herself on the burning body of her dead husband, were abolished; a university was founded, and a railroad, short though it was, constructed. Still, unrest and dissatisfaction with the Ranas was growing.

Nepal had sent 50,000 Gurkha soldiers to the First World War and continued to fill its three regiments in the British Army thereafter. In addition many served as mercenaries in the India Army. These returning soldiers were Nepal's major contact with the outside world, and came to form a core of resistance to the Rana rule.

Danish journalist Karl Eskerlund wrote, "but for the alliance between the British and the Ranas, the country would not have stagnated so long. The British left Nepal alone because they wanted a buffer between India and Tibet. It was in their interest to keep Nepal as primitive as possible."

After World War II, the liberal Prime Minister Padma Shamsher realized that the days of autocracy were numbered. He moved to create a city council for which there were open elections and a new constitution. As far as the other A-Ranas were

OPPOSITE: Young sentinel of the famed Gurkha force of soldiers. ABOVE: Gurkha unit of the Nepali Army on parade in Kathmandu.

concerned, however, the Prime Minister took his reforms too far when he proposed an independent judiciary system. In 1948 Padma Shamsher was forced to resign in favor of Mohan Shamsher, a conservative.

Meanwhile, a "liberation" army of political exiles had formed in India, as well as several underground opposition movements in Kathmandu. On November 6, 1950 King Tribhuvan Shah and his family succeeded in escaping from Rana custody by detouring into the Indian embassy on the way to a picnic. They then flew to New Delhi and joined their supporters in exile. To insure survival of the royal line in the event that the escape failed, Tribhuvan left his four-year-old grandson, whom Mohan Shamsher immediately placed on the throne.

For the next three months, Mohan Shamsher sought international recognition for the new child-king, while from his exile in India King Tribhuvan organized support for himself within Nepal. In February, 1951, liberation forces entered the Terai; there were demonstrations in Kathmandu demanding a new constitution; and a group of C-Rana army officers announced they would no longer support a government which excluded them from the right of succession. The power of the Ranas was broken.

INTO THE TWENTIETH CENTURY

On February 15, 1951, King Tribhuvan returned to Nepal and brought the Shah family back to power after 104 years. Mohan Shamsher remained as Prime Minister; half the cabinet positions went to revolutionary leaders. Mohan resigned soon after, and went into exile in India. Nepal had finally emerged from isolation to take its place among the nations of the world.

King Tribhuvan ruled for four more years with several different cabinets, and died March 1955 while undergoing medical treatment in Zurich. His son, Mahendra Bir Shah, ascended to the throne and saw the new nation through the establishment of a constitution and its admission to the United Nations.

King Mahendra's coronation marked the first time in history that Nepal opened its borders to foreign heads of state and the international press. It was a gala affair organized and catered by a flamboyant retired Russian ballet star, Boris Lissanevitch, and his Scandinavian wife, who had started the only western-style hotel in Nepal at the request of Mahendra's father.

The King instituted a constitution that established a parliament and allowed political parties. Elections were held from February to April, 1959. The two-month time for voting was essential in this young nation where no internal communications existed except footpaths. The elections were publicized and carried out by *gaines*, wandering chanters. B.P Koirala, leader of the liberation movement and supporter of the King's father, became Prime Minister.

The first parliament, however, was not long-lived. Locked in continual conflicts with his Prime Minister, the King dissolved Parliament, outlawed political parties, and imprisoned Koirala and several other ministers on December 15, 1960. Mahendra ruled the country until 1962, when he inaugurated a new constitution based on a system of *panchayats*.

The *panchayat*, still in use today, is a pyramidal system with locally elected villages and municipal councils at the bottom (over 4,000 in all). These elect members to the 75 district panchayats, which elect members to the 14 zonal *panchayats*. And these in turn elect representatives to the top-of-the-pyramid Rastriya or National Panchayat. The National Panchayat has the power to propose, debate, and draft legislation, but only the King has the power to promulgate laws.

In 1963 King Mahendra passed a new social code guaranteeing equality to all citizens, freedom of speech and religion, and the right of assembly. Castes were abolished, polygamy forbidden, and the marriage of minors prohibited. Mahendra opened Nepal's doors to foreign visitors, aid and investment, and fostered nationalism in this country where previously many citizens did not even understand the concept of a nation or the meaning of Nepal.

When Mahendra died on January 31, 1972, he was succeeded by his son, Birendra Bir Bikran Shah, who at his coronation pledged to improve the standard of living of his people. Under King Birendra's rule there have been new constitutional changes which have made the National Panchayat more like a traditional parliamentary form of government. The prime minister is now elected by the National Panchayat and the king's cabinet is also responsible to the Panchayat.

Despite constitutional changes, the government has remained stable and since the opening of its borders to foreigners international interest in Nepal has exploded.

palace in Kathmandu, and, like most visitors, fell in love with the country.

The number of visitors in Nepal has risen from fewer than 5,000 a year in 1960 to nearly 300,000 in 1990. Most come to trek the high country and stay between two to six weeks. Others make Kathmandu a short stop on round-the-world voyages. Kathmandu now offers a full range of tourist services, while the high-country remains an adventure for those seeking distance from the distractions of modern civilization. A study published by the American Medical Association in

Mountain climbers and journalists were among the first to arrive. There was only one western-style hotel and virtually no tourist amenities. Nonetheless, visitors found that the warm, welcoming nature of the Nepali people made trips a pleasure. The word spread and soon it was evident to the government that tourism would be a major source of foreign exchange.

Karl Eskelund said that before he left Copenhagen in 1959 the largest travel agency there did not have a single brochure on Nepal. "Anyway," they asked, "why are you so keen on going to an unknown country, which probably has no accommodations whatever for tourists?" True, but Eskelund and his family went anyway, rented a Rana

1989 happily reports that trekking in Nepal is one of the safest vacations to be had, and in fact it can be healthful.

Regardless of length of stay, few travelers are disappointed. A visit to Nepal has a uniqueness that can change one's vision of the world. As seasoned trekker Stephen Bezruchka has written:

Nepal is there to change you, not for you to change it. Lose your self in its essence. Nepal is not only a place on the map, but an experience, a way of life from which we all can learn.

ABOVE: Members of Nepal's royal family, including King and Queen, acknowledge the salute of the crowds from the balcony of a Kathmandu palace.

Abode of
the Gods

BUDDHA'S BIRTHPLACE

The world's only Hindu kingdom, birthplace of the Lord Buddha, Nepal today is ruled by a modern monarch, King Birendra Bir Bikram Shah Dev. The country is known as the "Abode of the Gods", for not only was the Lord Buddha born here, but the most eminent of Hindu deities, Lord Shiva, together with his consort, Parvati, is believed to live among the world's greatest mountains. The north summit of sacred Gaurisankar, 7,144 m (23,438 ft), represents Shiva; the south Parvati. Gaurisankar is also sacred to Buddhists, especially to the Sherpa people of this region who call it "Jomo Tsheringma". Gaurisankar did not yield easily. As recently as 1979, an American, and a Sherpa who was born in the mountain's shadow, were the first to reach the summit and gaze upon this haven of the gods.

Many other gods and goddesses make their home among the Himalaya: Sagarmatha atop Everest, and Annapurna, "Goddess of Plenty", atop the 8,091-m (26,545-ft)-high peak of Annapurna I; while Ganesh, the elephant-headed God, resides on top of 7,406-m (24,298-ft)-high Ganesh Himal I. All are living deities to most Nepalis.

Lumbini, in the Terai of southern Nepal, is the birthplace of Siddhartha Gautama Buddha. It is as sacred to the world's 300 million Buddhists as Mecca to the Muslims and Jerusalem to the Christians.

The Buddha was born in 540 BC in a garden under a grove of cool, leafy trees. His mother, Maya Devi, had been on her way to her mother's home in Devadaha when she went into labor and sought sanctuary in the garden. It was hot and humid and the grove of trees was welcome shade.

Son of King Suddhodhan, the Buddha wanted for nothing as he grew up at his palace home at Taulihawa, about 24 km (15 miles) from Lumbini. When he played in the garden within the palace walls his eyes often turned northward to the distant Himalayan peaks, then already an inspiration for the founder of what would become one of the world's major religious forces.

At the time of his birth, there was great poverty and hardship among the people, but Siddhartha Gautama, sheltered by royal privilege, knew nothing of this.

He was 29 before he set foot outside the palace, persuading his charioteer to drive him around the nearby countryside. So overwrought was the prince by what he saw that he quit the palace and became an ascetic, wandering around the countryside close to death most of the time from self-deprivation. Finally, he abandoned his wandering way of life and became a recluse. He spent his days meditating on life until, under a pipal tree at Gaya near Benares, India, he evolved the philosophy which would sustain millions through the next 2,500 years. Out of this came his name, "Enlightened One" — the Buddha.

He reasoned that the way to enjoy life to the full was to reject extremes of pleasure or pain and follow an "Eightfold Path" based on "Four Noble Truths". Mankind suffered, pronounced the Buddha, because of its attachment to people and possessions in a world where nothing is permanent. Desire and suffering could be banished by an attachment to rightfulness.

The individual, he theorized, was simply an illusion created by the chain of cause and effect, karma, and trapped in the cycle of incarnation and reincarnation. Nirvana, the highest point of pure thought, could only be attained by the extinction of self — and the abolition of karma.

The Buddha preached his doctrine for 45 years before attaining nirvana with his death at the age of 80.

AFTER BUDDHA

In the centuries that have followed the Buddha's death sectarian differences have caused schisms in Buddhism so that in India there is the Mayahana school of Buddhism and in Southeast Asia and Sri Lanka the Hinayana school. The latter more closely follows the Buddha's original teachings.

Another unique form of the faith is Tibetan Buddhism. It believes that the religion's leading figure, the Dalai Lama, is the reincarnation of his predecessor.

In Nepal the predominant form is the Mayahana school, subtly interwoven with

Tibetan and Tantric influence. Tantra is a Sanskrit word for weaving. Tantrism literally reiterates the Buddhist thought — all things and actions are part of a living, constantly changing tapestry — but is opposed to meditation. Devotees express themselves in actual experience and direct action.

One Tantric cult, the shakti, praises the female counterpart of a god. Some Tantric texts suggest that all sin is removed through wine, flesh, fish, women, and sexual congress — and some suggest that sex is not only the ultimate form of bliss and tranquil-

A GARRISON OF GODS

Almost to a man, Nepalis worship their gods and goddesses in temples that pepper the land from end to end. More than 98 percent of the people are Hindu or Buddhist.

New deities are constantly discovered or created. One source says that there are now more than 33,000 Hindu deities — and at most times the dividing line between the Buddhists, Tantrics, and Hindus is thin enough to be indivisible.

ity but also wisdom.

At his coronation, on 24 February 1975, King Birendra declared Nepal "an international zone of peace" — in keeping with the first tenet of the Buddhist religion — and 10 years later this zone had been endorsed by 75 of the world's nations.

Both the motif and the heart of this international zone is the Lumbini garden which was visited in 1967 by U Thant, the Secretary General of the United Nations. Many Buddhist nations have built their own commemorative shrines to the "Enlightened One" in Lumbini.

Giant statue of reclining Vishnu at Buddhanilkantha in Kathmandu valley, which measures 4.6 m (15 ft), undergoes daily cleaning by a priest or temple acolyte.

THE HINDU WAY OF LIFE

Hinduism, in fact, is an entire way of life cushioned against life's hardships by their philosophy, the seemingly happy-go-lucky outlook of the Nepali is not a matter of chance but a carefully evolved acceptance of destiny.

This sustains them so well that in the midst of dire poverty, the poorest people often display the most incredible cheerfulness.

Hinduism seeks no converts nor does it attempt to impose its tenets on non-Hindus. Live and let live is the Hindu credo — all living creatures are sacred. By the same standard, it abhors proselytism — the act of seeking converts to another faith. Evangelism is a criminal offense in Nepal, with stiff jail sentences for both proselytizer and proselyte.

The most popular gods are Brahma, the Creator, and his consort, Saraswati; Vishnu, the Preserver, and Lakshmi; Shiva, the destroyer, and Parvati. Each appears as incarnations in many different forms.

Worshippers belong to six main sects: Vaishnavas, Shaivas, Shaktas, Ganpatyas, Saurapatyas, and Smrathas; the last worship all Hindu deities.

In Nepal, the Shiva cult is the most

popular, above all in his most gentle manifestation as Pashupati, the shepherd, or literally "Lord of the Animals".

He is most often represented by the lingam, a stone symbol of his sexual organ. Most often the lingam is set inside a representation of the female sex organ, yoni, of Parvati, Shiva's consort.

One particular lingam in one of Kathmandu's oldest temples, at Pashupatinah, has five faces — one on each side and an amorphous one on top — and is said to be endowed with cosmic power.

ABOVE: Carved stone statue, Kathmandu.
OPPOSITE: Stone carving of Shiva as Bhairav, his most terrifying incarnation.

It's well-guarded and only priests are allowed to enter the precinct where it's kept, perhaps because Pashupati is believed to be an alchemist who can turn base metal into gold.

Shivaists — worshippers of Shiva — regard the lingam as the fountain of life and the source of pleasure, according to Nepali religious authorities. Swami Hariharannanda Saraswati in the 1941 treatise, Karaparati, says, "The symbol of the Supreme Being (Purusha), the formless, the changeless, the all-seeing eye, is the symbol of masculinity, the phallus or lingam. He adds:

"The symbol of the power that is Nature, the source of all that exists, is the female organ or the yoni."

Only under the shape of a lingam, could Shiva, the giver of seeds, be enveloped within in the yoni and be manifested.

For Shiva is the giver of enjoyment.

"Pleasure dwells in the sex organ [a statement few will be churlish to argue about]," writes Saraswati, "in the cosmic lingam and yoni whose union is the essence of enjoyment. In the world also, all love, all lust, all desire is a search for enjoyment. ... Divinity is the object of love because it is pure enjoyment. ... The whole universe springs forth from enjoyment; pleasure is found at the root of everything. Perfect love itself is the transcendent joy of being."

He seems to have got it just about right.

Hindus have many phallic symbols — one shaped like an egg, one that is a formless mass, one as an altar fire, one as an arrow, and another as a light. The Shiva lingam is always represented in erect form. Divided into three parts, the lowest part is square and concealed in the pedestal, the second is octagonal and set in the yoni, and the third is cylindrical and rises above the yoni.

THE HOLY COW

Sacred to all Hindus is the domestic cow, also Nepal's national animal. It plays a significant role in the country's religious rites. It is used to exorcise evil spirits and to turn an unlucky horoscope into one of good augury. Devout Hindus often touch a cow's tail in the belief that it will help them across the river Vaitarani on their way to paradise.

As in India, these bovids are left to wander freely in both town and country. The great Hindu religious epic, the Mahabharata, avers that those who kill, eat, or allow any cow to be slaughtered are condemned to hell.

When someone dies, families donate a cow to one of the Brahmans in the belief that the cow will reach their dead kin in heaven. These days the animal has been replaced by a token gift of one or two rupees to the presiding priest at the funeral.

SHAMANISM

In the isolated communities of the Nepal Himalaya, the creed of the Shaman — spirit-possessed holy men — still runs strong, as it did 15 centuries ago.

In Shamanism, all illnesses are believed to be caused by the wrath of gods or the mischievous soul of a dead ancestor.

Thus spirits with names like "Warrior King of the Black Crag" and "Great Lord of the Soil God" and "Fierce Red Spirit" are invoked from the shadows of eternity. These take hold of the Shaman and then exorcise evil and sickness from the patient.

Convulsive shaking during a ceremony known as *puja* is the key sign of possession. If the Shaman cannot find the lost soul of the patient then the victim will die.

Minor illnesses, however, are less traumatic, for both patient and witchdoctor. Then the *jhankri* invokes a magic formula called phukne, and caresses away the pain of the affliction with a broom while reciting sacred prayers, mantras.

THE NEPALI CALENDAR — AHEAD OF THE TIMES

Just like the rest of the world, except Ethiopia, Nepal has 365 days and 12 months in each year. But the length of the months differs — from 29 to 32 days. Nepal's first century began at the start of the Vikram era, the date on which King Vikramaditya of India defeated Saka in 57 BC. That was when the Nepali calendar, Vikram Samvat, began.

Abode of the Gods

Under the Vikram Samvat, the country is now more than half a century ahead of the rest of the world.

Thus, Nepal and its citizens celebrated the dawn of the twentyfirst century in splendid isolation. This auspicious event took place in April 1943 when the country's borders were still sealed, and the rest of the world — including some brave Gurkhas — was at war.

There are four other New Year days — one based on the solar calendar, two on the lunar calendar, and one on the Christian Gregorian calendar.

The Vikram Samvat, the official calendar used for administration and followed by all Nepalis, is based on a lunar-solar system of reckoning.

The second most popular of Nepal's calendars — no doubt because it is widely used by many professional astrologers — is the Shakya Samvat, which also follows a lunar-solar system of calculation. But, it can be confusing. It dates back to the accession of an ancient king, Salivahan. Under this calendar, Nepal has only just begun the second decade of the twentieth century.

What might be called Kathmandu's calendar, the Newar Samvat introduced by the Malla dynasty, is roughly 900 to 1,000 years behind the other two.

Perhaps the most confusing of all is the Tibetan calendar. Based on the cycle of Jupiter which works in spans of 12 and 60 years, it was established in Western Nepal about 1,400 years ago.

It does not begin with any given year nor is there any certainty about its dates.

But it's easily the most colorful, each year bearing the name of one of 12 animals: rat, bull, tiger, hare, dragon, serpent, horse, sheep, monkey, rooster, jackal and pig.

Most Nepalis therefore have a choice of three or four New Year days to celebrate but the universal choice, based on the official calendar, falls somewhere in mid-April.

The seven days of the Nepal week are named after the planets — Sun Day, *Aityabar*; Moon Day, *Somabar*; Mars Day (Tuesday), *Mangalbar*; Mercury Day (Wednesday), *Budhabar*; Jupiter Day (Thursday) or Day of the Lord, *Brihaspatibar*; Venus Day (Friday), *Sukrabar*; and Saturn Day (Saturday), *Shanisharbar*.

BUDDHIST AND HINDU ART FORMS

Nepal is perhaps the world's greatest treasury of Buddhist and Hindu art, and most art in Nepal is of a religious nature. More than 2,500 years of the Hindu and Buddhist faith have given Nepal an unrivaled collection of religious architecture and art, from the simple Buddhist stupas to the ornate Hindu pagoda temples.

The Indian Emperor Ashoka was one of the earliest known contributors to Nepal's artistic heritage. Not only did he construct stupas in Patan and Lumbini, and numerous monasteries or gompas, but he also established trade, cultural, and religious ties between the two areas. Ashoka's priests probably originally brought their own Indian artists (wood and stone cutters, carvers, architects, and painters); eventually a professional artist class developed in Nepal with its own style.

The development of a wholly Nepali form of artistic expression seems to have begun between the fourth and seventh centuries AD. Five centuries later, Tibetan influences began to appear in the native art forms: Tantric and Lamaistic themes filled with sinister and demoniac images such as Bhairav, the God of Terror.

In the thirteenth century Chinese influences became apparent, but the admiration for each other's art proved to be mutual. The Nepali architect Araniko was so highly venerated for his style that the mandarins of China invited him to Beijing to work for them.

The richest periods of Nepali expression were during the early Lichhavi dynasty, between the fourth and ninth centuries, and in the Malla epoch, from the thirteenth to eighteenth centuries. These royal houses were great patrons of the arts, as is the ruling house of Nepal today. Many of the art treasures from these periods were destroyed, not only in the recurrent earthquakes, but also by the Muslim invader Shamsu-din-Ilyas of Bengal, who swept with his armies through the valley in the fourteenth century, and desecrated virtually every temple and piece of religious art in Patan, Kathmandu, and Bhaktapur. But those that have survived are considered so priceless that in 1970 West Germany undertook to finance their renovation and preservation, and also to make an inventory of the major works, especially the temples.

It is said there are more temples in Kathmandu than houses, but the same seems to hold true outside the valley. And although much of this heritage from the Malla dynasty and that of other eras was destroyed in the great earthquakes of 1833, 1934, and 1988, an incomprehensible amount remains. Students of religion, art, or architecture need many months to absorb the wonders of Nepal.

THE PAGODA

Of the many architectural styles in Nepal, one of the most striking is the pagoda. The pagoda temple originated here, and is said to have its origin in the practice of animal sacrifice. One theory on the evolution of the pagoda argues that worshipers found it necessary to have an altar that was sheltered to keep the rain from extinguishing the fire. It was also necessary, however, to cut a hole in the roof in order to let out the smoke. To keep the rain

OPPOSITE: One of Nepal's treasured five-storied temples — Nyatapola — in the ancient city of Bhaktapur. When it was dedicated more than two centuries ago its doors were locked, never to be opened again.

from entering the hole a second roof was added atop the first.

Most pagodas stand on a square base, or plinth, of brick or wood, and have two to five roofs, each smaller than the one below. The uppermost roof is usually made of metal and gilded, as are frequently the lower ones. The buildings are richly adorned with carved pillars, struts, doors, and other woodwork. Most decorative carvings are of various deities of all sizes and shapes, such as gods with many arms or deified, humanized animals, often in erotic poses.

THE SHIKARA

Although the shikara is of northern Indian rather than Nepali origin, many of Nepal's temples follow its architectural form: a simple square tower of bricks or stones and mortar, with a small room at the base which houses the god or goddess. Variations on the shikara have pillars, balconies and surrounding interconnected towers, which may also house deities.

The Krishna Mandir in Patan is an excel-

The deity to whom the temple is dedicated is normally housed on the ground floor; the upper levels are more decorative than functional. Some art historians believe that the receding upper tiers are intended to represent the umbrellas that protect the deity from the elements. Above the main entrance is a semi-circular tympanum or torana usually with the enshrined deity as the central figure.

The Nyatapola temple in Bhaktapur is considered the most impressive pagoda in the country.

ABOVE LEFT: Bhuddist prayer stones, *mani,* on the trail to Everest, at Solu Khumbu.
RIGHT: Buddhist stupa at the village of Chaunrikharka on the approach to Everest.

lent example of a stone shikara, but the most interesting shikara in Nepal is the Mahabuddha, temple of One Thousand Buddhas, also in Patan. This shikara is built with bricks, each contain ing an image of Buddha.

THE GOMPA AND THE HINDU MONASTERY

Another form of architecture indigenous to Nepal and neighboring Tibet is the Buddhist monasteries of the high mountains, gompas. Although they follow a fairly simple floor plan, all are delicately adorned and embellished and many date back to the time of Ashoka. The most striking example of this architecture in Nepal is the Thangboche Monastery at Khumbu, near Mount Everest.

Abode of the Gods

There are about 400 Buddhist monasteries in the Kathmandu valley; those near the stupa at Bodnath are open to visitors.

Of a more intricate style are the Hindu monasteries, thirty of which are located in the valley. These serve as centers of Hindu study and learning. The most beautiful is probably the Pujahari Math in Bhadgaon.

THE STUPA

The Buddhist stupa is the oldest and simplest of the Nepali art forms. On its base,

DELICATE WORKMANSHIP

Most Nepali art is worked in stone, metal, wood, or terracotta. Compared to other art forms, there is very little painting in the history of the country's art, but the fine, filigree detail of Nepali sculptures, in these four materials, is as delicate as any brushstroke.

The earliest expression is Buddhist, from about the third century BC. Its surviving examples are four stupas in Patan, Kathmandu, and the Ashoka pillar at Lumbini.

usually a stepped pyramidal platform, is a solid hemispherical mound in white adorned by a spire. The mound represents the universe, and the pairs of eyes on the four sides of the spire symbolize the four elements of earth, fire, air, and water. The 13 steps between the dome and the spire represent the 13 degrees of knowledge needed to attain nirvana; the canopy that surmounts the top of the spire represents nirvana. Each stupa is usually ringed by prayer wheels, each of which is given a twirl by devotees as they circle the shrine clockwise.

The oldest known stupas in Nepal are those erected by Ashoka in Patan, but the most famous are those of Swayambunath and Bodnath.

Abode of the Gods

Nepali art reached a zenith in the Licchavis dynasty. Working in stone, local artists learned all that they could from India's Gupta, Deccan, and Pala schools of art. These they refined and presented in indigenous creations with distinctive Nepali features.

They also began to work in various metals, producing incredibly wrought bronzes of mythical and religious figures. Some of their 1,500-year-old works, exquisite in their detail and imagery, still survive in the Kathmandu valley.

ABOVE LEFT: Buddhist *mani* stones, adorned with prayer flags, in the high country of the Himalaya. RIGHT: A Bhuddist stupa at Thangboche Monastery, Khumbu, which stands at 4,267 m (14,000 ft) on the slopes of Mount Everest.

The metallic sculptures of Tara, Vajrapani, Maitreya, Umamaheshwara, and the Buddha are among the most illustrious, both for their style and their antiquity.

More latter-day examples of Nepali metal work exist in the hollow cast statues of kings and queens, in the gilded sculpted doors, and in other artifacts of the art cities of Patan, Bhaktapur, and Kathmandu.

Tibetan bronzes are notable for the holes set in them for paper prayers, mantras, votive offerings of grain and precious stones, or for religious icons.

Dating some of these masterpieces defies the art historian. Inscribed with the images of a pantheon of gods, both Buddhist and Hindu, most are believed to be from the Pala or an earlier era.

Even more detailed and expressive than stone and metal are the wood carvings which grace the buildings of Nepal, on struts, pillars, beams, doors, windows, cornices, brackets, and lintels inside and outside temples and private homes. The ivory windows of the Royal Palace in Kathmandu's Durbar Square are a well-known example of this art form, but countless others can be found in varying stages of repair and disrepair on the once-elegant Rana palaces and villas in Kathmandu. On a walk through the back streets of Kathmandu's Old Town, you can find windows peeking through the tail of a peacock, others grotesquely circled by skulls, and a variety of suggestive and erotic motifs.

Developed from the twelfth century as an integral part of Nepali traditional architecture, wood art has always been the purview of the Newaris.

The Newaris established a large vocabulary that included every component part and exact detail of traditional carving. These medieval texts have passed down through the generations and still serve as the instructional handbooks for today's wood carvers.

The skill of the Newar craftsman is seen in the absence of either nails or glue in his works. And the erotica that adorn the temples throughout the country leave no doubt about the vividness of their artistic imaginations. Given the Hindu philosophy that

worships Shiva's lingam, the religious of old considered the sexual nature of such art and temple decoration profoundly significant.

Nepal's history of terracotta art stretches back to the third century BC, but in Kathmandu it reached its peak during the sixteenth and eighteenth centuries. Outstanding examples of friezes and moldings decorate the buildings from this era in Kathmandu valley and can also be found in the museums. Notable are the bands of male and female figures, *nagbhands*, that stretch around some temples, depicting Hindu narratives and epics. The gateway of the Taleju temple in Hanuman Dhoka, Bhaktapur, and Patan's Mahabuddha and Maya Devi temples are outstanding examples of this art form.

Pottery-making has been practiced for over a thousand years in Nepal, and some fine examples survive. The pottery center of Kathmandu valley is Thimi, where potters turn out outstanding figurines, smoking pipes, lamp stands, and flower pots.

RELIGIOUS PAINTINGS

Most Nepali painting is of a religious nature and has existed since the ascendancy of the Lichhavi dynasty in the fourth century. The earliest surviving specimens, however, in the form of illustrated manuscripts, date back only to the eleventh century. These manuscripts were produced in Buddhist monasteries and, together with thangkas — a form of painting that features favorite gods and lesser deities and are inevitably subdued in form and color — represent the major form of painting in Nepal.

In recent years the government has asked donor nations and UNESCO to help in the restoration and preservation of Nepal's art works.

It has been estimated that at least half of Kathmandu's most priceless works from the last 2,000 years have been lost in the 40 years since Nepal opened its borders to the rest of the world, much of it spirited away in a vacuum of control by ruthless middlemen and art dealers acting on behalf of wealthy art collectors and museums in the West, thus robbing Nepal of its art.

Of the country's 200 most valuable paintings — all more than a thousand years old — only three remain.

Cairn of *mani* mark the entrance to Thangboche Monastery which guards the approach to Mount Everest, revered as, "The Mother of the Universe".

Nepali
People
and
Customs

THE NEPALI LANGUAGE

Each of Nepal's 35 different ethnic groups are characterized by their own dialect (any one of 22 major languages), locale, dress, and religion. Nepali society is a complex blend of two major religions, Hinduism and Buddhism. For centuries, the people have worshiped each other's gods and displayed mutual respect for one another — from the day more than 2,500 years ago when Gautama, the Buddha, was born.

Their customary way of greeting one another is to clasp their hands together, bow their heads in deference, and murmur, "Namaste" (pronounced Na-Ma-Stay) — "welcome". They believe that, invited or uninvited, "a guest is a god in disguise".

The lingua franca, Nepali is understood by virtually everyone but only spoken by about one-third of the population. It is derived from the North Indian vernacular, Pahori, which is related to Hindi. Nepali uses the Hindi alphabet, Devagnagari, and has borrowed heavily from Sanskrit, the Hindu religious language. But in Nepal there are almost as many local dialects as villages, although, after centuries of intermarriage, there is neither a pure tribe or race nor a pure language. The Tibetan language — another traditional vehicle for religious teaching — remains widespread in northern Nepal, both in its pure, classical form and in the local dialects, such as Sherpa and Thakali, that have evolved from it.

The dialects of the various peoples of the Terai stem from Indo-Aryan dialects. The majority speak Maithili, which originated in the eastern Terai.

English is widely spoken and understood in offices and hotels and most taxi drivers and shopkeepers in Kathmandu valley have a basic knowledge of it, as do most Sherpas. But English is little used or understood anywhere else and you may find difficulty in understanding — and being understood — though many younger people have acquired a smattering of English words.

OPPOSITE: Colorfully attired and bedecked in beads, this wizened old man seems to personify the spirit of Nepal's tribespeople.

Nepali People and Customs

ETIQUETTE

The idea that foreigners are wealthy is deeply ingrained in Nepali minds. Palms extended, children in the streets chant "Rupee! Paisa!" Ignore them and they usually smile and run away. And if they persist, adults normally send them away, for the idea of begging is abhorrent to the Nepali people.

The people are immensely friendly, and travelers, even lone women, can move almost everywhere with complete confidence. But bear in mind that the Nepalis have different values and standards from our own. For reasons that may be obscure to you, they may ask you not to enter a certain precinct or photograph a certain shrine. The fact is that they regard any foreigner as ritually "polluted".

Superstition and religion are indivisible, and are deep-rooted, in Nepali society. Never step over someone's feet or body when you can walk around them and never offer "polluted" food— food that you have tasted or bitten into.

In Nepali custom, the left hand is tainted and it is impolite to pass on things or offer something with the left hand. It is just as impolite to receive anything with the left hand. Always use the right hand — or both hands together. This will signify that you honor the offering, and the recipient or donor. Most Nepalis take off their shoes before they enter a house or a room, so avoid entering any house unless you wish to spend some time in it — for instance, to eat or to drink tea. The cooking and eating areas must be especially respected. Never enter these when wearing shoes — and remember that the fireplace in any home is regarded as sacred. Most Nepalis squat cross-legged on the ground to eat, so take care not to stand in front of them because your feet will point directly at their food.

VOODOO AND RITUALS

In the Terai, witch doctors, *jhankri*, invoke the timeless arts of voodoo — beating drums and sacrificing black chickens to drive evil spirits out of the sick. In some places, the placenta of new-born babies is preserved in an earthen pot for a few days — a potent omen for good. Astrologers cast horoscopes and traditional taboos are still honored. Some people won't eat garlic, onions, and chives. Others won't eat beef, but eat buffalo meat which is not considered sacred — hence the many cafés serving "buffburgers".

Rituals are particularly in evidence during births, marriages, and funerals. Special ceremonies are held six days after birth, for the christening, the first rice-feeding, the first hair cutting, and the

coming of age. Six days after a child is born, the door of the house is opened and lamps are lit — inviting God to enter and write the child's destiny. Marriage is celebrated early in Nepal — unborn children are sometimes pledged to another in an arranged marriage.

RACIAL GROUPS

The two main racial groups are Indo-Aryan and Mongoloid. The southern communities, Brahmins and Chhetris, are of Aryan stock. The Sherpas and Tamangs of the north are pure Mongoloid. In between come such groups as the Newars of Kathmandu, the Kirantis of the midlands, the Gurungs, and the Magars, who are a mixture of both.

The main ethnic groups of the midlands are the Kirantis (Rais and Limbus), Tamangs, Gurungs, Thakalis, and the Newar. Those of the Himalaya mountains are the Sherpas, Lopas, and the Dolpos of remote northwest Nepal who number just a few hundred people. On the lowlands, the main groups are the Tharus, Satars, Dhangars, Rajbansis, Danwars, Majhis, and Darais. Among the minorities are a Muslim population that numbers around two percent of the population and about 6,000 Tibetan refugees who have settled in Nepal and obtained citizenship.

Nepal's many diverse cultures have been shaped over thousands of years by the weather and the environment — and there is a direct living link between groups still in the Stone Age and the metropolitan elite of Kathmandu who have entered the Jet Age. The country's Stone Age groups, where people still make fire with flint and iron and use stone axes, are found in Bajhang and the high, hidden valleys of the west.

THE GURKHAS

Perhaps the best known of all these communities are the Gurkhas and the Sherpas. In fact, the Gurkhas are not an ethnic but a warrior grouping, with more than 300 years of tradition in the armies of Nepal and as mercenaries in the pay of the Indian and British armies. After tourism, military service in foreign armies is the country's second-largest single source of foreign exchange. Salaries, pensions, and related services bring between US$15 and $20 million a year.

The bravery of the Gurkha soldier who forms the elite force of the Royal Nepali Army, is legendary. Short and stocky hillsmen, they have fought and distinguished themselves in some of the greatest battles in military history. During the last two centuries, their daring feats have earned them endless awards, notably 13 Victoria Crosses, considered to be Britain's highest award for valor. Most recently, in the 1982 Falklands War between Argentina and Britain, their bravery was acknowledged yet again.

The name Gurkha denotes their status as the bravest of the brave. It originated from the Gorkhali community of central Nepal which raised the first two Gurkha battalions in 1763 to serve the founder of the present royal dynasty. Calling themselves the Sri Nath and the Purano Gorakh, these battalions first saw action against the British in 1768. They also took part in separate campaigns against Tibet.

By 1814 this force, made up mainly of Thakuri, Magar, and Gurung tribesmen, had slashed their way through the central Himalaya with the *kukhuri* — the fearsome, long, curved blade that by the end of the nineteenth century had become the most celebrated weapon in the arsenal of hand-to-hand combat.

Their derring-do during the two-year Anglo-Nepal War (1814–1816) impressed Western observers, and the British East India Company began recruiting Gurkhas on an informal basis. These casual contracts continued for another 70 years. When the Gurkhas were formally acknowledged, eight units were already in continuous service in India. Most were made up of Magar and Gurung tribesmen, but officers had already begun to draw other recruits from the Rais, Limbu, and Sunwar tribes of the east and from the Khasas in the west. During the 1857 Indian Mutiny, they demonstrated not only tenacity and bravery but also loyalty that would become equally as legendary. As Bishop Stortford, in a 1930 introduction to Ralph Lilley Turner's Nepali Dictionary, remembered:

" ... my thoughts return to you ... my comrades .... Once more I hear the laughter with which you greeted hardship ... . I see you in your bivouacs ... on forced marches or in the trenches, now shivering with wet and cold, now scorched by a pitiless and burning sun. Uncomplaining you endure hunger and thirst and wounds; and at last your unwavering lines disappear into the smoke and wrath of battle. Bravest of the brave, most generous of the generous, never had country more faithful friends than you."

In the last half of the nineteenth century, these warriors fought all across south Asia, from Malaya to Afghanistan — even in

Africa, in Somaliland — displaying remarkable endurance as well as courage.

Several Gurkhas have also stood out as mountain climbers. In 1894, Amar Singh Thapa and Karbir Burathoki climbed 21 major peaks and walked over 39 passes in the European Alps in an epic 86-day trek during which they covered more than 1,600 km (994 miles). Thirteen years later, Karbir Burathoki, with Englishman Tom Longstaff, completed the first major ascent of any Himalayan peak, 7,119-m (23,357-ft)-high Trisul. (Between 1921 and 1937, Gurkha

porters helped to mount five assaults on the then unclimbed Everest.)

By the end of World War I, more than 300,000 Gurkhas had seen service across Europe, Africa, and in the Indian Army. In a battle in Flanders in 1915, Kulbir Thapa won the first of the 13 Victoria Crosses; Karna Bahadur Rana won the second in Palestine in 1918. Certainly, without these doughty stalwarts, Britain would have been even more hard pressed to defend itself and its colonies in World War II. Expanded to 45 battalions, Gurkha troops distinguished themselves in

Women of the Tamang community OPPOSITE and ABOVE, one of the major ethnic groups of the Nepal midlands region.

action across the Middle East, the Mediterranean, and in Burma, Malaya, and Indonesia. Two battalions were formed into crack paratroop outfits. By war's end, the Gurkhas had accumulated another 10 Victoria Crosses.

In 1947, Britain began to dismantle its empire and the Gurkha regiments were divided. Six became the Indian Gurkha Rifles, and four the British Brigade of Gurkhas. Subsequently, the Gurkha regiments of the Indian Army fought against China in 1962 and in successive conflicts with Pakistan in 1965 and 1971. The British sector served

with distinction in Malaya, Indonesia, Brunei, and Cyprus and, in 1965, in action in Sarawak, Lance Corporal Rambahadur Limbu won the Gurkhas their 13th Victoria Cross, for "heroism in the face of overwhelming odds".

Today, the descendants of these brave men sign up for service in faraway British outposts — Hong Kong, Singapore, Brunei, and Belize in Central America. It was from there that the Gurkhas were rushed into action when war broke out in 1982 between Argentina and Britain. Described by the

Argentinian press as a cross between dwarfs and mountain goats, they presented such a ferocious mien as they advanced on the Argentinian positions that the Latin Americans dropped their weapons and fled — not wishing to discover the Gurkhas' legendary skill at disemboweling the enemy with their wicked-looking kukhuri blades.

The Kiranti hillsmen from eastern Nepal are now among the principal recruits to the Gurkha regiments. Of Mongoloid and Tibetan stock, they are said to have won the myth-shrouded battle of Mahabharat. Their religion is a blend of Animism, Buddhism, and Hindu Shivaism.

Numbering more than half a million, they speak a language that derives from Tibet.

Most Kirantis, military mercenaries or farmers, carry the Gurkha kukhuri tucked beneath the folds of their robes. Tradition says that once this is drawn it cannot be put back in its scabbard until it has drawn blood.

Until recently, Kiranti honor could only be satisfied by the slaughter of a chicken or duck. Now they settle for another compromise. It's cheaper by far simply to nick a finger and spill their own blood to satisfy this centuries-old belief.

THE SHERPAS

The Sherpas are a Nepali ethnic group that have earned fame as the world's most skilful high-altitude mountain porters and climbers. Of Mongoloid stock and numbering between 25,000 and 30,000 they migrated centuries ago over the Himalaya from Minyak in eastern Tibet. It was Sherpa Norgay Tenzing who, with Sir Edmund Hillary, conquered Everest; and it's the Sherpas who accompany every major mountain-climbing expedition. For endurance few are known to equal them. They are Buddhists and earn a living by trading, farming, and herding yaks.

It was A. M. Kellas who first used Sherpas in a mountain assault in 1907 in Sikkim. But renown came with the opening of the Nepal Himalaya in the 1950s; so courageous and skilful were they on the perilous slopes that the Alpine Club gave them the title, "Tigers of the Snow".

Sherpa Tenzing earned immortality from his ascent with Hillary, but he died penniless

ABOVE: Grizzled face of a veteran Sherpa mountain porter. OPPOSITE young Sherpa boy at Lukla, the community's high country "capital".

in exile in Delhi, India, in 1986. Others of his kin have since followed him to the top of the world. One, Pertemba Sherpa, has been there twice.

The high altitude of the Sherpas' environment has prepared them physically and mentally for the challenges of climbing 8,800 m (29,000 ft) into the sky.

Since the Mongol invasions 700 or 800 years ago, they have maintained much of their nomadic lifestyle; in summer they move up to the sparse pastures above 5,800 m (19,000 ft). In the past, they migrated to Tibet

in summer, returning in winter to the Khumbu region. Slowly, they settled in more permanent communities, tilling the fields and growing vegetables and root crops.

Made up of 18 clans, each speaking its own dialect, Sherpas follow tribal laws that prohibit intermarriage not only between members of the same clan but also between members of specific clans. Gifts of the Sherpa home-brewed beer, chhang, are exchanged between heads of families when their offspring become engaged. Weddings

are elaborate and lavish affairs with great feasting and drinking.

Traders and money-lenders are prominent in society. Usury is big business, loans at 25 to 30 percent interest not uncommon.

Yaks provide butter for the lamps which burn in the monasteries and private homes, and for the rancid Tibetan tea served in these parts. Arts and handicrafts are limited but images, scrolls, murals, and rock carving provide lucrative rewards for those Sherpa priests, or lamas, who have become skilled artists. They belong to the oldest Buddhist sect in Tibet, still largely unreformed.

The priests borrow freely from the arts of sorcery and witchcraft to sustain their authority, and sacrifice is a ritual tool to deal with the mythological demons and gods who inhabit every peak and recess of the region, and whose presence is confirmed in the Buddhist scriptures.

THARUS

The Tharus are the indigenous inhabitants of the most fertile part of Nepal, the southern corn and rice belt of the Terai. They number close to a million. Over the centuries they have been joined by many migrants from the midland valleys and the mountain highlands — the Terai is also host to the majority of Nepal's 300,000 muslims — lured to the plains by the fertile soil and climate.

The Tharus, especially those of high-caste birth, are much more conservative and rigid in their values than the rest of their countrymen. In the south they live, together with non-caste communities such as the Danuwar, Majhi, and Darai, along the Terai's northern edge and in the west; with the Rajbansi, Satar, Dhimal, and Bodo people in the east, and Morang.

The Tharus have lived there longest, building up a resistance to malaria and living in cool, spacious, airy houses with lattice-work brick walls to allow in any breeze. Besides farming, they hunt, breed livestock, and fish.

Their bejeweled women are noted for their stern demeanor. They marry early, but if the groom cannot afford the dowry he must work for the bride's family — up to five years — to be eligible.

ABOVE: Tamang man in the colorful market of Namche Bazaar on the slopes of Mount Everest and OPPOSITE two Newari girls from the Kathmandu valley.

Nepali People and Customs

They worship tigers, crocodiles, and scorpions in a form of Hinduism tinged with animism.

NEWARS

In Kathmandu valley, the oldest community is that of the Newars. Descended from the Mongols, they practice some form of the Hindu caste system, ranking hereditary occupations such as carpentry, sculpture, stonework, goldsmith, and others according to ritual purity. Their crafts adorn almost

When a man reaches the golden age of 77 years, seven months, and seven days, there's a re-enactment of the rice-feeding ceremony, pasni, which marks the seventh month of every male child.

He's hoisted on a caparisoned palanquin and paraded through the town, his wife following behind on a second palanquin. He's given a symbolic gold earring which marks him out as a wise one for the rest of his life.

Death is marked by cremation at any one of the many burning places near the holy Hindu bathing places, or ghats, which in

every corner of the valley and its cities.

To the Newars, every day is a celebration of life and death. Together with their extended families, they observe a constant round of rituals worshiping and placating the many deities whose blessings rule their daily lives.

Once a year they honor one of the family cows, usually a calf, which personifies Lakshmi, the goddess of wealth, treating it to grain and fruit. Windows are lit throughout the night to please the divinity who circles the earth at midnight and to bring her blessings on cash boxes and grain stores.

Each stage of a Newar's life is marked by colorful ceremonies. In a land where few people live more than 50 years, the old are venerated.

Kathmandu, in particular, line the banks of the Bagmati river.

Mourners walk around the body three times before setting the funeral pyre alight, while relatives shave their heads and ritually purify themselves with the slimy scum-laden waters of the river. After this, the ashes are scattered in the Bagmati and the wind-borne smoke carries the soul to the abode of Yama, the god of death, where it will merge with the divine.

Young Newar girls are symbolically married to Vishnu. Thus, "married for life", they escape any stigma if widowed or divorced from their earthly husband.

These little sisters also pay homage to their brothers — often their only source of support in old age — during the Tihar Bhaitika festival. The boys, seated behind decorative symbols of the universe, mandals, receive the mark of the *tika* and the blessing, "I plant a thorn at the door of death; may my brother be immortal."

OTHER COMMUNITIES

In the Dhaulagiri region, slashes of brilliant orange or white mark the farms of the Brahmins, Chhetris, Gurungs, and Magars. Their gardens are filled with the colors of poinsettias, marigolds, and other flowers, and shady banyan trees. Barley, wheat, millet, rice, and maize are grown in the valleys that lie between the mountains.

The people of the Manang valley, however, are famous for their trading. Tibetan in culture, they travel to many parts of the Orient — Singapore, Hong Kong, and Bangkok — to do business.

Another trading community is that of the Thakali people, whose colorful trade caravans of mules, loaded with sugar, kerosene, and rice, travel through the low-lying Kali Gandaki gorge, the deepest in the world, and, for centuries, one of the most important trade routes linking Tibet with Nepal and India. Like the Manang community, their settlements are distinguished by the flat roofs of their houses.

Of Nepal's many diverse communities perhaps the smallest is that of the Dolpos, a few hundred people who herd their yaks and goats in the sterile stony moors of Nepal's western Himalaya. They also grow wheat, barley, and potatoes. Lamaist Buddhists who speak a Tibetan dialect, are mainly traders who use pack beasts to move their goods in caravans from Tibet to the more populous areas of Nepal. They ride tough highland ponies and are adept horsemen.

NATIONAL EMBLEMS

Nepal's national bird is a rare, brilliantly-colored pheasant, of the species *Galliformes*, found between the 2,400- and 4,500-meter

(7,800- and 15,000-ft) contours of the Himalaya. It belongs to the same family as the peacock.

The ubiquitous rhododendron, of which there are about 32 species, most with red and pink flowers, rarely white, is the national flower.

Crimson-red, *simrik*, is Nepal's national color. Regarded as both sacred and auspicious it is considered a symbol of progress, prosperity, and action and is visible at all national and sacred occasions. Shiva is supposed to draw power from this dark red hue.

During Nepal's many Hindu festivals, red flowers are presented as votive offerings to the different gods and goddesses. Crimson is also the color that symbolizes married bliss, and virtually all Nepalis women wear red during festivals and other sacred occasions.

Usually red is the color of the country's national dress, *labeda suruwal*, which is made of homespun cotton. On other occasions color of this dress is gray or light brown.

It consists of a seamed, double-breasted tunic blouse that extends almost to the knees, fastened by two ribbons, and trousers that are baggy around the thighs but tight at the ankles, similar to the *shalwa qamiz* of India.

For some occasions sophisticated Nepali women wear the Indian sari.

Nepal's national flag is formed by two adjoining red triangles, symbolizing morality virtue and unity, bordered by blue. The top triangle contains a crescent moon emitting eight rays, the lower one, a sun emitting 12 rays. These are symbolic representations of the many legendary solar and lunar dynasties to which the royal family belongs.

The family's coat of arms includes some leaf-shaped decorative pieces to symbolize the title of *Sri Panch* — five times glorified. For the crest, the heraldic device uses the plume of a bird of paradise which is believed to have been introduced to Nepal by a former premier, Mathbar Singh Thapa. Below this are the footprints of Paduka, the guardian god of Gorkha, ancestral home of the ruling dynasty.

Crossed *kukhuris* represent the national weapon, the traditional, curved sword of the famed Gurkha battalions. On either side are the sun and the moon, symbol of enlightenment and eternity.

The shield depicts Nepal, from the Himalaya to the Terai, and at the center, hands

Tamang woman at Lukla. Highland people like the Sherpas, the close-knit Tamang are descended from Tibeto-Mongoloid stock. They number about one million and are mainly Buddhist.

clasped, sits Pashupatinah, creator as well as destroyer of the universe.

The Sanskrit motto avers that love of mother and motherland is superior even to love of heaven. The soldier recruit and veteran are also represented by a prayer exhorting them to defend their country, so long as the universe shall exist.

Nepal's national anthem wishes for the continued prosperity of the "excellent, illustrious, five times glorified King" and a similar fivefold increase in the number of his subjects.

and Sherpa food, for instance a gluey barley flour and spuds, or rancid tea, salted with yak butter and churned Tibetan-style with globs of grease floating on the surface, might be hard for the first-time visitor to swallow.

The national drink is *chiya*, tea brewed together with milk, sugar, and sometimes spices. It is served in glasses, scalding hot.

During festivals the standard vegetarian diet is relieved with dishes of chicken and goat meat. Arrange your trip to coincide with a festival when the community join hands to serve a greater variety of food.

FOOD AND DRINK

BASIC FARE

If you're eating out country style in Nepal, remember that most of the country is rural. Don't expect too much in the way of culinary adventure. It's basically vegetarian.

Home cooking keeps to simple essentials. The staple is rice, *bhat*, soaked in a gravy of pulse, *dhal*, with vegetable side dishes. You can spice these meals up with some of the country's tangy herbs and chutneys.

This basic fare varies according to the region and available seasonal fruits and vegetables. Some particular forms of Tibetan

Outside Kathmandu, travelers on day outings should carry their own food, either snacks from the Annapurna or Nanglo bakeries, or fresh fruit for a picnic. More cosmopolitan menus are available in Kathmandu.

The metropolitan Nepalis have acquired the culinary taste of their Indian neighbors so, in the capital, you can expect to enjoy a wide range of curries.

If you've never been to India, you should try Indian yoghurt, *lassi*, either salted or sweet, and confections like *halwa* and Indian ice cream, *kulfi*.

Basic fare in Nepal is flavored with seasonings such as chilies OPPOSITE laid out to dry in Kathmandu street, and garlic and shallots ABOVE sold by street vendor in Kathmandu.

Nepali People and Customs

Tea served in the lowland and midland regions is sweet and stimulating, but whatever you do, wherever you go, avoid drinking unboiled or unfiltered water.

Nepal's Star and Golden Eagle lager beers are excellent and there's a stronger, mountain brew — the Nepali equivalent of kill-me-quick — *chhang,* made from fermented barley, maize, rye, or millet. *Arak* (potato alcohol), and *rakshi* (wheat or rice alcohol), also have their adherents.

The local brewers also produce strong spirits — whisky, rum, and gin — but there's

brate popular myths or folklore. Seasonal festivals serve as occasions for offerings to the gods or thanksgiving for good harvests.

Though many festivals are celebrated regionally, major ones are national. Nearly all involve prayers and ritual exercises — purging, *puja,* either the family or some ethnic or religious group.

The Nepali word for feast, *jatra,* also signifies a procession or pageant. The Nepali word for birthday is *jayanti:* for fair, *mela;* and for fast, *vatra.*

Festivals are based on Nepal's official

no wine industry. Imported beers, spirits, and wines are available in most major tourist centers — at a price.

FESTIVALS

Nepal is the "Land of Festivals". Almost every week of the year a festival with religious, historical, mythical, or seasonal significance is celebrated.

The major religious festivals, staged by the Hindus or Buddhists and dedicated to one of their many gods and goddesses, are marked by fervor and jubilation. Historical festivals usually commemorate the royal family or an epic event from the past. Other festivals cele-

Vikram Samvat calendar or the movement of the planets, so equivalent western dates are only approximate.

One of the most fascinating festivals, celebrated only every 10 years or so, is the search for the vestal virgin, the reincarnation of Kumari, the Mother Goddess, who the Newars worship with offerings of money, food, and ornaments. There are more than a dozen of these virgins in Kathmandu valley.

The major one is the Kumari of Basantpur to whom even the Royal family pay homage. According to legend, there's every reason for them to do so.

When the last of the Malla kings, who thought his Kumari was a fraud with an "evil eye", banished her from the city, his queen was seized by convulsions, and declared that the spirit of the goddess had entered her body, too. At once, the virgin was called back to the city and publicly proclaimed by the King, who worshipped at her feet.

Thereafter he spent most of his time playing games of chance with her until, one day, overcome by her beauty, he was filled with desire. The goddess perceived his lust and vanished immediately— returning to him in a dream that night to warn him that his days were numbered. She commanded him to select a girl-child from a caste of

Newar gold and silversmiths, saying she would dwell in the virgin's body. "Worship her as the Goddess Kumari for to worship her is to worship me."

Not long after this, the Gorkha King, Prithvi Shah, founder of the present Shah dynasty, overthrew the Mallas and became ruler of Kathmandu and Nepal.

Chosen roughly once every 10 years, when the reigning Kumari reaches the age of puberty, the new goddess must be an unblemished virgin between three to five years old.

She needs 32 special qualities — physical and spiritual — said to be the sign of reincarnation, including prominent blue or black eyes, white teeth, small and sensitive

tongue, sonorous voice, long and slender arms, soft and delicate hands, and straight hair curled towards the right.

But all this means nothing if the child fails a final test — walking over severed animal heads in an underground chamber lit by flickering lanterns while masked demons leap and shriek.

The chosen one is installed in the temple, dressed in elegant brocades and silks, served by women attendants, bedecked in jewels, and crowned with a tiara as the guardian and ruling deity of Nepal.

Worshipped daily by visitors, she gives counsel on legal, social, and economic matters and in return is showered with gifts and cash. Every move or gesture she makes is considered either a good or bad omen.

But when the Living Goddess reaches menarche she returns home, an ordinary but wealthy citizen, free to marry if there's man brave enough. It's said he who takes a Kumari's virginity dies early!

FESTIVALS AROUND NEPAL

SPRING

TUNDIKHEL (Kathmandu)
Ghode Jatra (March). Held to appease Demon Gurumapa. The King of Nepal is the chief guest and there's excitement aplenty with horse races, acrobatic shows, and a procession of chariots of the goddesses.

JANAKPUR (and other places)
Ramavami (March). This spring festival commemorates the epic victory of Rama, hero of the Ramayana, over Ravana.

It's normally held around the end of March and beginning of April when elephants, ox-carts, and horses lead the thousands of devotees through Janakpur in a milling throng. Other Ramavami celebrations are held in Kathmandu and elsewhere for those unable to travel to Janakpur.

Not long after his wedding to Sita (see below), Rama was banished to 14 years exile in the forest — with his loyal brother Lakshman by his side. During this time the ugly sister of Ravana, his greatest foe, tried to seduce first Rama and then, having failed,

Lakshman, who snubbed her simply by cutting off her nose and ears. This so annoyed Ravana he raided Ayodhya — and made off with Sita.

Back in his palace, the brutal king lusted after Sita's unimpeachable beauty and tried to have his way with her, but she made it clear there was nothing doing and, pining for her beloved Rama, began to waste away.

Now enters, in this thousands-years-old epic, the forerunner of America's Superman, Hanuman, the loyal monkey, son of the Wind God. He also had the gift of being able to encircle the earth by flying through space like an orbiting satellite, and did so until he found where Sita was held hostage.

He then flew like the wind to Rama who swiftly quit the forest, and with the ever-faithful Lakshman by his side, traveled to Lanka where he met Ravana in terrible battle, ending in victory for Rama — and, of course, virtue.

KATHMANDU
Chaitra Dasain (March). One of the capital's most colorful festivals. The towering chariot of White Matsyendranath is pulled through the city for three days, and sacrifices are offered to Durga, Shiva's consort, in one of her most terrifying aspects.

BALAJU
Balaju Mela (March). Held at the full moon, this honors Vishnu. Worshippers purify themselves with the water from 22 taps.

BHAKTAPUR/THIMI/BODE/NATIONWIDE
Bisket Jatra/Balkumari Jatra
New Year's Day (April). Nepal's New Year celebration, which usually falls somewhere in mid-April, according to the position of the sun and the moon.

Derived from the Newari words for snake, *bi*, and slaughter, *syako*, the celebration is called Bisket.

It's an immensely colorful commemoration of the sacred battle of Mahabharata, the feast of snakes; and also honors Bal Kumari, the Virgin Goddess, when the chariots of Bhairav and Kali are pulled in procession through Bhaktapur, and the Bal Kumari's chariot is drawn in procession through Thimi.

Early in the morning, each New Year's Eve, hundreds of thousands gather outside the Nyatapola temple in Biratnagar, in Kathmandu valley, where two enormous vehicles of the gods, *raths*, with solid wooden wheels are waiting.

Long ago, there was a Bhaktapur king whose daughter, Bhadra Kali, was a nymphomaniac. So insatiable was her appetite that each night her father had to conscript a new man to serve her — for each morning the Royal stud was found dead — if not from exhaustion, then inexplicably. But one night a visiting Prince offered his services, thinking he might solve the mystery.

That evening, after the Princess fell into a deep and satisfied sleep, the Prince left her bed and hid himself, sword in hand.

Now he watched in horror as, from the Princess's nose, two threads of hair began to emerge as enormous serpents, writhing about, seeking their nightly victim. Swiftly, he left his hiding place and pounced upon them.

To their surprise the coffin bearers, who arrived the next morning expecting to carry away yet another corpse, found him deep in conversation with the enraptured Princess. Not unnaturally, the King and all his people — particularly the young men — were overjoyed.

The bodies of the snakes were draped from a tall wooden pole and the two lovers paraded around the town in their respective chariots before they were wed.

The victor, in fact, was Bhairav, the manifestation of Shiva in his destructive power, and the Princess, the Goddess Bhadra Kali.

Now, four days before New Year, her brass likeness is carried from its Bhaktapur shrine to the Nyatapola temple and placed in the smaller of the two chariots— and Bhairav's image in the other.

Together, these enormous, unwieldy vehicles are pulled through the town, up hill and down, past the Potters' Market, until they reach Khalna Tole, ready for the celebrations that begin on New Year's Eve.

The virgin Kumari OPPOSITE, living goddess of Kathmandu valley, is identified as the reincarnation of the eighteenth-century original through a process of ritual ordeal and despite her tender age is a revered oracle.

Dominating all is a 24-m (80-ft)-high representation of Bhairav's victorious lingam, draped with two banners representing the snakes, set in a massive circular 1.2-m (four-feet)-deep yoni.

Rival teams, each representing one of the deities, battle to dislodge the lingam and bring it crashing down. The lingam's fall signals the death of the old year and the evil serpents.

Next is a tug-of-war to see which group can win control of Bhairav's chariot: and the right to guard the great god for the next seven days of the Bisket festival.

For the winners it's an auspicious omen of good fortune. The following week, they sing and dance in the narrow streets with parades in honor of Brahma, Ganesh, Lakshmi, and Mahakali, the Goddess of Terror.

Five kilometers (three miles) away in Thimi, New Year is marked in spectacular fashion with a celebration for Bal Kumari, Thimi's Living Goddess. Throughout the day her temple is thronged with musicians and worshippers bringing offerings of rice, vermilion, burning oil torches, holy water, flowers, and garlands for Bhairav's consort.

The local folk believe that it's important to keep the four ceremonial oil torches, *chirags*, which guard her, alight. If they go out it means Thimi is doomed to suffer during the forthcoming year.

It's just after midnight, the start of New Year's Day, that Thimi comes to incandescent life. Then, like gladiators of old in the streets of Rome, their route lit by torches, teams of strong young men begin to carry immensely heavy palanquins — borne on thick bamboo poles — in a rowdy procession through the streets. So heavy are the palanquins that a sudden lurch sends them all stumbling. There are 32 of these palanquins, and each needs a team of 20 to 30 to carry them.

The heavy, wrought-iron, little temples, *khats*, carried on these palanquins, contain images of Bhaktapur's guardian deities with Kumari in principal place. It's said that the combined heat of the many torches — literally hundreds — which burn through the night and day will drive away winter and hasten summer's warmth to make their crops burgeon.

In each group, an attendant staggers with them, twirling a weighty ceremonial umbrella on a heavy bamboo pole above the deity ensconced within the *khat* — its pagoda-tiered brass roof decorated with fruit, ribbons, good-luck charms, garlands, and green shrubs.

Clouds of brilliant orange-red powder hang in the air, infiltrating into hair, teeth, eyes, and nose, and permeating clothing: the happiness is as infectious as the stain is ineradicable. It's said to be a very special token of respect and admiration reserved only for elders, close friends, and neighbors.

The climax of the mounting frenzy is when Ganesh, on a *khat* from Nagadish village — surrounded by several hundred supporters — joins the procession. Soon the rest of the palanquins join a wild chase down the main street — nothing more than a sun-baked earth road — after Ganesh when he turns for home, to persuade him to stay and thus ensure that the celebrations continue.

The chase over, the festival moves to its colorful close with the procession moving back to the Kumari temple, standing before the entrance to stop the Goddess's palanquin from entering — for with her departure the festival is ended.

Finally, amid much laughter, shouting and jeering, the palanquin bearers are triumphant. Bal Kumari disappears into her sanctum to rest another year while the others shoulder their deities and vanish through the thicket of lanes back to their homes.

Many carry sacrificial chickens and goats. The blood from their slit throats has already been drained and poured over the image of Bal Kumari to slake her thirst.

On this day enmities and rivalry are forgotten. None may refuse an invitation to eat or drink. But before this feasting begins, the crowds head across the patchwork countryside, over the dykes that divide their terraced fields and village from that of Bode.

There, each year, a member of the community is chosen by the village elders to undergo a traumatic ordeal as an act of penitence for the village. Tongue extended, a holy man, *pujari*, will pierce it with a thick needle.

On the day, the chosen one sits cross-legged and reclusive on a mat in a small courtyard outside his house. For four days he will have been living in solitude; beard, head, and eyebrows shaved, eating only one meal a day: no meat, garlic, or salt. For the last 24 hours he eats nothing.

The penitent sits with his mouth agape as the priest inserts the needle, forged eight months earlier during the festival of Jandraganar and kept in oil in the Ghantakarna.

Few actually see it pass through the tongue, but if he bleeds it's an ill-omen and taken as a sign of the penitent's impurity during his seclusion. The gods will punish him.

The ordeal is not yet over. After this, a giant bamboo candelabra, containing about 30 smouldering oil torches, is fastened over the penitent's shoulders. Tongue outstretched, shoulders bowed, he has to walk through the village for the next 90 minutes — a source of admiration for his virtue and stoic courage until, purged and purified, he enters the temple. There the *pujari* removes the needle and cauterizes the wound with mud from the temple floor.

All these celebrations are a noisy, boisterous melee of people, chariots, vermilion powder, and riotous happiness. Plus, more quietly, the King's message to his countrymen.

SANKHU (Kathmandu valley)
Bajrayogini Jatra (April). Held on the third day of the Nepali New Year, the image of Bal Kumari is drawn through the village in a procession.

PATAN (Kathmandu)
Rato Matsyendranath Jatra (April to May). Held in the first month of the New Year, the actual date is decided on the basis of propitious signs by Hindu priests. Then the chariots of Matsyendranath and Minanath are led through different parts of the town before the Patan Bal Kumari.

MATA TIRTHA (near Thankot)
Mother's Day (May). The motherless travel from all over Nepal to bathe and make offerings to the soul of their departed mother.

THAMI MONASTERY (Bhote Kosi valley)
Mani Rindu (May). A rarely witnessed Sherpa festival of prayer that takes place a few days before the new moon.

SWAYAMBHUNATH/BODHNATH (Kathmandu valley)
Buddha Jayanti (April to May). Butter lamps and electric lights blaze all night in late April or early May at the Swayambhunath stupa in Kathmandu valley, during the full moon celebration of Buddha's birthday.

Overshadowing hundreds of smaller images, a massive gilded figure of Buddha is carried in a colorful procession down the many steps to a cloister where religious rites continue throughout the day before the Buddha is returned to its hilltop shrine.

At the Bodhnath stupa, on the other side of the valley, an image of the Master is mounted on the back of an elephant and paraded around the dome. Ribbons of colorful flags stretch from the gilt-copper pyramid which surmounts the stupa, as the monks below blow their long copper horns. In the crescendo of the climax everyone hurls fistfuls of ground wheat into the air.

Centerpiece of these festivities is the large portrait of the Dalai Lama held head high and shielded under a large canopy.

JAISIDEVAL
Sithinakha (June). A Newar festival celebrating the birthday of the warrior God, Kumar, son of Shiva, and the advent of the rains with a feast of bean patties and pancakes.

BUDDHANILKANTH
Harishayani Ekadasi (June). Held just before the full moon, Hindus celebrate Vishnu with worship and praises of honor. Sacrifices and meat are banned.

SUMMER

SWAYAMBHUNATH
Gunla (July to August). A month-long celebration marked by massive pilgrimages to the Buddhist shrine at Swayambhunath.

PASHUPATINAH/NATIONWIDE
Nagpanchami (July). Hindus paste pictures of the snake gods and mermaids on their front doors and worship them.

FOLLOWING PAGES: Flour fills the air as Buddhist monks at Kathmandu valley's famed Bodhnath stupa celebrate yet another religious festival.

KATHMANDU

Ghantakama (July). One of and most riotous of Newar celebrations when, on the last day before the new moon, worshippers place tripods of fresh reed stalks at various crossroads and indulge in cheerful obscenities. At twilight, amid much good humored banter and jostling, an effigy of the demon, Ghantakamna, is symbolically drowned.

KHUMBHESHWAR (Patan)/**NATIONWIDE**

Janai Purnima (July). Full moon Hindu cele-

KRISHNA TEMPLE (Patan)/**NATIONWIDE**

Krishnastami (August). Birthday celebrations honoring Krishna.

PATAN/SWAYAMBHUNATH

Panchadan (August). At the new moon, devotees bring offerings of rice to the Buddhist priests.

GOKARNA/NATIONWIDE

Father's Day — Gokarna Aunsi (August). Children give their father sweets and fruit. Those whose fathers are dead, purify

bration of the renewal of the sacred thread (Janai) by Brahmins and Kshatriyas. The *jhankris* (witch doctors) mark the occasion by making a pilgrimage to Gosainkund, the sacred lake at the head of Trisuli valley, 4,300 m (14,000 ft) above sea level.

KATHMANDU VALLEY

Gai Jatra (July). Held the day after the full moon, in memory of those who died during the preceding year. At Patan the crowds impersonate cows, holy men, sadhus, or madmen as they walk around the city. Singing, stamping, joking, and shouting characterize the festival atmosphere in neighboring Bhaktapur.

themselves in the waters near Gokarna temple.

AUTUMN

PASHUPATINAH

Festival of Women — Teej Brata (August to September). An immensely colorful ceremony when the banks of the Bagmati are crowded with hundreds of thousands of Nepali women, all dressed in striking dresses of various hues of red.

Married women wear their scarlet and gold wedding saris, and the unmarried sing and dance in their brightest clothes to pray to Shiva and his consort Parvati for a long and happy marriage.

They all bathe in the Bagmati in honor of their husbands or husbands-to-be. Throughout the Kathmandu valley, there is feasting on the first day and fasting on the second and third.
Balachaturdashi (October). Held on the eve of the new moon, Hindus commemorate the memory of their departed relatives by scattering seeds in the forests of Pashupatinah.

BASANTPUR/HANUMAN DOKHA

Indra Jatra (September). Starting four days before the full moon, Indra Jatra is one of Kathmandu's largest festivals, eight days of noise and color, celebrating the release of Indra, the King of Gods, who, disguised as an ordinary mortal, was arrested for stealing flowers in Kathmandu. When his mother came down to earth to find him, the people, overcome with remorse, fell down before them and then carried them in triumph through the streets in a week-long festival.

It also marks the conquest of Kathmandu valley by Prithvi Narayan in 1768. The demon god, Bhairav, is also venerated.

Before the event starts, King Birendra consults the Bal Kumari for assurance that all augurs well. The Kumari anoints the King on the forehead with the Hindu's sacred red mark, the *tika*, and he presses his forehead on her feet. Then, watched by foreign and Nepali dignitaries, she is carried from her temple to a large chariot, for her feet must not touch the ground.

King Birendra and his queen watch from the balcony of their Durbar Square palace, opposite a three-story temple that has beautiful carved windows— including a seventeenth-century peacock window of matchless detail— as the Kumari's chariot, accompanied by images of Ganesh and Bhairav, is drawn through Durbar Square and the streets of old Kathmandu.

Sheep or goats are laid in the path of the juggernaut's wheels, sacrifices to save those who may stumble or fall before the giant vehicle.

NATIONWIDE

Dasain (Durga Puja) (September). Starting at the new moon and lasting for 10 days,

this is the biggest of Nepal's national festivals in worship of the Goddess Durga and celebrating the start of the good season. Friends and family welcome each other into their different homes for feasting and drinking. Outside there is much entertainment and social recreation, particularly kite-flying. And, of course, frequent visits to the temple.

Ashwin (September to October). The Ganesh Festival at the September full moon honors the pot-bellied elephant god without whose blessings no religious ceremony, be

it private or public, is ever begun. Nepalis believe that even Surya, the sun god, offers *puja* to Ganesh before he journeys across the heavens.

Tihar Bhaitika (October). A Newar celebration, when sisters pay homage to their brothers. The boys, seated behind decorative symbols of the universe, mandalas, receive the mark of the *tika* and the blessing,

Clad in rich scarlets, reds and golds, women OPPOSITE purify themselves in the waters of a sacred river at Kathmandu's Pashupatinah temple during the Teej Festival in a ritual of bathing and ABOVE feasting as they pray for the continuing love and devotion of their husbands.

Nepali People and Customs

"I plant a thorn at the door of death; may my brother be immortal".

Tihar Dipawali (October). Hindus and Buddhists honor Lakshmi, Goddess of Wealth, with a blazing display of light throughout the Kingdom, and worship their livestock, pets, and the crow, for three consecutive days.

KATHMANDU

Mha Puja (October). Held at the new moon, this day of self-worship is celebrated in a big — and presumably selfish — way.

WINTER

JANAKPUR

Bibaha Panchami (November to December). This week-long festival commemorates Rama and Sita's wedding.

On the first day, everybody joins the great procession from Rama's temple. Rama's idol, dressed as a bridegroom, is placed in a gaily-decorated sedan chair that rides on the back of an elephant, just as elegantly bedecked in brocades

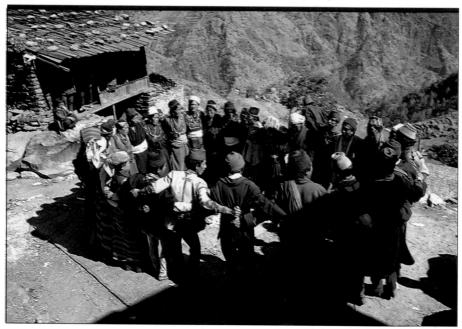

BUDDHANILKANTH

Buddhanilkanth Mela (October). Celebrating the ritual awakening of the Hindu God, Vishnu, three days before the full moon, after four months' immersion in water.

THANGBOCHE MONASTERY (Khumbu)

Mani Rindu (November). Sacred Buddhist ritual held in the shadows of Everest at this monastery, 3,800 m (12,500 ft) high, near Khumbu.

and silks and led to Sita's temple, Naulakha Mandir. Next day, Sita's idol is carried with great fanfare to the side of Rama in a symbolic re-enactment of their marriage.

BAGMATI (and other rivers)

Maghesnan (January to February). A Hindu purification ceremony when hundreds of thousands swarm along the banks of the Bagmati in Kathmandu and elsewhere at the full moon of the 10th month of the Nepali year.

They pay visits to their temples. At Sankhu, celebrants soak themselves in the Salinadi river to wash away their sins.

Folk dance of a remote Tamang community in ABOVE Langtang valley's remote Bharku village. A flower seller OPPOSITE parades his blooms through the streets of ancient Patan during the annual Matsyendranath Jatra festival.

Nepali People and Customs

BUTWAL (on the road to Bhairawa)
The **Tribeni Mela** (January to February). Coinciding with the Devighat Fair, it marks the transition from winter to spring with ritual bathing and traditional religious songs. Soon after, at the next new moon, the fair of Tribeni Mela, on the banks of the Narayani river, is characterized by colorful religious ceremonies and much feasting and happiness.

DEVIGHAT (near Trisuli Bazaar)
The **Devighat Mela** (January to February). A colorful Hindu fair that starts several days before the full moon and ends on the night of the full moon. Celebrants soak themselves in the Trisuli river and worship at the local temples.

HANUMAN DOKHA/SWAYAMBHUNATH (Kathmandu)
Sri Panchami (Basant Panchami) (January to February). This lively celebration of spring, on the fifth day of the new moon during the 10th month of the Nepali year, celebrates Saraswati, Brahma's consort and the Goddess of Learning, and Manjushri, legendary Buddhist patriarch of Kathmandu valley, regarded as the God of Learning.

At Kathmandu's Hanuman Dhoka palace, the King is anointed with a *tika* and slices of coconut while a 31-gun salute is fired and poems and songs are performed in honor of spring.

Temples are decorated with flowers, and schoolchildren parade in the streets, carrying their text and exercise books for blessing by Saraswati. The next day new primary students start their lessons. Older students go to Swayambhunath or Chabahil to ask Saraswati for success in their examinations.

And this being the time of the first plowing farmers perform special *pujas* in their fields to obtain a good summer crop.

KATHMANDU
Yomadhi Puni (December). A Newar festival, Yomadhi Puni is celebrated by worship and a banquet of cookies, *yomadhi*, made of rice flour stuffed with molasses and sesame seeds.

NATIONWIDE
Tribhuvan Jayanti — National Democracy Day (February). Nationwide parades, colorful processions, and cultural programs in honor of the late King Tribhuvan.
Phagu/Holi (February). Incredible, incandescent displays everywhere as Hindus and Buddhists celebrate the festival of light at the full moon, with colorful parades and ceremonies all over the country, especially commemorating the victory of Narsingha over the demon, Hiranya.
Constitution Day — Mahendra Jayanti

(December). National celebration in honor of the 1962 constitution that brought democracy to newly-awakened Nepal. Colorful processions and parades.
King Birendra's Birthday (December). Parades and pageantry as Nepal's 19 million citizens celebrate the birth of their monarch (47 years old in 1991).
National Unity Day — Prithvi Jayanti (December). Honors King Prithvi's seventeenth-century conquest of Kathmandu and the unification of Nepal.

PASHUPATINAH (and other places)
Makar Sankranti (January to February). A colorful Newar festival celebrated on the first day of Magh in honor of the sun, Vishnu, Shiva, Swasthani, and Bhagmati. Worshippers eat only clarified butter and refined molasses.
Shivratri (February). Prayers and devotion in honor of Shiva.

The Cities of Kathmandu Valley

KATHMANDU VALLEY

There's something about Nepal's mountain regions that make the far-fetched and fanciful believable. But perhaps, too, given the millenniums in which the Hindu faith has flourished in these parts, it's part of the national ethos — nowhere more so than in the fabled **Kathmandu valley,** seat of the Malla kings and repository of all Nepali art and culture.

Set 1,350 m (4,425 ft) above sea level, Kathmandu valley is ringed by gentle, evergreen hills touching about 2,370 m (7,800 ft), slate-blue in the misty haze of spring and summer. The eternal backdrop is the Himalaya. From the top of 2,200-m (7,175-ft)-high Nagarkot, you can see the Annapurna massif and Dhaulagiri in the west and Everest in the east.

BACKGROUND

Technology's graft on ancient in Nepal however is only skin deep. Aeons ago the valley was a lake which, perhaps in one of the cataclysmic earthquakes which occasionally shake this region, suddenly drained itself. Legend says it happened when the sage Manjushri used his sword to slash a gorge — now bridged by a Scottish-built suspension bridge — at Chobar about eight kilometers (five mile) south-west of the modern capital where the Bagmati, one of Kathmandu valley's major rivers, begins its plunge to the Ganges. There's a temple, of course, right by the gorge — Jal Binayak — that pays homage to the myth. Whatever the cause, the waters left behind a loam so rich that Kathmandu farmers can count themselves blessed. Abundant rains and sunshine combine with the loam to ensure that everything grows with profligate ease in the valley. No land goes fallow.

The ox-plough keeps dominion still over the grain and paddy fields and, among the brown-brick houses scattered across the fields without any perceptible form of planning, except in the built-up metropolitan area, most of Kathmandu's 300,000 people seem to have a small patch of ground to till. Indeed, from a distance, this richly fertile basin must look much the same as it did

when it was first farmed. Before then, the only communities lived near the shrines and pilgrimage sites which lay on the slopes of the encircling hills. The earliest settlements in the valley go back well beyond 2,500 years, their beginnings shrouded in ancient myths and legends.

Those that remain, such as the Buddhist stupas, evoke eras long before Kathmandu itself came into existence. Kathmandu valley is peppered with these stupas, of which the two most visible are Swayambhunath and Bodhnath.

KATHMANDU

Though Kathmandu came late to the western world's twentieth century — and its own twenty-first century — it has adapted gracefully. Tribhuvan International Airport, built in the 1960s, marks Nepal's emergence as one of the world's great tourist destinations, though the homey buildings of the terminal reflect the rural tempo of the people.

The capital has a network of broad malls, many lined with graceful avenues of trees, and a 27 km (17 mile) long ring road built by the Chinese during the 70's. Well-maintained highways connect Kathmandu with Patan, Bhaktapur and other towns in the valley.

GETTING AROUND THE TOWN AND VALLEY

Trolley Buses
A fleet of quiet, pollution-free trolley buses, provided by China, ply the 18 km (11 miles) between Tripureshwar and Bhaktapur and carry passengers for a virtual pittance.

Public Scooters
Kathmandu's three-wheel public scooters can carry up to six passengers. They always ply the same route, starting from Rani Pokhara. Black-and-yellow metered scooters are also available for private hire on payment of a full surcharge of 10 percent.

Rickshaws
Kathmandu's gaudy, honking rickshaws form part of the capital's vibrant street canvas.

OPPOSITE: Lush and verdant Kathmandu valley.

These large tricycles accommodate two passengers under cover in the back. Be sure that you agree on the fare before you set off and that the driver knows your destination. They should not cost more than taxis.

Taxis

Taxis, with white on black registration plates, ply throughout Kathmandu valley. Check that their meters are working and expect to pay an official surcharge of 10 percent. You can negotiate special half and full day rates.

Cycling

Cycling is one of the most popular means of exploring the capital and the valley. Bicycles can be hired from many shops in old Kathmandu and near the main hotels. Check that the bell, brakes, and lights work. If there are no lights carry a flashlight as the law is enforced. For a few coins children will take care of the bicycle when you visit a popular tourist spot. Elsewhere, it is safe to leave it unattended (but locked) while you go sightseeing.

Buses

In Kathmandu the main bus station is opposite Kanti Path, next to Tundikhel parade-ground. Minibuses depart from near the post office. For Pokhara, they leave from the Madras Coffee House (near Bhimsen Tower). In Pokhara, the bus terminal is close to the post office.

BUS SERVICES

TO: **Patan Gate:** 7 am to 7 pm FROM Ratna Park (in front of Indian Airlines office).

TO: **Jawalkhel, Lagankhel:** 7 pm FROM National Stadium.

TO: **Bhaktapur:** 7 am to 8 pm FROM National Stadium (trolley bus) and Baghbazar (local bus).

TO: **Pashupatinah, Bodhnath:** 6 am to 6 pm FROM Ratna Park.

TO: **Dhulikhel:** 6 am to 6 pm FROM Main Bus Station.

TO: **Barabise** (Chinese Road): 5:40 am to 4:45 pm FROM Main Bus Station.

TO: **Kodari** (mail bus): 6 am FROM near Post Office.

TO: **Balaju:** 7 am to 7 pm FROM near Post Office and Rani Pokhari.

TO: **Trisuli:** 7 am and 12:30 pm FROM Pakanajol.

TO: **Pokhara and Jomosom:** (trekking) 6:30 am to 9 am FROM near Post Office Main Bus Station.

TO: **Birganj** (connections to **Raxaul**, India): 6:30 am to 9 am FROM near Post Office Main Bus Station.

TO: **Janakpur** (connections to Indian border at **Jaleshwar**): 5 am FROM Main Bus Station.

TO: **Biratnagar** (connections with **Jogbani,** India): 5 am FROM near Post Office.

TO: **Kakar Bhitta** (connections to **Siliguri** and **Darjeeling**): 5 am FROM Main Bus Station.

TO: **Pokhara to Bhairawa** (connections to **Nautanwa,** India) 6 am to 9 am FROM near Post Office in Pokhara Town.

ACCOMMODATION

In Kathmandu city area accommodations range from deluxe to guest house standards. See ACCOMMODATION, page 195, in the TRAVELERS' TIPS section for general advice and tips on accommodation. The listing below is a selection based on value for money.

LUXURY

Hotel de l'Annapurna (221711. Burgarg Marg, Kathmandu. In the city center with 150 rooms, swimming pool, and tennis courts.

Hotel Yak and Yeti (413999 or 228255 or 228780, fax (997) 1 227782. PO Box 1016, Durbar Marg, Kathmandu. In the city center with 110 rooms, two suites, swimming pool, tennis courts, and shopping plaza.

Soaltee Oberoi (272550/5, fax (997) 1 271224. Tahachal, Kathmandu. 15 minutes from the city center, with 300 rooms, 10 suites, casino, swimming pool, tennis courts, and four restaurants.

The Everest Hotel (220667, fax (997) 1 226088. PO Box 689 Baneswar, Kathmandu. On Airport Road, with 155 rooms, rooftop bar and restaurant with fine mountain views, swimming pool, tennis courts, and shops.

FIRST CLASS

Hotel Kathmandu (418494 or 410786. Maharajgunj, Kathmandu.

Hotel Shangri-la (412999. Lazimpat, Kathmandu. Fine gardens, and friendly service.

Hotel Shankar (410152 or 410151. Lazimpat, Kathmandu. Converted from a former Rana palace, with 135 rooms and extensive gardens.
Hotel Sherpa (222585 or 228898. Durbar Marg, Kathmandu.

MODERATE

Hotel Woodlands (222673 or 220123 or 220623, fax (977) 1 226650. PO Box 760, Durbar Marg, Kathmandu. Centrally located and upgraded from its previous bed and breakfast only status.

Hotel Mount Makalu (223955 or 224616, telex 2489 ckcint np. 65 Dharma Path, Kathmandu.
Hotel Vajra (271545 or 272719. Bijeswori, Swayambhu, Kathmandu. Near Swayambhunath, is more a cultural experience than a hotel. It has a Tibetan painted rooftop bar, the October Gallery.
Ambassador (410432 or 414432, fax (977) 1 415432. Lazimpat, Owned by the same management as the Kathmandu Guest House, and is friendly and convenient.
Kathmandu Guest House (413632 or

Hotel Yellow Pagoda (220337 or 220338 or 220392, telex 2268 pagoda np. PO Box 373, Kantipath, Kathmandu. In the city center with 51 rooms.
Kathmandu Village Hotel (470770 or 472328, fax (977) 1 225131.PO Box 469, Kathmandu. 19 rooms, with carvings and antiques, in traditional bungalows, and rare, if remote from Kathmandu charm.

INEXPENSIVE

Hotel Blue Diamond (226320. PO Box 2134, Jyatha, Thamel, Kathmandu.
Hotel Garuda (416776 or 416340, fax (977) 1 223814 Att: Garuda. PO Box 1771, Kathmandu.

418733. Thamel. A longtime favorite of veteran travelers, with a splendid garden in the heart of Thamel.

RESTAURANTS

MAIN HOTEL RESTAURANTS AND BARS
Al'Fresco Restaurant (Soaltes Oberoi) (272550/6. Italian cuisine, including pizza. Open 11 am to 11 pm.
Arch Room (Hotel de l'Annapurna) (221711. Nepali and Continental cuisine. Rhapsody band nightly except Mondays.

Rickshaw operators ABOVE wait for customers in a Kathmandu street.

Open 7 to 10 am, 12:30 to 3 pm and 7 to 10:30 pm.

Arniko Chinese Room (Hotel de l'Annapurna) (221711. Szechuan and Cantonese cuisine. Open 12:30 to 3 pm and 7 to 11 pm.

Bugles and Tigers (The Everest Hotel) (220567. Bar. Open 4 to 11 pm.

Casino Nepal (Soaltes Oberoi) (272550/6. Games: Flush, Baccarat, Paplu, Roulette, Pontoon, Blackjack and Jackpot.

Chimney Restaurant (Hotel Yak and Yeti) (228255 or 228780. Continental and Russian cuisine. Large fireplace. Open 6:30 to 11 pm.

Damara (Hotel Woodlands) (222683 or 220123 or 220623. Discotheque every night, free for guests and members Rs 350 per couple. Open 9 pm to 1 am.

Explorer's Restaurant (Hotel Vajra) (271-545 or 272719. Continetal, Tibetan and Nepali cuisine. Open fireplace, classical and folk music on the *yang-jin*. Open every day.

Far Pavillion Restaurant (The Everest Hotel) (220567. Indian cuisine; *ghazals* singer nightly except Tuesday. Open 7 to 11 pm.

Ghar-e-Kabab (Hotel de l'Annapurna) (221711. Indian cuisine, live classical music from 7 to 8:30 pm; *ghazals* singing by Zulfikar until 11 pm. Open noon to 3 pm and 7 to 11 pm.

Gurkha Grill (Soaltes Oberoi) (272550/6. French and continetal cuisine. Live contemporary music. Open 7 pm to 1 am.

Himalayan Tavern (The Everest Hotel) (220567. Drinks and live entertainment. Open 6:30 to 10 pm (closed Sundays).

Himalchuli Restaurant (Soaltes Oberoi) (272550/6. Indian and Nepali cuisine. Nepali Folk dancing 7 to 9 pm, *ghazals* until 11 pm except Tuesdays.

Juneli Bar (Hotel de l'Annapurna) (221711. Drinks and snacks. Jazz band plays nightly except Mondays. Open 9 am to midnight.

Kokonor Restaurant (Hotel Shangri-la) (412999. French cuisine. Open 7 pm to midnight.

Naachghar Restaurant (Hotel Yak and Yeti) (228255 or 228780. Nepali Indian and international cuisine. Traditional dancing nightly at 8:15 except Wednesdays. Open 6:30 to 11 pm.

Pazeeka (Hotel Kathmandu) (418534. Mughlai, Tandoori and Dum Pakt. Open 7 to 11 pm.

Rooftop Garden and Pagoda Bar (Hotel Vajra) (271545 or 272719. Alfresco lunch and dinner. Open noon to 10 pm.

Sherpa Grill (Hotel Sherpa) (222585 or 228898. Continental and Indian cuisine, dance band every night. Open noon to 3 pm and 7 to 10 pm.

Sherpaland (The Everest Hotel, rooftop) (220567. Tibetan, Manchurian and Chinese cuisine, nightly barbecue. Open noon to 2 pm and 7 to 10 pm.

Tian-Shan (Hotel Shangri-la) (412999. Cantonese and Szechuan cuisine. Open noon to 2:30 pm and 7 to 11 pm.

OTHER RESTAURANTS AND BARS

Coppers Restaurant (417095. Tridevi Marg, Thamel, Kathmandu. Continental cuisine. Open 7 am to 10 pm (breakfast, lunch and dinner).

Koto Restaurant and Bar (226025. Thamel, Kathmandu. Japanese cuisine. Open 11:30 am to 3 pm and 6 to 10 pm (closed Sundays).

Newari woman vending fresh fruit ABOVE on curbside. OPPOSITE TOP View of Kathmandu and its varied architecture; BOTTOM shops in a Kathmandu bazaar.

Kushi-Fuji (220545. New King's Way, Kathmandu. Japanese cuisine (sukiyaki, tempura and teriyaki).

La Dolce Vita (419612. Thamel, Kathmandu. Italian cuisine and bar.

Mero Pub (226016. Durbar Marg, Kathmandu. European style bar; light meals.

Omni Restaurant and Bar (226412. Tridevi Marg, Thamel, Kathmandu. Pekinese and Cantonese cuisine. Open 11 am to 10 pm.

Ras Rang Chinese Restaurant and Bar (416086 or 410432. Lazimat Plaza, Lazimat, Kathmandu. Szechuan and Hakka cuisine.

Rum Doodle Thamel, Kathmandu. Steaks and burgers, also vegetarian dishes. Bar.

Sunkosi Restaurant (226520. Nepali and Tibetan cuisine.

SEEING THE CITY

Kathmandu itself is neatly divided into two separate districts distinguished by their different architecture. In the west there is the **Old City** and **Tundikhel**, Kathmandu's Hyde Park, at its easternmost periphery. The division between the two districts is marked by the Kanti Path, or King's Way, which runs from north to south, skirting the Royal Palace and cutting across the diplomatic precinct of Lazimpat to continue as far north as the reclining Vishnu of Buddhanilkanth. Kathmandu city's most visible landmark is **Bhimsen Tower, Dharahara**, a 70-m (200-ft)-high edifice. Built as a watch station, it was damaged in the 1934 earthquake that rumbled through Kathmandu, and later rebuilt. For safety reasons, however, it's now closed to the public — thus denying what was a popular and spectacular 360 degree panoramic view of the city.

Between the Tower and the Singh Durbar— built by the Ranas and once the world's largest private palace — is the **Martyrs' Memorial,** an impressive modern archway honoring those who gave their lives to overthrow the Ranas. There are also four black marble busts of rebel leaders — Shukra Raj Shastri, Dharma Bhakta, Dasharath Chand, and Gangalal — executed in 1940, either by hanging or firing squad, when Juddha Shumsher was premier.

Tundikhel

Tundikhel, with its royal pavilion, is where the nation celebrates state occasions and festivals with colorful parades, horse races, and acrobatic shows. It's decorated with statues of the six Gurkha VCs of the two world wars and around the park are equestrian statues. The park, says local lore, was the home of a mythical giant, Guru Mapa, and each year, during the Ghode Jatra festival, a buffalo and mounds of rice are laid out in supplication to Guru Mapa, to keep the peace.

Narainhiti Royal Palace and Singh Durbar

Two buildings of the twentieth century deserve mention, the imposing **Narainhiti Royal Palace,** built during the reign of King Rana Bahadur Shah and extended in 1970 to mark the wedding of Crown Prince Birendra who is now the king, and Kathmandu's most impressive architectural work, the **Singh Durbar.** With the restoration of Royal power in 1951, its 1,000 rooms, set in 31 hectares (77 acres) of ground, were put to use as government offices. Sadly, much of it was burnt down in 1973. Its most impressive feature, the mirrored Durbar hall furnished with a throne, statues, portraits of dead rulers, and a line of stuffed tigers, still survives. Today the Nepali Parliament, the Rastriya Panchayat, meets in the Singh Durbar which is also the headquarters of the national broadcasting system. Radio Nepal has been on the air for some years but television came late. The first transmissions began in May 1986.

Swayambhunath

The stupa of Swayambhunath looks down from the top of a 100-m (350-ft)-high hill in the west of the city, the rays of the rising sun setting fire to its burnished copper spire as it floats above the sea of early morning mist that fills the valley. Buddha's all-seeing eyes, in vivid hues, adorn all four sides of the base of the Spire, keeping constant vigil over Kathmandu. Many believe this sacred ground protects the divine light of Swayambhunath, the Self Existent One who, when the waters drained from the valley, emerged as a flame from a lotus blossom atop this hill.

Man worshipped here long before the advent of Buddhism, perhaps at a projecting stone which now forms the central core of the stupa. Here, it is said, Manjushri discovered the Kathmandu lotus which floated in its ancient lake.

The earliest known work was carried out in the fifth century by King Manadeva — confirmed by an inscription dated AD 460, some 600 years after emperor Ashoka is reputed to have paid homage at the site. Destroyed by Bengali troops in the mid-fourteenth century, it was rebuilt by the seventeenth-century Malla monarch, King Pratap, who added a long stairway leading to

which, when they dropped to the ground as he had his hair cut, sprang up as monkeys. It is also said that each strand of his hair which fell also sprang up again — as a tree!

On the stupa, only Buddha's all seeing eyes are depicted; disdaining the sounds of praise, ears are omitted, and abjuring the need for speech, so is the mouth. There is no nose, but only the Nepali letter which symbolizes both oneness and virtue, *dharma*.

Mounted on a brass pedestal before the stupa is the thunderbolt, or *vajra* — so powerful that it can destroy anything —

it, two adjoining temples, and a symbolic thunderbolt at the top.

The stupa is shaped like a lotus flower and in the last two thousand years saints, monks, kings, and others have built monasteries, idols, temples, and statues which now encircle the original stupa and the entire hilltop. Today pilgrims and the curious climb laboriously up King Pratap's 365 flagstone steps. Even if you have no sense of religion or history, you'll find the antics of the monkeys, which inhabit the temples and the shops, fascinating — they use the handrails of the steps as a slide — and the views over Kathmandu as breathtaking as the stiff climb. Nepali legend says the monkeys are descended from the lice in Manjushri's hair

representing the divine strength of Lord Indra, King of the Heavens, in contrast to Buddha's all-pervading knowledge. Beneath the pedestal stand the 12 animals of the Tibetan zodiac: rat, bull, tiger, hare, dragon, serpent, horse, sheep, monkey, rooster, jackal and pig.

There's a daily service in the monastery, or gompa, facing the stupa — a rowdy and, to western ears, discordant clanking of instruments, blaring horns, and a melee of saffron-robed worshippers. The eternal flame, Goddesses Ganga and Jamuna, is enshrined in a cage behind the stupa where a priest makes regular offerings.

Opposite, on a neighboring hill, the serene image of Saraswati, Goddess of Learning, gazes on the often frantic throng around Swayambhunath in benign astonishment.

Bodhnath

Yet for all its size, the stupa takes second place to the one north-east of the capital. Dedicated to Bodhnath, the god of wisdom, it's the largest stupa in Nepal—an immense mound surrounded by a self-contained Tibetan township and ringed by the inevitable prayer wheels, each given a twirl as devotees circle the shrine clockwise. Most worshippers here are from Tibet. The Bodhnath lama is said to be a reincarnation of the original Dalai Lama, for the stupa's obscure origins are tenuously linked to Lhasa, ancestral home of the now exiled spiritual leader.

Legend says it was built by the daughter of a swineherd, a woman named Kangma. She asked the King of Nepal for as much land as the hide of a buffalo would cover on which to build the stupa. When the king agreed, Kangma sliced the hide into thin ribbons which were joined into one and laid out to form the square in which the stupa stands. A relic of the Buddha is said to lie within the solid dome which symbolizes water and is reached by 13 steps, again symbolizing the 13 stages of of enlightenment from which the monument derives its name, *bodh* meaning enlightenment and *nath*, meaning God.

Saffron and magenta-robed Tibetan monks celebrate their colorful rituals with worshippers chanting prayer verse, mantras, and clapping their hands as travelers, especially those heading for the high Himalaya, seek blessings for their journey.

With about 5,000 exiles living in the valley, Kathmandu has a distinctly Tibetan ambience with a number of new monasteries around Bodhnath and one, in the form of a castle, on the wooded slopes beside Gorakhnath cave. This guards the footprints of a fourteenth-century sage who lived in the cave as a hermit. Not far from this cave, the Tibetans have built another monastery — commemorating Guru Padma Rimpoche Sambhava, a saint who rode down to Kathmandu from Tibet to conquer a horde of demons. But Tibetans are just one of the many colorful communities who have made their home among the original inhabitants of the Kathmandu valley, the Newars. These hardy folk and their extended families observe a constant round of rituals worshipping the many deities whose blessings, and curses rule their daily lives, a complicated mix of Hinduism, Buddhism, and animism.

Natural wealth, also, blossoms in this fecund spot like a second Eden. Nepal's flora enchanted early European visitors who exported it lock, stock, and root to their own climes. In the words of Nobel laureate Rudyard Kipling:

Still the world is wondrous large —
seven seas from marge to marge —
And it holds a vast of various kinds of man;
And the wildest dreams of Kew
are the facts of Kathmandu

Godavari Royal Botanical Gardens

Though sadly deforested during the last half century, perhaps the easiest place to see much of Nepal's unique flora is **Godavari Royal Botanical Gardens,** at the foot of the valley's highest point, 2,750-m (9,000-ft)-high Pulchoki Hill, where the sacred waters of the Godavari spring from a natural cave.

Buddhist monks OPPOSITE at Bodhnath stupa in Kathmandu valley and novice monks ABOVE at a Kathmandu monastery.

But Godavari's real majesty is its forests and floral sanctuaries.

Godavari has some 66 different species of fern, 115 orchids, 77 cacti and succulents, and about 200 trees and shrubs as well as many ornamentals — only a small proportion of the country's 6,500 botanical species. It also has orchid and cacti houses, and the fern, Japanese, physic, and water gardens. Throughout, by lily ponds and on grassy slopes, the visitor finds rest and shade in thatched shelters.

Every 12 years, thousands of pilgrims

journey from all over Nepal and India to bathe in the divine waters of the Godavari.

Changu Narayan temple

On another hilltop stands Kathmandu's oldest temple, Changu Narayan, in almost derelict splendor; its struts and surroundings are detailed with hundreds of delicately-carved erotic depictions. Founded around the fourth century AD, it represents the very best in Nepali art and architecture. It's hard indeed to imagine a more stunning example of what the Kathmandu valley is

ABOVE: A woman prostrates herself in prayer at Swayambhunath. OPPOSITE: Giant Buddha statue at the ancient Swayambhunath temple, Kathmandu.

all about. Woodwork, metalwork, and stonework combine in dazzling harmony nowhere to more effect than in the sculptures of Bhupatindra, the seventeenth-century Malla king, and his queen. There's also a man-sized figure of Garuda with a coiled snake around his neck, close to the country's oldest stone inscription, to record the military feats of King Mana Deva who ruled from AD 464 to 491. Though fire and earthquake have often damaged Changu Narayan and its environs, this link with its ancient past still remains close to an image of a lion-faced Vishnu ripping the entrails out of his enemy.

Life's rhythms here in the cobblestone square are unchanged, too, with its pilgrim's platforms and lodges, *dharmsalas,* surrounding it and the central temple. Cows, chickens, pye-dogs and snot-nosed urchins wander around while women hang their saris out to dry in the warm evening sunlight, which like some pastoral idyll of old, bathes the red brick in glowing orange.

Pashupatinah

From the high point of the hill Kathmandu's majestic panorama unfolds in a 360 degree sweep — and down there, at **Deopatan,** is Pashupatinah, holiest and most famous of all Nepal's Hindu shrines.

Set on the banks of the Bagmati, where it leaves a once-forested gorge, it's reserved exclusively for Hindu worshippers. For a better perspective, there's a series of terraces on the opposite bank — thickly populated with hundreds of rhesus monkeys, regarded by Hindu believers as kin of the gods, sun, and stars — where it's possible to study the classic proportions of the pagoda's gilded copper roof, sadly surrounded by tatty, corroded tin roofs and despoiled by higgledy-piggledy power lines. There was a temple here as early as the first century AD and long before then— in the third century BC — what may well have been the valley's first settlement.

In the age of mythology Lord Shiva and his consort lived here by this tributary of the holy Ganges and it's reckoned a more sacred place of pilgrimage than even Varanasi on the Ganges. The Hindu holy men, sadhus, dressed in loin cloths and marked with cinder ash, looking immensely wise and benign — but still wanting cash for picture sessions — sit cross-legged everywhere meditating, surrounded by the temple's delicate gold and silver filigree work.

To the visitor, the most astonishing thing about almost any Hindu shrine is its shabbiness. It's best to bear in mind that after centuries of use these are not monuments or museums but living places of worship, in many cases sadly in need of immediate work to preserve their glories. Pashupatinah is no exception. Much of the exterior is close to collapse, stained with the patina of centuries

well-planned but strongly fenced natural sanctuary. The tiger, a notorious maneater, once terrorized villagers on the Terai Plains.

New Road (Juddha Sadak)

Old Kathmandu has remained virtually unchanged throughout the centuries except for New Road built over the devastation caused by the 1934 earthquake. Running west from the Tundikhel, it ends at Basantpur and the Durbar Square, in front of the old palace. New Road — Juddha Sadak — is the pulsating mainstream of this fascinating city,

and with litter lying everywhere. Its most precious treasure is its carved Shivalings or Shiva's phallus, stepped in a representation of the female sex organ, or yoni, of Parvati, Shiva's consort.

Royal Game Sanctuary

Pashupatinah is not far from the forested slopes of Gokarna, close to the open glades and myriad birds of a Royal Game Sanctuary that's now a safari park for citizen's recreation. For those who fancy a touch of Maharajah-style travel, a lone elephant plods across the nine-hole golf course among herds of grazing chital, rare blackbuck and other deer, rabbits, monkeys, and pheasants. There's also a Royal Bengal tiger in a

where you can find everything from the latest electronic appliances, cosmetics, expensive imported food and drugs, to jewels and priceless antiques.

Halfway along is a small square shaded by a pipal tree, where intellectuals meet to philosophize and debate. Facing the Crystal Hotel at the end of New Road is a supermarket close to a small isolated shrine. There's also a statue of Juddha Shamsher Rana, prime minister from 1932 to 1945, who masterminded the building of New Road.

Running off this thoroughfare are a series of paved alleys, each with their squares with corner *patis*, central *chaityas*, and occasional temples, between traditional terraced houses. The medieval ambience is an

authentic time warp, save for the gossiping crowds and the whine of transistor radios. Westward is **Basantpur** — it takes its name from a large tower looming over the massive Hanuman Dhoka Palace — a large open space where the royal elephants were once kept. But when New Road was completed, the square turned into a marketplace, to be replaced by a brick platform built for King Birendra's coronation celebrations in 1975. Touts sell an assortment of cheap bric-a-brac — local trinkets, bracelets, bangles, religious images, swords, and knives — all over the square.

Famous **"Freak Street"**, the end of the rainbow for the dropouts and the hippies of the '60s, who strummed Beatles and Beach Boys numbers on their guitars, is in Basantpur, just off New Road which leads into the main Durbar Square opposite the Kumari Bahal. Pause a while to gather your breath when you enter the square, but not from the exertion of getting there. It's a sweep of incredible instant images: shuttered, carved, leaded windows and timbered gables, metal and stone statues of man and beasts and gods and goddesses, in every material including gold and silver, and buildings both oriental and baroque and many other styles, all quite unlike anything anywhere else in the world. The only equals this place has are just a few kilometers down the road in **Patan** and **Bhaktapur** — and nowhere else. There's scholarly dispute about some of the historical detail of each of these pristine works of art and architecture, but that should be of no concern to the visitor.

Durbar Square

Immediately you enter the square there's a **Narayan temple** with a raised seventeenth-century grey-stone statue of Vishnu's personal, mount Garuda, in a kneeling position outside. What's inside nobody's quite sure since the inner sanctum has long been closed.

Facing it is the **Gaddi Baithak,** an ornate annex of the old Royal Palace built early in the twentieth century by a Rana premier, Chandra Shamsher, during the reign of King Tribhuvan Bir Bikram Shah Dev. It's here that Nepal's top brass gather with the Royal Family to celebrate Indra Jatra and other festivals and state occasions. There's a

throne for King Birendra in the main room which is lined with portraits of his ancestors.

On the other side of the square, behind the Narayan Mandir, is a temple dedicated to **Kamdeva,** God of Love and Lust, built by King Bhupatindra's mother, Riddhi Laxmi, and adorned with an immaculate sculpture of Vishnu with Lakshmi. Close by, on a flank of Vishnumati Bridge, is the fourteenth-century wooden **Kasthamandap** built from the wood of a single tree from which it derives its Sanskrit name: *Kastha*, wood, and *mandap*, pavilion. Renovated in the seventeenth century, it's from this structure also that Kathmandu takes its name. Built in the pagoda-style, with balconies and raised platforms, it was for many years a place for Tantric worship but is now a shrine with an image of Gorakhnath, a deified yoga disciple of Shiva, as its centerpiece.

On the corner of Chikan Mugal, opposite this inspiring fountainhead of the capital, is the lion house, **Singha Satal** — built from the surplus timber left over from the Kasthamandap — with a second-story balcony and several small shops on the ground floor. Standing in the shadows of the Laxmi Narayan is a small nineteenth-century temple, built by King Surendra Bir Bikram Shah Dev and dedicated to **Ganesh,** the elephant-headed God, where the kings of Nepal worship before their coronation. Near the temple to the God of Love and Lust is an eighteenth-century temple dedicated to **Shiva** and **Parvati, Nava Yogini**, guarded by lion statues. Opposite this is another dedicated to the **Goddess Bhagvati.**

Move along past the Big Bell, and a stone temple dedicated to Vishnu, and you'll come to a **Krishna temple** where you will be diagonally opposite the entrance of the Durbar Square's inner treasury, the **Hanuman Dhoka** piazza, which derives its name from a large statue of Hanuman the monkey-god and the Nepali word for gate, *dhoka*.

All this is something of a Royal mall. For three centuries or more, the kings of Nepal have been enthroned here. The first most noticeable feature is the house on the corner

OPPOSITE: A treasury of ornate medieval architecture adorns the cities of Kathmandu valley including TOP the priceless carved windows of a palace in Kathmandu.

overlooking the Durbar Square which has three distinctive carved windows on one side where the Malla kings used to watch processions and festivals. Two of them are carved from ivory, a discovery made in 1975 during preparations for King Birendra's coronation.

Next door you'll find another large, latticed window with a gargoyle of a face — a grinning mask in white of Bhairav — carved in the eighteenth century by Rana Bahadur Shah to ward off evil. It's still there offering benedictions. Each Indra Jatra festival thou-

sands clamor to siphon off sanctified rice beer, *jand*, from the back of its mouth as it's poured through the grinning orifice. They'll be particularly blessed, it's believed, even if cursed with a hangover next day.

The old **Royal Palace** — some parts of it have withstood the ravages of six centuries — stands next door and is difficult to miss not only for its scale and form but also because of its massive golden door, guarded by stone lions. Elaborately decorated with intricate motifs and emblems, it's a fitting entrance for kings-to-be. In the courtyard inside, on 24 February 1975, King Birendra was crowned King of Nepal. At each corner of the palace stands a colored tower representing one of Kathmandu's four cities — the fourth is Kirtipur.

The Hanuman statue stands at the gate and just by its right-hand side a low fence guards an inscribed seventeenth-century dedication to the Goddess Kalika on a plaque set into the wall. The inscription in at least 15 different languages — among them English, French, Persian, Arabic, Hindi,

Kashmiri and, of course, Nepali — was written by King Pratap Malla, a gifted linguist and poet. Facing the Hanuman Dhoka there's the sixteenth-century **Jagannath temple**, outstanding for the erotic carvings on its struts.

But all these are trifles compared to the **Taleju temple** that rises from a mound to the right of the palace, considered the most beautiful in Kathmandu. Dedicated to Taleju Bhavani, the tutelary goddess of the Malla dynasty who was a consort of Shiva, the three-story temple reaches about 36 m (120 ft) high, and each of the three pagoda roofs is gilded with copper and embellished with hanging bells. Only open to the public once a year, nobody but members of the Royal family are allowed to enter the main sanctum. For anything its equal you'll have to move on to Bhaktapur or Patan and, unless you want a surfeit of erotica in temples and statues, by the time you've walked around both you'll have enough memories of Kathmandu's man-made treasures to last your lifetime.

Durbar Square Environs

Some distance south of the Durbar Square, faced in ceramic, there's a three-storied temple to **Adko Narayan** one of the four main Vishnu temples of Kathmandu, guarded by an image of Garuda and lions, and liberally adorned with erotic carvings on the struts that support the second story. Nearby there's a small temple dedicated to Shiva, **Hari Shanker.** Walk on to a crossroad where the struts of the three-storied seventeenth-century Shiva temple, **Jaisi Dewal,** on top of a seven-stepped pyramid, has very finely carved erotica. Set in a yoni behind it is a massive, free-shaped lingam — truly erect stone. It's thought the lingam may date back to the Lichhavi era.

Not far away is more classic erotica, on the struts of the **Ram Chandra Mandir** — tiny, delicately but explicitly detailed carvings. Next you come to a stupa ruined in the fourteeenth century the Takan Bahal, a round stucco mound covered by a brick building.

From here you can wander around the narrow streets and alleys of the southern end of the **Old Town,** discovering ancient houses and more ancient religious shrines.

One, **Machhendra temple** plays a significant role during the Seto Machhendranath festival when the deity's chariot must be driven three times around the temple as part of the final ceremony, after which the chariot is dismantled and the image returned in a colorful palanquin to its principal temple near Asan Tole.

South-west of Durbar Square, near the Bishnumati bridge, is a revered shrine dedicated to Bhimsen, the god of traders and artisans, whose shops occupy its ground floor. Another manifestation of Shiva, Bhim-

fourteenth-century carvings of the female form. It faces a painted metal door with two figures, one with four eyes, while above, an attractive woman's face appears out of a carved window frame, entrance to the house of the deity, Kanga Ajima.

Indra Chowk

The Indra Chowk, an area noted for its silk bazaar with many fine blankets and textiles, including woolen shawls, north-east of Durbar Square, is approached through the six-meter (20-ft)-wide Makhan Tole, flanked by

sen has been worshipped in the valley since the seventeenth century. In the days when Nepal's main commercial trade was with Tibet, every 12 years this was carried to Lhasa on the Silk Road. There are some Buddhist stupas next to the temple.

In the opposite direction, to the north of Durbar Square, is a popular three-storied temple, the **Nara Devi,** guarded by red and white lions, dedicated to one of the Ashta Matrikas. Inside women prostrate themselves surrounded by dazzling ceramic tiles and paintings. Nearby is the three-tiered **Narsingha temple** with its image of Vishnu with a lion's head. Along the same road is an open courtyard with a Swayambhunath-like stupa, **Yaksha Bahal,** with four sensual

a many-hued facade with wooden balconies and columns. Six streets radiate out of Indra Chowk. Various peddlers wander among the cloth and flower sellers, past a dried-fish market into the bead bazaar where the colors of the tawdry bangles and necklaces dazzle the eye. The Chowk is noted for its three temples, of which the most important is a three-storied house to the south, with white, purple, and green ceramic tiles, yellow windows and two balconies, from one of which hang four gilded griffins. The temple holds a highly revered shrine to Akash Bhairav. During the Indra Jatra festival a

Erotic carving OPPOSITE on an ancient Kathmandu valley temple. ABOVE: Religious icon in front of Kathmandu's Jagannath temple.

The Cities of Kathmandu Valley

large image of Bhairav is displayed in the square when a huge lingam pole is raised in the center. Other important shrines and buildings in the Chowk include a highly venerated shrine to **Ganesh** and the **Shiva Mandir,** a simpler version of Patan's Krishna temple. This solid stone building is set above a four-stepped plinth where carpet sellers lay out their wares.

Beyond Indra Chowk, the open space of **Khel Tole** is a fast and furious Nepali bazaar area, a never-ending bedlam and hubbub, with a constant stream of shoppers

and peddlers, sightseers, even cars, forging through the narrow street watched by families from the balconies of their houses.

Seto Machhendranath

At the other end of the Chowk, to the east, past a small shrine smeared with blood, is one of Nepal's most revered temples; Seto Machhendranath is at the center of a monastic courtyard, its entrance guarded by two splendid brass lions. Each evening, beneath the porch that leads to the courtyard, musicians gather and chant sacred verses, gazing at the temple as it rises behind a foreground of steles, chaityas and carved pillars, its gilt-copper roof glowing in the evening sun.

The shrine guards the image of Kathmandu valley's most compassionate deity, Padmapani Avalokiteshwara, also known as Jammadyo or Machhendra. Once a year, around March and April, this is taken from the temple for chariot processions through the city during the Seto Machhendra festival. Built at an unknown date, the temple was restored in the early seventeenth century. Around the inside courtyard are many shops selling a variety of goods — wool, paper prints, cloth, string, ribbons, beads, curios, Nepali caps, and pottery. Near the temple, on a street corner, is a small, Tantric temple, the three-storied **Lunchun Lunbun Ajima** which carries, between portraits of the king and queen, erotic carvings.

Asan Tole

North-east from here is Asan Tole, the capital's rice bazaar, where mountain porters gather seeking employment. It's a large open space with three temples, including the three-storied **Annapurna temple**, notable for the upturned corners of its gilded roofs. Many come to pay homage at its shrine, which contains nothing more than a pot. There's a a mini-Narayan shrine near the center of the square and a smaller Ganesh temple.

Kanti Path

Leaving Asan Tole to wander through the fascinating narrow alleys and byways of this ancient Old Town you eventually come to **Kantipath,** one of the city's main thoroughfares, with a notable *ghat* on one side of it, the **Rani Pokhari**. In the sixteenth century the wife of the Malla King Pratap built a temple in the center to honor her young son after his death, but it later collapsed. Since then a new shrine has been built. On the side of the lake stands Trichandra College, built by the Ranas, with its **clock tower** and the wide expanse of the Tundikhel and the landmark column of the **Bhimsen Tower**.

If you head north-west from Asan Tole through the city's vegetable and fruit market, the street becomes narrower and narrower until you reach a door that opens into the **Haku Bahal** courtyard. This has a notable carved window balcony, supported by small carved struts, and an exquisitely

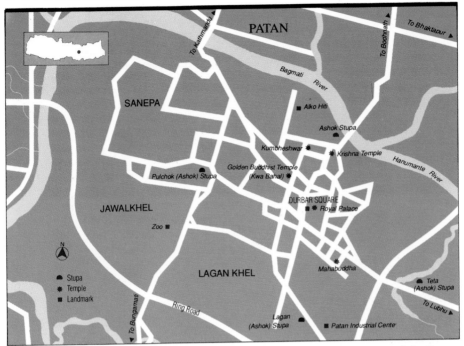

carved door frame, all of the seventeenth century. Nearby is the three-storied **Ugra-tara temple** dedicated to the relief of eye infections and ailments. The temple wall is adorned with reading spectacles that have been donated to whatever Hindu deity cares for the gift of sight.

Walk on now until you see the two-storied **Ikha Narayan temple** with its magnificent four-armed Sridhara Vishnu, dating from the tenth to eleventh century, flanked by Lakshmi and Garuda. There's another monument to a healing deity, Viasha Dev, the God of Tooth-ache, opposite this shrine. The idea is that you hammer a nail into this large piece of wood and thus nail down the evil spirits causing the pain. If all this fails, there's a street of friendly, neighborhood dentists, complete with off-the-peg molars of all shapes and smiles, in the nearby lane.

If you continue north, past a sixteenth-century Narayan temple, you'll find one of the capital's oldest and most remarkable antiquities — a carved black stone **fifth-century image of Buddha;** and beyond that a **bas-relief Shiva-Parvati** as Uma Maheshwar set in a brick case. On now to a passage guarded by lions that leads into a monastery courtyard containing the **shrine of Srigha**

Chaitya, a miniature likeness of the Swayambhunath stupa. It's believed that those too old or sick to climb the hill to Swayambhunath can earn the same merit by making pilgrimage here.

PATAN

ACCOMMODATION AND RESTAURANTS

Most visitors stay in Kathmandu city area and the selection of accommodation in Patan is limited. However the following can be recommended:

INEXPENSIVE
Aloha Inn (522796, telex 2489 aloha np. PO Box 1562 (Kathmandu) Jawalakhel, Patan.
Hotel Himalaya (523900. Patan.
Laxmi Hotel (523968 or 521138. Jawalakhel, Patan.
Summit Hotel (521894 or 521810, fax (977) 1 523737. PO Box 1406, Kupondole Height, Patan. Near the city center, with 30 traditional-style rooms, spectacular mountain views,

Shiva OPPOSITE in his most terrifying aspect, on a mask carved in the eighteenth century as an incarnation of Bhairav.

conference facilities, swimming pool, and craft shop.

Chalet Restaurant (Hotel Himalaya) (523900. Serves a selection of Indian, Chinese and European dishes (Japanese on request) from noon to 2:30 pm and 7 to 11 pm.

Base Coffee Shop (Hotel Himalaya) (523900. Breakfast and light snacks. Open 7 am to 11 pm.

Pasha Restaurant (Aloha Inn) (522796. Chinese, Indian and European dishes. Open noon to 10 pm.

Blue Fox Restaurant Jawakhel, Patan. Noted for *momos* and cakes.

SHOPPING

To discover the variety as well as relative values and prices travelers should first survey the products and visit the shops.

The best of **Tibetan carpets,** old and new, are found at Jawalkhel, near Patan, in the **Tibetan Refugee Center,** and many shops.

The **Cheez Beez Bhandar, (Nepali Handicraft Center)** near Jawalkhel, sells **handicrafts** from all parts of Nepal.

Excellent quality **antiques and rare art objects** are on display at the **Tibet Ritual Art Gallery,** Durbar Marg, above the Sun Kosi restaurant, run by two experts in the subject.

Woodcarvings, metalwork, and thangkas religious paintings can be seen at **Patan Industrial Estate,** and the **Bhaktapur Crafts Center** in Dattatraya Square.

The main shops in Kathmandu for **imported articles** are in and around New Road. Shops selling handicrafts to tourists are centered around Durbar Marg and the big hotels.

It is forbidden to export thangkas and bronzes if they are more than 100 years old.

SEEING THE CITY

Durbar Square

Right at the entrance to this city's Durbar Square, another Royal mall, is an octagonal **Krishna temple,** nearby an immense copper bell cast in the eighteenth century by Vishnu Malla and his Queen, Chandra Lakshmi. Traditionally, it's deep sonorous clanging summoned worshippers, but it was also used as an early warning system in the event of emergencies: fires, earthquakes, and raiding armies. How the people of Patan distinguished the difference between the call to divine duty and the need to make a getaway remains unexplained.

Set next to the Krishna temple is a three-storied **Vishnu temple** notable for its tympanums, the ornate triangular recesses set between the cornices of its low gables. One

Patan's Durbar Square holds matchless treasure of medieval architecture and art.

of Patan's oldest temples, **Charanarayan,** is believed to have been built around 1566 by King Purendra, although lately architectural historians suspect it belongs to the seventeenth century. The struts of this two-storied pagoda building, embellished with lively erotica — either inspiring or inspired by the Kama Sutra — will impress enthusiasts of gymnastics.

The centrally placed **Krishna temple** is unmistakable. One of the most beautiful temples in the country, generally regarded as a masterpiece of Nepali architecture, it's

tury Royal Palace was badly damaged, but its ornate gates, delicately-carved struts, statues, open courtyards, and many rooms — conference halls, sleeping chambers, kitchens and so forth — remain to recall the glory of Malla architectural splendor. One of these many splendors is the eighteenth-century **Taleju temple,** built as an additional storey to the palace itself and tragically destroyed in 1934. Now rebuilt, it's open only 10 days each year, during the September to October Chaitra Dasain festival. It's smaller temple — **Taleju Bhavani**

built entirely of limestone, a legacy of King Siddhi Narsimha Malla, who reigned for 41 years in the seventeenth century. The focus of thousands of devotees each year celebrating Krishna's birthday around August to September is the narrative carving on the frieze, depicting the stories of the epic Mahabharata and Ramayana. It was the king's son, Shri Nivasa Malla, who in 1682 restored the undated Bhimsen temple after it was damaged by fire. Since then, following the 1934 earthquake, it's been restored once more. The gods make Kathmandu tremble frequently.

Not only the gods. When King Prithvi Narayan Shah swept into the valley in 1768 to oust the Mallas, Patan's fourteenth-cen-

— though not as impressive, is held more sacred.

Of its statuary, Patan's most imposing monument is the sculpture of **King Yoga-narendra Malla** seated on a lotus atop a six-meter (20-ft)-high pillar in front of the **Degatule Taleju temple.** He ruled at the beginning of the seventeenth century and is the subject of a still popular belief among Patan folk that one day he will return to take up his rule again. For this reason, one door and one window in the palace always remain open to welcome him.

Patan's treasures are not confined to the immediate precincts of its Durbar Square. Five minutes walk away there's a **Golden Buddhist temple,** and another Buddha shrine, Mahabuddha, two kilometers (1.2 miles) distant. There's also **Kumbhesh-war,** one of the two five-storied temples in Kathmandu valley where Shiva is believed to stay for six months every year during the winter before leaving to spend his summer with Parvati on the crest of Gaurisankar.

Around Patan
At the southwestern edge of Patan is **Ja-walkhel,** site of the valley's largest Tibetan refugee camp. This area is a center for Ti-

South of Patan, various vehicle and walking tracks line settlements and sacred sites of the one-time capital. West of the Bagmati river are **Kirtipur** and its satellite hamlets, **Panga** and **Nagaon.** The twin settlements of **Bungamati** and **Khokan**a lie on either side of the sacred Karma Binayak site. There is a road leading to the **Lele valley,** and a trail to **Godavari** and **Phulchoki,** passing through **Harisiddhi, Thaibo,** and **Bandegaon.** An eastern lane takes travelers to **Sanagaon** and **Lubhu.** All these villages have close links to Patan.

betan handicrafts. In two large buildings, 200 men and women are always busy carding wool and weaving carpets. In the first building, five rows of women in traditional costume sit on the floor, one to three on a carpet, weaving traditional patterns, chatting and singing. In the next building, old men and women comb the wool and spin it into threads. Shops display these handicrafts for sale. Portraits of the King and Queen of Nepal and the Dalai Lama look down from the walls on a maze of carpets, blankets, woven bags, and small coats.

Jawakakhel Zoo, near the craft shops in the industrial area, has a selection of exotic south Asian animals, especially Himalayan species. Open daily.

About 16 km (10 miles) from Kathmandu is Bhaktapur, eastern gateway of the valley. In its present form the city dates back to the ninth century when King Anand Malla made it his seat in AD 889.

Mainly a Hindu town, its Durbar Square is probably the most visited of the three historic cities, nicely compact and only a

OPPOSITE: Ornately carved windows testify to the skills of the famed Newari craftsmen of Kathmandu valley. ABOVE LEFT: Stone carving of Buddha and RIGHT intricately made door to Buddhist temple, both in Patan.

The Cities of Kathmandu Valley

brief walk from the tallest and most popular of Nepal's pagoda temples, Nyatapola.

ACCOMMODATION AND RESTAURANTS

As in Patan the selection of accommodation in Bhaktapur is limited. However the following can be recommended:

INEXPENSIVE
Bhaktapur Guest House and Restaurant (211670. Outside the city, 15 minutes walk from the bus station.
Nyatapola Inn Old Newar house converted to a lodge. Hot shower but no bath en suite.

The **Cafe Nyatapola** opposite Nyatapola temple serves pies, cakes, pizzas and snacks and the **Restaurant Bhaktapur**, also opposite the Nyatapola temple, has passable food and great views from the restaurant balcony.

SEEING THE CITY

Nyatapola Pagoda
Durbar Square is dominated by Nyatapola Pagoda and is usually overrun with tourists who sometimes stand in the square stunned not only by the incredible dimensions of the temple but also by the nonstop hurly-burly of hawkers, pedestrians, and children who occupy the place day and seemingly night. Most seek sanctuary in the tea room opposite where a good hour can be spent sipping the piquant local tea and studying the erotica on the tea room struts. Built in similar style to the temple but more recently, the tea room building has been restored and preserved, and perhaps fittingly so, by West Germany in its concern for their historic nature.

Nyatapola is one of two five-storied temples in the valley. (Kumbheshwar is the other, see page 91). From as far back as you can stand it looks like a fretted pyramid climbing up to the clouds, reaching a height of more than 30 m (100 ft). Its inspiration is said to have been a form of appeasement to the terrifying menace of Bhairav who stands in another temple. There seems to be more than just fancy to this tale. Now more than 200 years old, its doors were sealed and

bolted when the builders finished their job and have never been opened since. What's inside is anybody's guess. Certainly, no menace terrifies the hordes who swarm over its plinth and up its steps which are guarded on each side by legendary sentinels, Jaya Mal and Patta, two wrestlers said to have the strength of 10 men at the bottom; next two huge elephants, each 10 times stronger than the wrestlers; then two lions, each as strong as 10 elephants; now two griffins each as strong as 10 lions; and finally, on the uppermost plinth, two demi-goddesses—

Baghini in the form of a tigress, and Singhini, as a lioness — each 10 times stronger than a griffin. It's a pattern of guardian sentinels found nowhere else in Nepali temple architecture and considered significant evidence of the measure of appeasement required to placate Bhairav.

Durbar Square
You'll need time to digest all this ambience, both exotic and enthralling, before walking on to Durbar Square to feast on its treasures which begin at its very gate, built of lime-plastered brick in the eighteenth century by Bhupatindra. Its arch is a depiction of the face of glory, Kirtimukha, guarded on either side by two wooden carvings: one of Bhairav, the other of Hanuman. The gate looks out on three remarkable temples of different styles, whose divine proportions are concealed by all being huddled together: one, the single-storied Jagannath, housing an

OPPOSITE: Carved stone sentinels guard the secrets locked inside the temple of Nyatapola in Bhaktapur. ABOVE: Bhaktapur after rain shower.

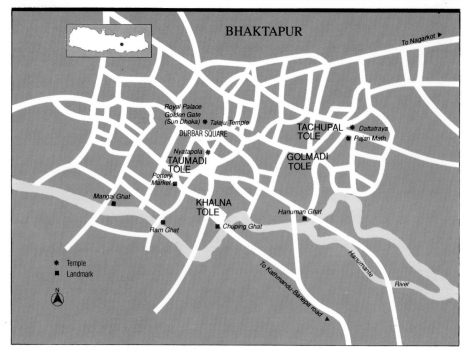

BHAKTAPUR

To Nagarkot ▶

Royal Palace
Golden Gate
(Sun Dhoka) ✳ Taleju Temple
DURBAR SQUARE

TACHUPAL ✳ Dattatraya
TOLE ✳ Pajari Math

Nyatapola ✳
TAUMADI
TOLE
Pottery
Market ■

GOLMADI
TOLE

Mangal Ghat ■

KHALNA
TOLE

Hanuman Ghat ■

Ram Ghat ■ ■ Chuping Ghat

Hanumante

To Kathmandu-Banepa road ▶

✳ Temple
■ Landmark

N

River

image of Harishankara; the second, a two-storied Krishna temple standing in front of it and housing images of Krishna, Radha, and Rukmani; and the third, the Shiva Mandir, built in the shikhara style with four porticoes each with a niche above them for plated images of gods.

Now stand here and the evening sun falls, as does the morning sun, on the north-facing **Golden Gate,** entrance to the **Palace of 55 Windows.** Though more than dross, the Golden Gate, alas, is only bronze, but when it catches the sun's rays it glitters and sparkles like the precious metal itself. Ranjit Malla commissioned it in 1754 to adorn the outer entrance to the Taleju temple within the Royal Palace, a one-storied shrine with many struts. During the Vijaya Dashami festival the Goddess is believed to take up residence in the south wing of the building. It's an extreme example of the artwork of Kathmandu valley, regarded by many as its finest. One of the carved windows is believed to be the personal handi-craft of Bhupatindra whose bronze statue — with him sitting, hands folded reverently before Taleju — faces the Golden Gate. Each of the corners has images of Hindu goddesses, Devashri and Lakshmi, and in the

temple area there's a large bell cast out of copper and iron. The temple opens its doors only once a year — between September and October — during the Dasain festival celebrations when Taleju's golden statue is placed on the back of the horse which is stabled in the courtyard and led around the town in a procession.

The adjacent palace is renowned mainly for its 55-windowed Hall of Audience, an elaborately carved balcony, and its collection of priceless wood carvings, some damaged in the 1934 earthquake but still considered priceless. Originally built in the fifteenth century, the palace was remodelled by Bhupatindra. Again, this Durbar Square also boasts a large bell that was used both to summon worshippers and to give alarms, particularly if there was a night curfew when it was rung to send citizens scurrying home. There are many more temples in Bhaktapur's Durbar Square: to **Kumari, Vatsala, Durga, Narayan, Shiva,** and **Pashupatinah.** The last is the oldest in the city, built around the end of the fifteenth century by the widow and sons of King Yaksha Malla to honor his memory though some argue it was built much later in 1682 by Jita Malla, father of Bhupatindra.

Bhaktapur legend says Lord Pashupatinah appeared before him in a dream and ordered him to build the temple. Another legend has it that the king wanted to visit the temple at Deopatan but was unable to cross the Bagmati since it was in full flood and so ordered another temple to Pashupatinah to be built in Bhaktapur.

THIMI

Just three kilometers (1.9 miles) west of

smaller dome shaped shrine is a brass likeness Bhairav.

But Thimi is more renowned as the location, along with two other adjacent villages — **Nade** and **Bode** — of the most riotous of Nepal's New Year (Bisket Jatra) celebrations. Nade is noted for its multicolored, three-storied Ganesh temple, while across the dykes that meander through the rice paddies Bode boasts a famous two-storied seventeenth-century Mahalakshmi temple. It stands on the site of an early temple built according to local legend in 1512, after Maha-

Bhaktapur is **Thimi** — Kathmandu valley's fourth-largest settlement. Founded by the Malla dynasty, it takes its name from the Nepali word *chhemi* which means "competent". It's an honor bestowed upon Thimi's residents by the Bhaktapur monarchs for their skill in fighting the forces of the rival kingdoms in the valley. It's a town of potters where families, taught skills handed down from generation to generation, turn out handsome chinaware fashioned from the red clay of the valley fields — vessels for domestic use and art works such as peacock flower vases and elephant representations. The colorful sixteenth-century **Balkumari temple** is the town's main shrine and nearby in a much

lakshmi appeared in a dream to the king of Bhaktapur.

Every year on New Year's Day, the square around the Bal Kumari temple in Thimi witnesses a spectacular gathering of 32 deities carried in elaborate multi-roofed palanquins under the shade of ceremonial umbrellas after which the Nade idol of Ganesh arrives. Later the crowds move across the field to Bode to witness another strange New Year's ritual (also see FESTIVALS 58).

Potters shape their vessels in traditional fashion ABOVE LEFT and RIGHT at the village of Thimi, close to Bhaktapur in Kathmandu valley.

LAND OF THE NEWARS

KIRTIPUR

About five kilometers (three miles) southwest of Kathmandu, perched on a twin hillock, twelfth-century Kirtipur was to become an independent kingdom and ultimately the last stronghold of the Mallas when Prithvi Narayan Shah rode into Kathmandu to conquer the valley in 1769–70. It withstood a prolonged siege, during which the Malla army taunted Prithvi's Gorkha forces as they hurled them back down the fortress-like hill.

It was a mistake. When Kirtipur finally fell, the vengeful Gorkha ruler ordered his men to amputate the nose and lips of all Kirtipur's male inhabitants — the only exception being those musicians who played wind instruments.

Now only the ruined walls remain to remind Kirtipur's 8,000 residents of this epic battle and Kirtipur is a place of trade and cloistered learning. Part of nearby Tribhuvan University's campus now sprawls across the former farmlands.

The traditional occupations, apart from farming, are spinning and weaving. At Kirtipur's **Cottage Industry Center,** 900 handlooms spin fine cloth for sale in Kathmandu.

Though it has withstood the savage earthquakes that have caused so much damage elsewhere in the valley, Kirtipur has been unable to withstand the ravages of time. Although decayed and neglected, a walk beneath the exquisitely-carved windows of its multi-storied houses, laid out on terraces of different levels all linked by ramps and sloping paths, its ambiance seems that of the middle ages.

The main approach is a long flight of steps that enter the town, settled on the saddle between the two hills, beside a small lake. On top of the hill to the south there's a huge stupa, the **Chilanchu Vihar,** encircled

Woman OPPOSITE preparing traditional Nepali bread, *roti,* in the village street.

by eight shrines decorated at their cardinal points by stone images. There are many Buddhist monasteries around the stupa also. On the hill to the north, which is higher, Hindus have settled around a restored temple dedicated to **Uma Maheshwar.**

The three-storied **Bagh Bhairav temple** stands at the high point of the saddle between the two hills, a place of worship for both Hindus and Buddhists. It's decorated with swords and shields taken from its Newar troops after Prithvi Narayan Shah's eighteenth-century victory. It contains an

image of Bhairav, manifested as a tiger, and the torana above the main sanctum shows Vishnu riding Garuda, and Bhairav attended on either side by Ganesh and Kumar. From the temple there are striking views of the valley and the brightly colored patchwork of farm fields below, with the villages of **Panga** and **Nagaon** in the south-east.

You can take a path through the rice fields from Kirtipur to Panga which was established by the Mallas as a fortress town to stall invaders from the north. None of its six or so temples, date beyond the nineteenth century. The path continues from

Panga to Nagaon, a name that means "new village".

The sixteenth-century Malla who ruled Kathmandu from Patan, concerned that his subjects might move too far from the city to serve its defence, established the twin settlements of **Bungamati** and **Khokana,** near the Karma Binayak shrine, amid fertile fields. During a major drought, the king sought the blessings of the rain god, Machhendra, at a temple in India, inviting the deity to come and settle in the valley. He built a shrine at Bungamati where, in the last decade of the sixteenth century, it became the custom to keep the image of the Rato Machhendra during winter, moving it back to Patan by palanquin in summer.

Many small votive *chaityas* line the processional way from Patan to Bungamati which nestles against a hillside, surrounded by terraced rice paddies and small copses of trees. The village is noted for its stronglystated, *shikhari*-style **Rato Machhendranath temple**. The adjacent Lokeshwar shrine contains an image of Bhairav's massive head in full, demonic fury.

There's another shrine, **Karma Binayak,** on a tree-clad hill and beyond that, 10 minutes walk away, is a brick-paved village famous for the manufacture of mustard-oil, **Khokana.** It has a temple dedicated to the nature goddess Shukla Mai, or Rudrayani. Rebuilt after the 1934 earthquake, its main street is noticeably wider than in similar villages.

TO THE WEST

Many interesting rural communities, with fascinating temples and shrines, are close to the capital, Kathmandu. In the west, on the old "Silk Road" to Tibet, stand the villages of **Satungal, Balambu, Kisipidi,** and **Thankot.** The first three cluster together within walking distance, no more than six kilometers (3.7 miles) from the city.

Satungal, Balambu, Kisipidi

The first, **Satungal,** was built in the sixteenth century as a fortress to thwart

Guardian elephant ABOVE outside a temple at Kirtipur village in Kathmandu valley.

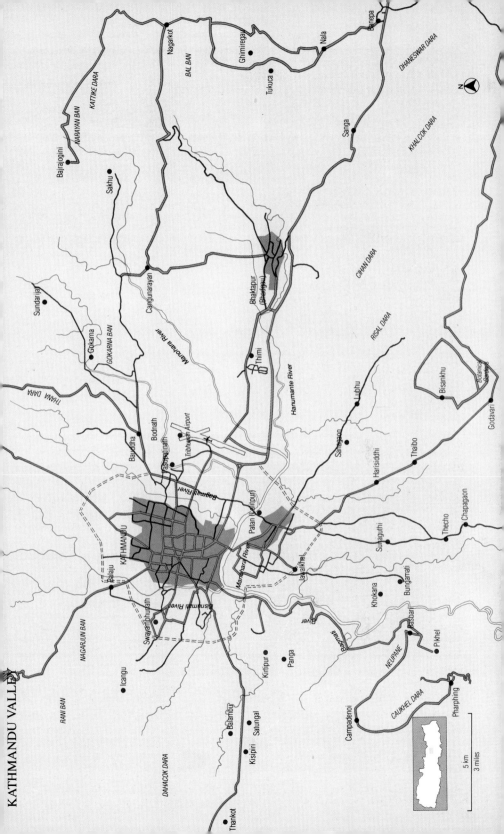

KATHMANDU VALLEY

invaders from the north. Many of its 1,000 residents work in Kathmandu. Its **main square** is notable for the two meter (6.5 ft) stone image of a seated Buddha on a free-standing platform. Nearby, to the north of the square, steps lead through an embellished gate to a **Vishnu Devi temple.**

Several inscriptions testify to the antiquity of the second village, **Balambu,** built more than a thousand years ago at the time that the Lichhavi dynasty ruled Kathmandu valley, but fortified later. Its main feature is the two-storied **Mahalakshmi temple,** in the central square, and some smaller temples. Among the three-storied houses that line the square is one dedicated as the god house of Ajima Devi.

The third village, **Kisipidi,** with its lush green trees and small, stone-walled gardens, is renowned for the two-storied **Kalika Mai temple** in its center.

Thankot

Travel on along the main highway, the Raj Path, and after two kilometers (1.2 miles) you come to the fourth village, **Thankot,** built by the Mallas, and later made a fortress by Prithvi Narayan Shah — its name, in fact, translates as "military base". On a hill above the village stands an impressive two-storied **Mahalakshmi temple,** much admired for its carved tympanum and columns, erotic carvings, open shrine, and images of kneeling devotees.

Four kilometers (2.5 miles) to the southwest of Thankot stands the 2,423 m (7,950 ft) peak of **Chandragadhi,** "The Mountain of the Moon", reached by a trail through a dense forest of bamboo, pine, and sal trees. At the crest there's a small Buddhist *chaitya* and splendid views of Kathmandu valley.

Back on the Raj Path look for the **monument to King Tribhuvan,** built to commemorate the re-establishment of royalty after the Rana regime. It has a raised hand. There's another monument along the road that honors the men who built it between 1953 and 1956 — Indian engineers and Nepali laborers. Before then goods were moved laboriously from India to Nepal by railway, and then from the Terai by ropeway to Daman, and by porters to Kathmandu.

The Lele Valley Road

Two of the valley's most ancient villages, **Chapagaon** and **Lele,** date back to Lichhavi times. The road to them cuts through a green and yellow quilt of mustard fields and rice paddies stretched out beneath the hazy gray-blue foothills of the mighty Himalaya.

Sixteenth-century **Sunaguthi,** standing on a high plateau at the edge of another valley, has a **shrine to Bringareshwar Manadeva** which houses one of the most sacred lingams in Kathmandu valley. Next

to the shrine is a two-storied **Jagannath temple.** Now the path climbs gently upward through the emerald, terraced fields to **Thecho** with its brightly-decorated **Balkumari temple.** There's another one, to **Brahmayani,** in the north of the village guarded by the deity's vehicle — a duck, of all things — atop a column, with the usual lion on the steps of this two-storied temple.

ABOVE: Ancient, yet elegant house in Patan. Typical village sights in Kathmandu valley include: OPPOSITE TOP: Serene bathing ghat in Bhaktapur. BOTTOM: A market stall in Nala village.

Two kilometers (1.2 miles) beyond Thecho, guarded by a metal Ganesh shrine and a statue of Brahma beside a huge yoni, the road enters **Chapagaon** where, says a famous valley legend, one of the Malla kings sent his son into exile for founding a caste of his own. The central square contains two temples, both two-storied, dedicated to **Narayan** and **Krishna**. The struts carry incredibly-detailed erotic carvings. Close by, in a single-storied building, is an image of **Bhairav**, the village's major deity. South of Chapagaon

are the two small hamlets of **Bulu** and **Pyangaon**.

TO THE EAST

King Anand Malla, founder of the Bhaktapur dynasty, is said to have built seven new villages in the east of Kathmandu valley, but of these, three were already in existence — Banepa, Nala, and Dhulikhel. The four that he did build are Panauti, Khadpu, Chaukot, and Sanga. But, in fact, some lie outside the valley. Nonetheless King Anand Malla's vision gave Banepa and Dhulikhel, situated, as they were, on the main Silk Road from Kathmandu to Tibet, a much greater status and strategic value.

SANGA AND THE ARANIKO HIGHWAY

The road climbed out of the valley over a pass, five kilometers (three miles) east of Bhaktapur, where it cut through **Sanga**. There's a small lane to the north, off the Araniko highway, that takes you into **Sanga**, where a vantage point offers an incredible panorama of the entire valley. Despite its antiquity, the only object of historical merit is a small **Bhimsen shrine** to commemorate a Kathmandu legend that, when the valley was a lake, Bhimsen crossed it by boat, rowing from Tankhot in the west to Sanga.

From Sanga, the Araniko highway zigzags steeply down into the lush **Banepa valley** and the village from which it takes its name. Standing at the foot of a forested hill, much of the village was razed by fire in the early 1960s but it remains the main center of commerce for the surrounding hill areas. Banepa's **Chandeshwari shrine** overlooks the valley from the top of a hill to the northeast of the town. North-west, there's a rough trail to **Nala** seat of a Buddhist meditation site, and **Lokeshwar**, about 100 m (330 yards) west of Nala, by the old Bhaktapur road. Pilgrim shelters surround the temple which has a water tank in front of it. A steep alley in the village center takes you to the four-storied **Bhagvati temple** in the center of a square — the locale for many colorful processions during the village's annual festivals.

DHULIKHEL

Back on the highway at Banepa, you drive on to Dhulikhel, which commands a prominent location on top of a high hill. There are several other sights worth seeing in Dhulikhel.

Dhulikhel's main square contains a **Narayan shrine** and an **Harisiddhi temple**. The village houses are renowned for their beautiful, carved woodwork. On a northern hill above the village stands a magnificent three-storied **Bhagvati temple**, famous for its ceramic tiled façade. It's also a major vantage point for views of the major peaks of the Himalaya. The mud-and-thatch

Main Street of Chapagon village ABOVE in Kathmandu valley where legend says a famous Malla king exiled his son for founding a caste of his own. OPPOSITE: Traditional scene in Chane village en route to Annapurna.

102

The Cities of Kathmandu Valley

houses in the sweltering valley below are home for a community of low-caste Nepali. Dhulikhel remains one of the trade gateways between Kathmandu valley, eastern Nepal and Tibet.

ACCOMMODATION

MODERATE
Dhulikhel Mountain Resort, reservations in Kathmandu, (220031 or 216930. PO Box 2302 Kathmandu. Only 34 km (21 miles) east of Kathmandu, in the direction

Panauti
One of the most fascinating Newar towns in this area, Panauti stands at the confluence of two rivers south of Banepa in a small valley surrounded by mountains. There used to be king's palace in the main village square and the town is noted for two fine examples of Malla temple architecture. Both the three-storied sixteenth-century Indreshwar **Mahadev temple** and a **Narayan shrine** have been restored.

Architecturally and historically, the Indreshwar Mahadev temple is one of the

of the Chinese border, the resort captures all the atmosphere of the Himalaya in just an hour's drive. Its location, high on a cliff, commands spectacular views making an ideal setting for sunrise breakfasts or dinner at sunset.

Seven chalet-style cottages provide 12 rooms.

INEXPENSIVE
Himalayan Horizon Sun-N-Snow Hotel (city office, Kantipath (226092). It's **Terrace Garden** serves Nepali, Indian, Italian and Chinese dishes (6 am to 10 pm). Meals and snacks are available at the **Panchkanya Restaurant** also from 6 am to 10 pm.

most important Newar shrines in Kathmandu valley and is thought to have replaced an earlier one built in the eleventh to twelfth centuries. The carving on its struts convey the profound serenity of Shiva, in his many incarnations. Two shrines guard the courtyard; one is to Bhairav, another to an original nature goddess. This is simply a symbolic stone. There's another **Krishna temple** on a peninsula at the confluence of the two rivers, with several Shiva lingams nearby and a sacred cremation ghat. On the other side of the Bungamati river is a famous seventeenth-century temple, also restored, where a chariot festival is held each year. It's dedicated to **Brahmayani,** chief goddess of Panauti after Indreshwar Mahadev.

The Cities of Kathmandu Valley

THE ROAD TO TIBET

KODARI

Just because it lies no more than 50 km (30 miles) from the crest of 8,013-m (26,291-ft)-high Shisha Pangma, or Gosainthan in the west, and much the same distance from 8,848-m (29,028-ft)-high Everest, in the east, Kodari would be remarkable.

But this tiny settlement is still more extraordinary because it's only 1,800 m (5,800 ft) above sea level, yet only 100 km (60 miles) from Kathmandu.

Though this short distance takes between four and five hours to cover by car the time passes swiftly, for this is a wonderland of raging rivers, valley towns, and forested slopes.

ARANIKO HIGHWAY (RAJMARG)

You set out along the valley highway in an early morning sun. Diffused by the soft spring haze of April, it casts a golden halo over the surrounding hills. Casual brickworks dot the fields and the buildings display the earthy color of the material.

Suddenly you're over the hills and the road plunges several hundred meters in a series of hairpin bends. Like most roads in midland Nepal, the Araniko highway was built by the Chinese. Although fairly new, it is already badly damaged by the frequent landslides and washaways that send whole sections of road — and sometimes the vehicles on them — plunging to the swollen torrents below.

Though it winds through the foothills of the greatest mountain range in the world, these hills themselves are so high and sheer that views of the snow-capped peaks are rare. The exception is **Dhulikhel** at the top of the narrow ridge just below the pass out of the valley — a thin ribbon of road with steep drops on either side — which offers a stunning vista of the Himalaya, including Everest.

Drive on, and after a few kilometers, at **Dolalghat** a long low bridge crosses the wide bed of the Sun Kosi, just below its confluence with the Indrawati river. It's

almost half-a-kilometer-long and the crystal-clear waters, abounding with trout and other fish, are inviting in the spring sunshine. The bridge, built in 1966, is a reminder of Nepal's progress in the 35 years since it reopened its borders. Not long after Dolalghat, on the Sun Kosi, is one of the country's first hydro-electric schemes, built in 1972 with Chinese aid.

The power station lies less than 900 m (3,000 ft) above sea level between Lamosangu and Barabise, and it's north of bustling Barabise that the road begins to climb upwards. All along the road the sparse winter and spring waters are tapped for irrigation and domestic use through ancient but well-kept aqueducts, models of traditional engineering dug out above the side of

the streams and lined withstone, with the fast-flowing water taken off the main body which soon descends below the level of the aqueduct.

Many visitors stop at **Tatopani,** where hot springs from the raging cauldron beneath the Himalaya have been tapped, pouring forth day and night in an everlasting supply of running hot water.

At occasional intervals there's the inevitable temple — and at **Chakhu,** only 15 kilometers (nine miles) from Tibet, there's an improbable circus pitched on a river bank just below the edge of the road. Eight kilometers (five miles) beyond, at **Khokun,** a temple occupies a rock in the middle of the gorge — with no indication of how worshippers climb up its sheer rock faces on all

sides — and a wonderful waterfall leaps and jumps like scintillating diamonds hundreds of meters down the sheer lush green wall of the mountain.

The perpendicular rock walls of the gorge press inexorably closer and closer. They seem to lean over the narrow ribbon of road that clings so precariously to the hillside. The road cuts beneath a cliff and you can almost reach out and touch either side of the gorge. Round one more bend and there's the immigration post and beyond the police post. Finally you reach the border spanned by the **Friendship Bridge.**

Annapurna's majestic beauty dominates the landscape of Nepal's midlands and provides a breathtaking backdrop for its many small villages.

It's already the source of a thriving tourist trade. Day trippers disgorge themselves from their coach to be photographed with the Tibetan town of **Khasa,** 600 m (2,000 ft) higher up the gorge, and the snows of 6,000-m (19,550-ft)-high Choba-Bahamare in the background. To the east, directly in line with Kodari, mighty Gaurisankar, only 35 km (21 miles) distant, remains invisible beyond the rise of the gorge wall.

A yellow line across the middle of the bridge marks the border between China's Tibet and Nepal. Nepalis can cross un-

that buttress the bridge foundations suggest the power they deflect.

THE ROAD TO POKHARA AND THE WEST

PRITHVI–TRIBHUVAN HIGHWAY

South-west of Kathmandu, the Trisuli gorge meets that of the Mahesh Khola river. From the capital to the confluence of the two rivers you take another of Nepal's major

hindered. Visitors must get a visa — a fairly easy process — in Kathmandu. (See VISAS, page 184) Khasa's Zhangmu Hotel runs an enviable occupancy rate on European and American guests eager to stay overnight on a two-day visa that marks the magic China immigration entry into their passport.

Where the border actually crosses — which side of the hill is Tibet or Nepal — is anybody's guess. On the other side the road winds back into what, hypothetically anyway, must be Nepal. The waters of the Bhote Kosi rage down the gorge between with a thunderous roar even though it's the dry season. It's an awesome thought to think of the Bhote in spate during the monsoons and thaw. Thick, strong walls

roads, the **Prithvi–Tribhuvan highway,** as scenic as it is dramatic. A memorial to those who died building both highways stands at the top of the pass close to a Hindu shrine.

PRITHVI HIGHWAY

The pass out of the valley leads down the almost sheer escarpment in a series of tortuous and terrifying hairpin bends to the Prithvi highway which starts at the town of **Naubise,** leaving the older Tribhuvan highway heading southward to Hetauda. The building of the Prithvi highway — in 1973 with Chinese aid — is marked at Naubise by a stone tablet set in the side of the rock wall.

Hamlets and villages — the main highway being their one street — abound along the road. On the level sections on either side are emerald-green rice paddies. Cultivating rice is a family affair — the men bullying the oxen teams with the plows, the women and children planting the young green shoots with astonishing speed and dexterity. Paddies cling to the mountain hundreds of meters above, protected from sliding away only by a fragile buttress of precious topsoil. Fields end abruptly at the edge of a gully or cliff. Many disappear in

dedicated to a Hindu deity with the power to make dreams come true.

During the clear season there are stunning views of Annapurna and its sister mountains from Gorkha, but nothing beats the panorama that awaits you in the trekking and climbing capital of Pokhara where the mirror reflection of sacred Machhapuchhare shines in the still, crystal waters of **Phewa lake.** Just 50 km (30 miles) from the village street at 900 m (3,000 ft) above sea level, Annapurna and its surrounding peaks stand up clear another 7,176 m (23,545 ft).

the monsoons, leaving only a void where once stood half an acre of sustenance.

Charoudi, the most popular "put-in" place for shooting the Trisuli's rapids, is a small one-street hamlet after which the road drops quickly to **Mugling,** veering westward over the elegant suspension bridge. Not long after Mugling there's a northward turn off the highway that leads to **Gorkha,** ancestral seat of the Shah dynasty, rulers of Nepal since the eighteenth century. King Prithvi Narayan Shah's old Palace still stands on a mountain ridge overlooking this ancient capital from which the Gurkha soldiers derive their name. There are some famous and distinctive temples in the town, including the pagoda-style **Manakamana**

POKHARA VALLEY

Like Kathmandu, Pokhara valley is blessed with fertile soil and an average of more than 420 mm (155 inches) of rain a year. The land burgeons with lush vegetation: bananas, cacti, rice, citrus trees, mustard fields, bounded with hedges of thorny spurge spiked with red blossoms, walls studded with ficus. The patchwork terraces are cut

OPPOSITE: Verdant rice paddies of the Suikhet valley near Pokhara. Women harvest grain ABOVE at Pokhara. FOLLOWING PAGES: Above the verdant rice fields north of Pokhara rises (left) Machhapuchhare and (right) Annapurna IV and Annapurna II.

through by gorges channeled by the Seti river and studded with lakes that glitter like diamonds in the spring sunshine. The ocher mud-and-thatch homes of the Hindu migrants from the Terai contrast to the white-walled, slate-roofed homes of the native Lamaistic tribes from the flanks of the mountain.

POKHARA AND PHEWA LAKE

Thirty years ago, Pokhara was an insignificant, little-known town. The first motor vehicle, a Jeep, arrived in 1958 — by plane. Progress since then, encouraged by tourists and climbers, the advent of hydro electric power in 1967, and the completion of the Prithvi highway in 1973, has been swift. Within a decade Pokhara's population doubled to 50,000. There's even a movie house and amusement park.

Local legend says Phewa lake covers an ancient city engulfed during a cataclysmic earthquake millenniums ago. Today local fishermen ply their *donga* (long dug-out canoes, fashioned from tree trunks) on the placid waters, ferrying pilgrims to the **shrine of Vahari,** a golden temple nestling on an island. There's also a **Royal Winter Palace** for winters on the lake shore.

ACCOMMODATION

There are many bed and breakfast lodges along the northern shore of Phewa lake, generally more pleasant than those on the airport road, from which you can hire boats and dugouts to sail on the lake.

With only two flights a day arriving in Pokhara, airport activities are more entertaining than disturbing. Two good hotels (listed below) face the airport: the New Hotel Crystal and Hotel Mount Annapurna.

FIRST CLASS

New Hotel Crystal (227932 or 228561 (Reservations in Jyatha) Pokhara. 46 rooms and a 24-room annexe. It's part of Kathmandu's Crystal Hotel group.

MODERATE

Fish Tail Lodge (20071. Reservations in Kathmandu at Hotel de l'Annapurna (221711 or 225242. Lakeside, Pokhara. Along the shores of Phewa lake, standing on a rocky promontory at the eastern end, accessible only by raft from the opposite shore. It offers spectacular views.
Hotel Dragon (20391 or 20052. Damside, Pokhara.
Hotel Kantipur Resort (21226. Lakeside, Pokhara. Opposite the Fishtail, it has 15 bungalow rooms and an excellent restaurant.
Hotel Mount Annapurna (20037 or 20027. PO Box 12, Airport, Pokhara. Tibetan ambience: Tibetan murals in the dining room and bar, and Tibetan management.

INEXPENSIVE

Hotel Tragopan (20910, bookings in Kathmandu (5225898, telex 2521 altlinc np. 24 hour coffee shop.
Hotel Garden (20870. Damside, Phewa Lake.
Hotel Hungry Eye (20908 or 20394. Lakeside, Pokhara.
Hotel Mandar (20732. Mehendra Pul, Pokhara.
Hotel Monalisa (20863. Pardi, Pokhara.
Himalayan Tibetan Hotel Another Tibetan hotel close to the airport — the with cheap Tibetan and Nepali food in modest surroundings.

RESTAURANTS

Baba Lodge and Restaurant Southernmost along Phewa Lake. Good breakfasts.
Bhutovi Lakeside, north to Hungry Eye. Japanese cuisine.
Don't Crass Me Lakeside, south of Hungry Eye. Chinese and European cuisine.
Fish Tail Restaurant (Fish Tail Lodge) (20071. European and Nepali cuisine. Live Nepali music and dance every evening.
Flying Dragon Restaurant (Hotel Hungry Eye) (20908 or 20394. Tibetan, Chinese, Nepali, Continental cuisine. Open 6 am to 10 pm.
Hotel Gerden Restaurant (Hotel Garden) (20870. Nepali style *dal bhat tarkari* dishes.
Hotel Kantipur Restaurant (Hotel Kantipur Resort) (21226. Continental, Indian, Chinese and Nepali cuisine. Great chicken dishes.

OPPOSITE: Evening settles on Phewa lake, Pokara.

Hotel Tragopan Restaurant (Hotel Tragopan) (20910. Indian, Continental and Chinese cuisine. Open 6 am to 10 pm.

Hungry Tiger Restaurant and Bar (Hotel Hungry Eye) (20908 or 20394. Exotic Continental, Italian, Chinese, Mexican, Indian and barbecue dinners. Perhaps the best place to eat in Pokhara. Open 6 am to 10 pm.

Solo Restaurant (Hotel Dragon) Chinese, Japanese, European cuisine and local *thakali* style *dal-bhat-tarkari.* The Mandala Folk Troupe performs traditional Nepali dances.

per half day, from **Pokhara Pony Trekking.** For those who like to cruise the lake, *dongas* are for hire at Rs 25 per hour — a a bit more if one of the boat-boys does the paddling. Modern boats are also available.

On Phewa lake you may be drawn to a small pagoda-style temple situated on the lake's tiny island. This temple is dedicated to goddess Barahi and is one of the most famous places of pilgrimage and animal sacrifice of the region. You may swim and fish in the lake.

There are three natural sites of interest in

SHOPPING FOR CRAFTS

Near to the Himalayan Tibet Hotel, and to the Airport is **Pokhara Craft,** a shop specializing in local handicrafts and featuring nettle fabric (made from the stinging hill nettle) and woodcrafts where you can see local craftsmen at work during the day.

SIGHTSEEING

There is much to do in and around Pokhara, and a pleasant way to sightsee is to hire a bicycle, pony or *donga.*

Bicycles are available for hire at just over Rs 10 per hour. Ponies cost just over Rs 100

the area. **Devlin's Falls** is located southwest from the airport along the Siddhartha highway. This dramatic but seasonal waterfall, known locally as *Patle Chhango,* is created when a a small stream flows out of the lake and suddenly collapses and surges down the rocks into a steep gorge. **Seti Gorge** is equally fascinating. To get there, drive to the middle of the first bridge along the Kathmandu highway. Look down below and you will see the four-and-a-half-meter (15-ft)-wide gorge carved more than 14 m deep by the flow of the Sati river. The third interesting natural site is at **Mahendra cave,** north of Shining Hospital and the University campus near **Batulechaur** village. It is one of the few stalagmite and stalactite caves in Nepal, known locally as a "holy" place. Carry a flashlight.

AROUND POKHARA

Ram Bazaar
East of Pokhara, Ram Bazaar is a small but picturesque village with shops, a school and artisans.

Tibetan Villages
The most interesting, lying just north of town in Lower Hyangja, is **Tashi Phalkhel.**

Southwest of the airport, beyond Devlin's Falls, is **Tashiling**.

Batulechaur
A few miles north of town, Batulechaur is famous for its *gaine* singers who tell of the rich history of Nepal in their rhapsodic songs. They play a small four-string, violin-like instrument (*Sarangi*) with a horse hair bow to accompany their voices.

Sarangkot
At the peak of the 1,600 m (5,250 ft) Sarangkot, are the remains of a fortress used by King Prithvi Narayan Shah the Great during the eighteenth century. Going west of Pokhara, past Kaskidanda Ridge to Gyarajati village, you climb to the summit.

Muktinah
One of many places of pilgrimage in these hills that line the Kali Gandaki basin, is **Muktinah**. At 3,800 m (12,460 ft), its eternal flame draws Hindu and Buddhist alike. Black ammonite fossils, thought of as the embodiment of Vishnu, are found in profusion, and pilgrims travel long distances over rugged trails to collect these.

Kali Gandaki Gorge
The deepest gorge in the world, Kali Gandaki gorge, is flanked on one side by the daunting massif of Annapurna and on the other side, only 35 km (22 miles) away, by 8,167-m (26,795-ft)-high Dhaulagiri I. In between, almost eight kilometers (five mile) below, at only 1,188 m (3,900 ft), sits the village of **Tatopani.** (See also page 105).

With Dhaulagiri and Annapurna you are at the frontier of the highest land in the world. The peaks of Annapurna and its sister cohorts form the world's greatest natural amphitheater. Its only equal — in scale, form, and drama — is directly opposite, across the Kali Gandaki valley, where Dhaulagiri's six peaks, and those around them, form another breathtaking amphitheater.

MAJESTIC MOUNTAINS

On Nepal's western border, the Himalaya curve southward enfolding the country and dividing it physically from the northernmost reaches of India. The highest of these western peaks is **Api.** Though small by comparison with its sister peaks in central and eastern Nepal, few mountains in the world outside Asia rise as high as Api's 7,131 m (23,396 ft), forming a formidable massif in the far west. Peak to peak, directly in line with Api, only 60 km (37 miles) away is its easterly neighbor, **Saipal,** just 97 m (318 ft) lower. The actual border is marked by the Kali river that flows down beneath lonely Api.

Api dominates a range of magnificent but rarely seen and little-known peaks including **Jetibohurani,** 6,848 m (22,468 ft); **Bobaye,** 6,807 m (22,333 ft); **Nampa,** 6,755 m (22,163 ft); and **Rokapi,** 6,466 m (21,214 ft). Close to Saipal stands the jagged peak of **Firnkopf West** of 6,683 m (21,926 ft); to the north is the lonely **Takpu Himal** gazing down on the lovely Humla valley and its remote capital of **Simikotat** from 6,634 m (21,766 ft).

Minnows compared to the peaks of central and eastern Nepal, these mountains remain relatively untouched by climbers.

Japanese teams conquered Api in 1960, Saipal in 1963, and Nampa in 1972. A major trade route from the plains — a long trek through tough country — winds between these two massifs, cresting a saddle more than 5,500 m (18,000 ft) high between Nampa and Firnkopf West, before entering Tibet over the Urai pass.

Eastwards of the remote western regions the Himalaya climbs steadily higher. In the little-known Kanjiroba Himal, a cluster of mountains that takes its name from the highest peak, 11 peaks rise above 6,000 m (20,000 ft), including 7,409-m (22,583-ft)-high Kanjiroba Himal. The mountains encircle the ancient **Kingdom of Dolpo** and the sacred **Crystal Mountain** (see OFF THE BEATEN TRACK page 133), forming the natural boundaries of the 3,540 sq km (1,388 sq mile) **Shey-Phoksondo National Park.** Dolpo came into the kingdom in the eighteenth century as a result of King Bahadur Shah's conquests.

Eastward, across the fortress of Langtang Himal's peaks, lies the **Rolwaling Himal,** that little-known and overshadowed annex of the great Everest massif. Accessible only from the west, it is considered as beautiful as Langtang.

At the far end of the Bhote Kosi gorge, 7,180-m (23,557-ft)-high **Menlungtse** and the slightly lower 7,144-m (23,438-ft)-high mass of **Gaurisankar** stand sentinel, like Lhotse and Nuptse, guarding Sagarmatha, Everest, hiding her massive pyramid from prying and curious eyes.

The twin citadels of Gaurisankar and Menlungtse are the westernmost bastions of the Everest massif. Peak to peak, a distance of about 70 km (43 miles) separates Shiva's abode from that of Sagarmatha, Goddess of the Universe. In between, and around and about, are literally dozens of lesser ramparts extending to the central pinnacle, most rising above 6,100 m (20,000 ft). Thirty kilometers (18 miles) distant from Everest, 8,153-m (26,750-ft)-high **Cho Oyu** guards the north-west approach while, fewer than eight kilometers (5 miles) distant from the pinnacle of the world, 8,511-m (27,923-ft)-high **Lhotse** guards the eastern flank and 7,879-m (25,850-ft)-high **Nuptse** the south-western flank. Sixteen kilometers (10 miles)

beyond Lhotse, 8,481-m (27,825-ft)-high **Makalu** and its four other peaks barricade the approach from the south-east. Thus, well-guarded, from the ground or the air, Everest hides herself, almost demurely, behind her cluster of courtier peaks with Nuptse and Lhotse serving as ladies-in-waiting.

The first major assault on Everest took place in 1924 when George Mallory and Andrew Irvine disappeared on the mountain close to the summit. Their bodies still lie somewhere beneath Sagarmatha's eternal snows. They took a route along the north-east ridge

from Tibet. It was only when Nepal opened its borders that the south face, the line taken by Hillary and Tenzing, was approachable.

Leaving the shadows of the brave and foolish who still lie on Sagamartha's slopes — including an English religious zealot without any mountain experience who fell to his death in the 1930s — leaving behind in his diary this epitaph: "Off again. Gorgeous day." — it's 125 km (78 miles) eastward from Everest as the crow flies to the top of 8,598-m (28,208-ft)-high **Kanchenjunga** astride Nepal's border with India's Sikkim State. Here too is a massif of giant peaks — 15 of them are above 7,000 m (23,000 ft).

ABOVE: Village craftsman weaving rush baskets.
OPPOSITE: Decorated house in Central Nepal.

The Terai

WILDLIFE AND RICE PADDIES

Along Nepal's southern border with India lies a narrow band of fertile plains, the Terai. Flat, and nowhere wider than 40 km (19 miles), it covers 24,000 sq km (9,500 sq miles). In addition to providing a dramatic contrast to the rest of the terrain of the world's most mountainous nation, the Terai has a charm all its own.

During the monsoon season, tributaries of the Ganges flood the Terai's fields and

The recently completed Mahendra or East-West highway links the major towns; footpaths connect everywhere else. Buses travel the main route and can get you to the birthplaces of Buddha and Sita and the jungle wildlife parks, but your feet or a bicycle are the only ways to get off the beaten track.

BIRATNAGAR

On the eastern reaches of the Terai lies Biratnagar, Nepal's second largest city with over

paddies, depositing soil eroded from the Himalayas. Often rivers and streams change course, uprooting stilted huts and villages, washing out roads, and destroying communication links. In the months that follow, crops are planted — rice, wheat, cane, jute, tobacco, beans and lentils — and harvested before the scorching desert winds arrive, preceding the next year's monsoons. Home for more than half Nepal's population and most of the national industries, this one sixth of Nepal's land area produces more than 50 percent of the gross domestic product and provides habitat for the country's remaining tigers and rhinoceros. In October and November, the ideal months for visiting this part of Nepal, the countryside is lush and a hub of activity.

100,000 people. A major industrial center with sugar, textile and jute mills, small- and medium-scale factories for timber products, and rice mills, in itself it is a town to pass by rather than through, but the attractions of its environs make it a worth a stopover.

ACCOMMODATION

Gaida Cottage, along the river opposite Narayanghat, can accommodate 60 guests. There's a restaurant, prices are reasonable, and the proprietor speaks English well.

There are seven other hotels in Biratnagar, the **Milan Holiday Home, Atithi Sadan, Birat Lodge, International Hotel, Dobhan** and **Bisauni.**

Reservations are best made from Kathmandu with the help of the travel and trekking agencies listed in TRAVELERS' TIPS, page 197.

AROUND BIRATNAGAR

To the west are the attractions of the area: green paddies, jute fields, floodplains, and marshes. On the Indian border, the massive Kosi Dam impounds the Sun Kosi river, which is fed by the Tamar river from the slopes of Kanchenjunga and the Arun river

from the snows of Makalu. Built by India, the dam is one of Nepal's major hydroelectric projects. Besides controlling unpredictable floods and generating much of the country's energy, it has created new wetlands that now form the **Kosi Tappu Wildlife Reserve**. Here you can see one of the few remaining herds of wild buffaloes and thousands of migratory birds. There are no tourist accommodations in the reserve. The nearest accommodation is in Biratnagar.

JANAKPUR

Of more interest is Janakpur, 120 km (74 miles) west of Biratnagar, on the Indian border. With 40,000 Maithili-speaking inhabitants, Janakpur is reputed to have been the ancient capital of Maithili and birthplace of Sita, consort of Rama (one of Vishnu's incarnations and hero of the epic Ramayana). It is a major pilgrimage center for Hindus from all over the subcontinent.

An eight-kilometer (five-mile) brick-paved road encircles the city and its many sacred Hindu shrines and ponds, of which **Gangasagar** and **Dhanushsagar** are the most outstanding. Pilgrims to its two famous festivals, commemorating Rama and Sita's wed-

ding and Rama's epic victory over evil, immerse themselves in these sacred waters and flock to **Janaki temple** to pay homage to Rama and Sita. Built by a Queen of Tikamgarh (in Madhya Pradesh, northern India) in 1900, its delicately-carved marble traceries were inspired by seventeenth-century Mughal architecture. The delicate filigrees shaped with exquisite beauty are seen at their best on the elaborate cupolas, ceilings, and tiles. Nearby is the **Vivah Mandap** where legend holds that Rama and Sita were wed.

The town is also famous as the main stop on one of the worlds shortest railways —

Farm workers tend the fertile fields of the Terai using the ubiquitous oxen for ploughing OPPOSITE and ABOVE for transportation.

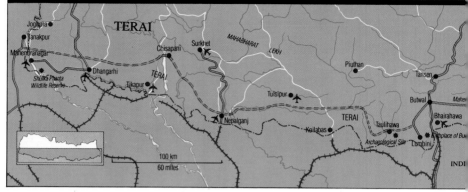

the 52 km (32 mile) narrow-gauge **Nepal Railway** that links Nepal with Jayanagar, India. The line is a colorful anachronism that delights inveterate travelers, a time-serving echo of the old British Raj.

BIRGANJ

Eighty kilometers (50 miles) west of Janakpur, the Mahendra highway links up with the Tribhuvan Rajpath, for many past years the country's main trans-Asia link. To the south is the border town of Birganj; to the north, through Amlekhganj and across the Mahabharat Lekh hills, is Kathmandu valley. Along the route is a dramatic view at Daman.

Birganj has seen better days. In the sixties and seventies, western hippies and mystics queued for clearance into Nepal on the Indian side at Raxaul, and spent the night in one of Birganj's many cheap lodging houses before taking the high road to Kathmandu.

It is, however, still a bustling industrial area with timber yards, a sugar mill, match factory, and a raucous bus depot where itinerants jostle each other in their eagerness to catch the next, often over-crowded, coach to Kathmandu. It is also a jump-off point for visitors to Royal Chitwan National Park and Parsa Wildlife Reserve.

ROYAL CHITWAN NATIONAL PARK AND PARSA WILDLIFE RESERVE

The highlight for most visitors to the Terai is a visit to Royal Chitwan National Park and Parsa Wildlife Reserve, wilderness retreats recreated out of the once fertile rice and wheat fields that swiftly covered the Rapti valley after the fall from power of the Rana dynasty in the 1950s.

Royal Chitwan, covering 932 sq km (360 sq miles), was the first of Nepal's extensive network of wildlife sanctuaries that now protect over seven percent of its territory. The valley in which it lies forms the flood plains of the Narayani river, joined here by the waters of the Rapti and other streams and feeders to become the second largest tributary of the sacred Ganges that flows approximately 200 km (125 miles) to the south.

Before the Park's creation in 1973, Nepal's population explosion had pushed migrants down from the hills, forcing the indigenous Tharu tribes into this area formerly reserved as royal hunting grounds. Using slash-and-burn techniques, they opened up the forests and planted rice and grain.

Concerned with the destruction of its traditional hunting grounds, the Nepali royal family planned new strategies for the protection of its wildlife, and in 1973 King Mahendra established Chitwan. The grasslands were rehabilitated, along with the sal (*Shorea robusta*) forests, and slowly the game began to creep back from the uncertain havens it had found outside. An exemplary model of wildlife management, Royal Chitwan and its denizens have continued to prosper. Subsequent extensions, Parsa Wildlife Reserve, have given it a much larger area, embracing smaller forests of khani (*Acacia catechu*), sisso (*Dalbergia sisso*), and simal (*Bombax malabaricum*) — all valuable indigenous woods.

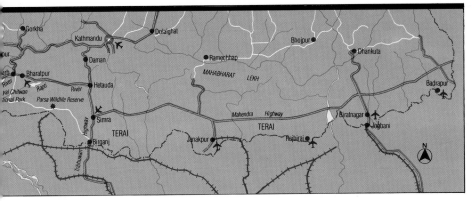

Monsoon fluctuations in the course of the rivers have created new ponds and lakes in a park/reserve that now covers an area of 1,200 sq km (470 sq miles) of subtropical lowland, bounded by the Rapti river in the north, the Reu river and the Churia or Siwalik Range in the south, and the Narayani river in the west.

Several animal observation blinds have been constructed next to water holes where patient visitors might see tigers and leopards and where most will sight rhinoceros, wild boar, deer, monkeys, and a multitude of birds. Throughout the Park, small fenced enclosures contain different kinds of grasses from which agronomists and conservationists hope to fine the ideal pastures for Chitwan's wild animals.

On clear winter days this jungle has one of the most dramatic backdrops in the world: the stunning ice slopes of Annapurna, Ganesh Himal, and Himal Chuli stand out on the horizon in magnificent detail. Needless to say, travel in the park is difficult during the monsoon season (May to September), and the best animal viewing is from February to April. Any stay shorter than two days is probably not worth the effort as the key to enjoying the game park is calm and patience. Accommodations should be arranged before leaving Kathmandu or from Birganj, if you are entering Nepal from India.

Riding an elephant has proven the best form of transport in the park. The Royal Nepali Army, which polices the Park and enforces conservation laws, makes its patrols by elephant, and Park workers move about in similar fashion.

It is not uncommon to come across a small work force resting in the shade of a clump of bombax trees around midday, the elephants relentlessly foraging with their trunks; their handlers, mahouts, even sleeping on their backs, many with umbrellas raised as protection against the sun.

Elephants can usually be rented at the Park offices or at one of the lodges listed below. Each beast has its own handler and individual gait. For most, these game rides are the memories that will last longest. The handler, astride the elephant's neck, brushes the lianas and the giant ferns aside with his steel goad, and the seemingly ungainly three-ton steed steps nimble-footed over fallen logs.

In the dark shadows of a thicket, a sudden flash of fawn reveals the flight of a startled sambar deer. Giant butterflies flit from leaf to leaf and beyond the wall of leaves shadows move — perhaps a tiger, a leopard. However briefly, you can be the last of the Maharajahs. Out on the plains the great Asiatic one-horn rhinos are moving with steadfast purpose, cropping the grass as a herd of chital — timid, fawn-like deer, edge nervously away from the young elephant. Back in the forest, a jungle fowl suddenly struts across the trail, and from a low-lying branch a wild peacock takes off in a technicolor cascade of feathers.

It is also possible to travel part way down the Rapti river and its streams by canoe, to view crocodiles basking in the sun, as well as a variety of riparian flora and fauna. Arrangements for a canoe trip can best be made at the Saura park office, four miles south of Tadi Bazaar (on the

Mahendra highway between Marayangarh and Hetauda).

Hiking is allowed in the jungle, but an experienced guide is a must as trails are not marked and the wildlife can be dangerous. Rather than being an encumbrance, a guide is an asset who can usually find and identify the wildlife and many can reel off with computer-like accuracy the names of many of the sanctuary's prolific yet rare bird species.

ACCOMMODATION IN AND AROUND CHITWAN NATIONAL PARK

If Tiger Tops pioneered the jungle safari in Chitwan, there are now many lodges, camps, and numerous teahouses in and around the sanctuary that developed in its wake. Best known are **Gaida Wildlife Camp,** and its tented Chitwan Jungle Lodge set in the darkest, deepest jungle, **Jungle Safari Lodge, National Park Cottages,** and **Wendy's Lodge.**

Outside the park, guests at the **Tharu Village Resort** can sleep in the traditional Tharu tribal longhouses, see Tharu dances, eat Nepali food, and visit local villages.

Demand for rooms in and around Chitwan is high. Book well in advance.

A more remote wildlife jungle can be experienced in far West Nepal, five hours drive from Nepalgunj, in the Royal Bardia Reserve. (See page 123).

Adventure Jungle Camp (Chitwan National Park) reservation office: Lekhnath Marg, PO Box 4100, Kathmandu. (416834 or 412116, telex 2654 gst np.

Chitwan Jungle Lodge (Chitwan National Park) reservation office: Durbar Marg, PO Box 1281, Kathmandu. (222679 or 228918, telex 2558 nepex np. Park fee $12. First and second night $100 per person (lodge; $70 per person (tented camp). Single supplement $60 (lodge); $45 (tented camp). Reduction for additional nights. extras: $2 for government tax and for camping.

Elephant Camp Chitwan reservation office: Durbar Marg, PO Box 4279, Kathmandu. (223976 or 222823, telex 2576 mass np.

Gaida Wildlife Camp and Jungle Lodge reservation office: Durbar Marg, PO Box 2086, Kathmandu. (220940 or 410786, telex

2659. First night $100 (lodge); $90 (tented camp). Single supplement $55 (lodge); $45 (tented camp). Reduction for additional nights.

Hotel Chitwan (200. Bharatpur Height, PO Box 12, Chitwan.

Island Jungle Resort – tented camp Park fee: $10; first night $115; additional nights $100; Single suppliment $75. Extras: $2 government tax and for camping.

Jungle Safari Camp (Chitwan National Park) reservation office: PO Box 2154, Kathmandu. (222055, telex 2375 np.

Machan Wildlife Resort (Chitwan National Park) reservation office: Durbar Marg, PO Box 3140, Kathmandu. (225001 or 227001 or 227099, telex 2409 alpine np. Park fee $12; first and second nights $126 (lodge); $66 (tented camp). Single supplement $75 (lodge; $66 (tented camp). Reduction for extra nights. Extras: $2 extra charge for government tax and $1 for camping.

Sunrise tourists take an early morning game trek abroad an elephant in Royal Chitwan National Park OPPOSITE TOP where park workers BOTTOM rest in shade during the midday heat. ABOVE: Threatened survivor of the greatest of the world's cats, the Royal Bengal tiger, pads through Chitwan's lush grasslands.

Narayani Safari (130, telex 2262 np. PO Box 1357 Bharatpur.

Temple Tiger Wildlife Camp reservation office: Kantipath, PO Box 1173, Kathmandu. (221585 or 225780, telex 2637 temtis np. Park fees $12. Per night $150. Single supplement $75. Extras: government tax $1.50; camping charge $4.

Tiger Tops Jungle Lodge (Chitwan National Park) reservation office: Durbar Marg, PO Box 242 Kathmandu. (222706, telex 2216 tigtop np. Park fees $12. Per night $250 (lodge); $180 (tented camp). Single supplement $160 (lodge); $90 (tented camp). Extras: government tax $7.80 (lodge); $6,60 (Tharu Village), and $4 (camp); camping charge $4 (camp and Tharu Village). Rates for full board — US$150 — include transportation by elephant or four-wheel-drive vehicle from Meghaulj airfield, elephant jungle safaris, boat trips, and guided nature walks. Tiger Tops also runs a tented camp to capture the romance of the golden days of the Raj. Tharu Village is out of the ordinary in that guests can sleep in the traditional Tharu tribal longhouses, see Tharu dances, eat Nepali food, and visit local villages.

BHARATPUR AND NARAYANGHAT

The twin towns of Bharatpur and Narayanghat are the nearest urban centers to Chitwan.

Bharatpur's role in the lowland infrastructure is as an airfield for what the domestic air carrier rashly promises are the daily flights to Kathmandu. Renowned for the reliability of its international schedules, Royal Nepal Airlines has an equal reputation for the erratic timekeeping of its internal flights: understandable in mountain regions where weather suddenly closes in but perplexing to passengers waiting in the balmy and reliable climes of the Terai.

Narayanghat, lying on the banks of one of Nepal's three largest rivers, the Narayani, and known as the "Gateway to Chitwan", is in fact the major junction on the Mahendra highway with a spur climbing up through the hills along the east bank of the Narayani to **Mugling,** the main junction town between Kathmandu and Pokhara on the

Prithvi highway. It is also a vital administrative and commercial center of the Terai, and indeed the ethnic capital of the indigenous people of this region, the Tharus.

Bustling Narayanghat, with sizable industries and flourishing markets, is also something of a pilgrimage spot. Each year, in January, tens of thousands flock to the nearby village of **Deoghat** when a major fair is held and immerse themselves at the confluence of the Kali Gandaki with the combined waters of the Trisuli-Marsyangdi.

Travelers continue their westward journey from Narayanghat over the modern bridge that spans the river, veering south-west along the Narayani's flood plains and over the shallow crest of a spur of the Siwalik Hills to join the **Siddhartha highway** — a direct India–Pokhara link — at **Butwal,** on the banks of the river Tinau. This market town, with 25,000 to 30,000 inhabitants, is famous for its market gardens and fruit orchards.

TANSEN

Northward of Butwal, a small eastward spur of the Siddhartha highway doubles back on itself as it climbs, in just a few kilometers, to **Tansen** — a town of 15,000 souls famed for the erotic carvings on its **Narayan temple.** Tansen is also justly renowned — for the sheer beauty of its panoramic vistas of the foothills around it — as a landscape artist's *El Dorado*. Craft industries and the traditional Newar houses also make the town a worthwhile stopover. Its **Bhairavnath temple,** legend says, was carried — lock, stock, and timber beams — all the way from the Kathmandu valley by King Mani Kumarananda Senior: one of history's biggest removal jobs. For anglers, Tansen's leaping streams provide fine sport.

BHAIRAWA

Hugging the Indian border 40 km (25 miles) southward as the Himalayan crow flies, in sharp contrast to Tansen, Bhairawa, the Terai's second largest industrial center, turns out the hard stuff of Nepal's liquor trade from a modern distillery, and also refines sugar, rice, and oil. There's also another British base, five kilometers (three miles) outside the town, which signs up more of the stout Gurkha military stock.

ACCOMMODATION

MODERATE
Pahupati Lodge ((071) 20139. Siddhartha Nagar, Bhairawa.
Lumbini Hotel (271. Bhairawa.
Hotel Himalayan Inn (347. Bhairawa.

INEXPENSIVE
Hotel Kailash across from the Post Office.
Annapurna Lodge west of the Post Office on the same road.
Mamata Lodge across from the bus terminal at the border with India.
Jai Vijay Lodge restaurant, across from bus terminal at border with India.

LUMBINI

Nineteen kilometers (12 miles) southwest of Bhairahawa is Lumbini, the birthplace of Siddhartha Gautama Buddha in 540 BC. Since 1958 Lumbini has been in the hands of an international committee established by the Fourth World Buddhist Conference and initially funded by a substantial contribution from King Mahendra.

At the turn of the century, German archaeologist, Dr. Feuhrer, began excavating the ruins of the area, including the Lumbini palace and gardens, several shrines, and a monastery. He discovered a sandstone nativity sculpture depicting Buddha's nativity (now in the National Museum, and a soaring obelisk erected to honor Buddha by Mauryan emporer Ashoka when he visited the Lumbini gardens in 249 BC. The pillar, inscribed in Brahmin, "Buddha Sakyamuni, the blessed one was born here," had been split in two probably by a stoke of lighting.

Later excavation have revealed a brick temple, Maya Devi, said to mark the exact spot where the Buddha was born.

TILAUROKOT

When Buddha was born, his father King Suddhondhan had as his capital Tilaurokot,

27 kilometers (17 miles) west of Lumbini. Although the stupas, monasteries, and palaces that Chinese travelers wrote about over two centuries ago no longer exist, the Nepalis have preserved it as a heritage site. — what does this mean? To the visitor very little distinguishes this site from the rest of the present-day Terai.

NEPALGUNJ

The western-most city in Nepal and capital of its region, Nepalgunj is an industrial

center on the Indian border. It has a population of approximately 40,000 and little to commend it to the tourist.

ROYAL BARDIA RESERVE AND SHUKLA PHANTA WILDLIFE RESERVE

Few tourists yet visit the lesser-known trails of western Nepal despite the presence of the Royal Bardia Reserve and the Mahendra highway linking the east and west will inevitably encourage more visitors to the region.

Karnali, part of the Royal Bardia Reserve, located on the eastern bank of the Karnali river, is a sanctuary for the endangered swamp deer. Here, Tiger Tops run **Karnali Tented Camp** with accommodation for 16 guests at US$100 a day each, fully inclusive.

Shukla Phanta, in Kanchanpur district in the westernmost reaches of Nepal, is one of the few places in the country where the endangered blackbuck are found.

ABOVE: Engaging wild monkey at Chitwan.

The Eastern Midlands

ILAM AND THE ILAM VALLEY

In the narrow neck of land that connects north-east India with the rest of that vast country — and also divides Nepal from Bhutan, another tiny Himalayan kingdom — is West Bengal and Sikkim. From **Siliguri** the road crosses the **Mechi river,** a tributary of the Ganges, to **Kakar Bhitta** in Nepal. You can also take an alternative hill road from **Darjeeling** through the **Mane pass** and down to the rolling tea fields of Ilam.

Set at around 1,300 m (4,000 ft), the tea fields are particularly lovely, rolling away from either side of the road in every direction, a carpet of vivid green laid out at the feet of Nepal's north-eastern mountains with dramatic views of mighty Kanchenjunga, the world's third-highest mountain, astride the Sikkim-Nepal border.

With its weathered brick houses, **Ilam** is a gracious town, by Nepali standards, of about 12,000 people. Its principle industry is tea and you can visit the factory where the leaf is cured before it is shipped to Kath-

ABOVE: Colorful market stall.
OPPOSITE TOP: Worn brick facades provide a pleasant backdrop to village life.
BOTTOM: Weaver works handloom.

mandu and to the rest of Nepal. Villagers also run cottage industries turning out a wide and attractive range of handmade cloth, blankets, sweaters, and carpets.

ACCESS

By bus from **Biratnagar** or **Dharan** to **Birtamodh** and another bus from **Birtamodh** to **Ilam.** Also one hour by bus from **Bhadrapur (Chandragadhi).**

DHANKUTA REGION

DHARAN BAZAAR

Focal point of this region, lying at the base of the ever-green Vijaypur Hills, is Dharan Bazaar. An unusual feature of town life is the Union Jack that flies over one of the squat single-storied buildings. This is one of the British Army Gurkha recruiting centers in Nepal. Wiry teenagers from the hills continue a long and noble tradition, enlisting — usually for life — while older generations, now retired, make the long trek each month from the same hills to pick up their pensions.

A tough physical examination limits the number of recruits but those who succeed are fitted out with new uniforms and flown to Hong Kong for 10 months' basic training, thereafter returning home for their first leave to a heroes' welcome from their relatives and neighbors.

The new recruits walk through Dharan smiling proudly at their success and browsing among the market stalls in the old town where vendors peddle oranges, butter, and herbs. The orchards of the Vijaypur Hills are rich and productive, and surplus fruit is preserved in a recently established canning factory. Access is by bus from Biratnagar.

DHANKUTA

Dhankuta, stands on a ridge in the hills above Dharan, pleasantly cool at an elevation of 1,200 m (4,000 ft), and famous for its orange groves and its leafy scenery punctuated by many mountain streams, their

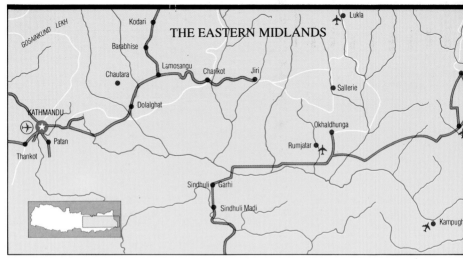

crystal clear-waters dancing between grassy banks lined with pine and oak forests. Its streets are lined with myriad tea houses, the market town itself serving as a commercial, banking, and government center. One modern wonder for townsfolk has been the arrival of electric power. Its gabled black-and-white houses, and dreamy ways are strikingly reminiscent of an Alpine village. A modern motor road winds its way from Dharan to Dhankuta. By foot it takes about five hours to climb 32 km (20 miles), via Bijaipur to this ancient Newar town.

TUMLINGTAR AND THE ARUN VALLEY

Close to the ridge on which Dhankuta stands lies one of Nepal's most remote and beautiful regions. Nowhere are the country's stunning scenic contrasts more sharply defined than in the **Arun valley,** lying in the shadows of the Khumbu Harkna Himal, below Makalu's daunting 8,481-m (27,825-ft)-high peak with the wide and lazy Arun river meandering along the valley floor.

The river bestows a mantle of verdant green and nourishes the cool leafy trees which provide shade all along this enchanted valley and its many companion valleys, equally as lovely. Its villages have remained unchanged for centuries.

Royal Nepal Airlines Twin Otters touch down in the meadow at **Tumlingtar,**

the Arun valley's main settlement, on scheduled flights from Kathmandu or the Terai. There is access by road from Biratnagar.

Though only a short distance northward above the tree-clad hills rise the world's mightiest mountains, at its lowest levels the valley could be part of Africa.

The red bare earth is dotted with stunted sparse semi-arid savanna grassland. Groves of succulents and stands of banana trees repeat the African image. The heat of the sun's rays, funneled into the valley by the rising hills, is merciless. Brickmakers use the heat to bake their product for the thatched Tudor-like cottages of the hamlets that dot the valley and perch on the hillsides.

In the north, the valley is bounded by the snow-covered 4,100-m (13,500-ft)-high Shipton pass — beyond which lie the mountain ranges surrounding the three great peaks of Everest, Makalu, and Lhotse.

Anglers delight in the **Ishwa valley,** its slopes thick with rhododendrons and magnolias, and its mountain streams alive with fish.

Barun, another valley, its walls a tangled jungle of undergrowth, with rushing streams and plunging waterfalls, forms an amphitheater with distant Makalu centerstage.

It was in one of the rivers in this area — at a height of almost 5,000 m (17,000 ft) — that a wildlife expert discovered what may well be the only high-altitude salamander in the world.

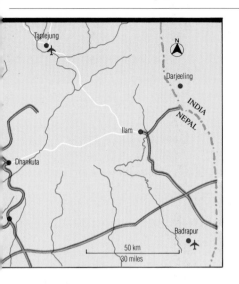

RUMJATAR

A stiff two- to three-day trek over the western ridge takes the fit and the active out of the Arun valley and down into **Rumjatar,** set at 1,300 m (4,500 ft) in the valley of the **Dudh Kosi river.**

OKHALDUNGA REGION

Some kilometers away, **Okhaldunga,** a pleasant unspoilt village with an old fortress, has given its name to this lyrical essay of hill and valley, river and lake.

Many of the birds, which give Nepal one of the most richly varied collections of avifauna in the world, are found on the forest-clad 3,000-m (10,000-ft)-high crests of the **Neche Dahuda Hills,** overlooking the valley floors. Flocks of them, some vividly-colored, flit from tree to tree — their dawn chorus in springtime a hosanna to life reborn.

Okhaldunga lies directly at the foot of Everest but few attempt the exhausting trek through these foothills to the roof of the world.

CHARIKOT AND THE ROLWALING VALLEY

West by north-west from Okhaldunga as the Himalayan crow flies, **Rowaling valley** (*rolwaling* is a Sherpa word that means "the furrow")

lies in the shadows between the Everest region of Khumbu Himal and Langtang Himal.

Long has this valley, shaped by the flood-waters that burst out of a nine-meter (30-ft)-wide opening in a sheer rock wall on the east bank of the Bhote Kosi river, fascinated those who visit it. Many pilgrims believe that this is the spot where Shiva thrust his trident into the mountainside to let the waters cascade down to the holy Ganges. It's in the upper reaches of the Rolwaling valley that members of the Sherpa and Tamang communities talk about the yeti — that elusive Abominable Snowman which has been seen so often by the Sherpa guides who live in the valley.

Perched at around 2,000 m (6,500 ft), just a few hours drive from Kathmandu, the small pleasant village of **Charikot,** with hotels and shops, is gateway to this region. But progress through Rolwaling valley from there-on is solely by foot (*see* TREKKING, page 137).

Three dining chairs stand outside the tea house in the tiny 10-house hamlet of **Piguti,** its quietness broken only by the scurry of pye-dogs chasing a lone trekker through its one street.

Here too trekkers are few, leaving Rolwaling's many splendors — including the magnificent amphitheater of Gaurisankar — to delight only the rare visitor.

Higher up, one-, two-, and three-storied houses cling to the edge of the precipitous paddy fields, now brown, awaiting the monsoons, as cotton wool clouds dab the little knolls and grassy shoulders with a chill-like balm to ease the sting of the sun.

The paths that climb up the mountain slopes veer left and then right, across perilous-looking rope or steel-hawsered suspension bridges, many run on a toll basis.

Slowly the trail winds through the forests to the highest settlement — a small close-knit Sherpa community. The 200 families of **Beding** live in small but striking stone houses with elegantly painted and carved exteriors.

There's also a monastery. Among the many holy places of the Himalaya, Beding is remembered as the refuge of Guru Padma Sambhava, the mystic Tantric recluse who chose the small cave in the cliff, about 150 m (500 ft) above the monastery, as his place of meditation 1,200 years ago.

Soon after this the trail passes beyond the tree line to the land of the yeti... .

Off the Beaten Track

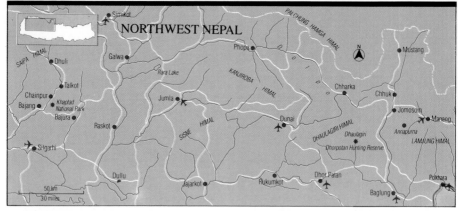

JUMLA AND LAKE RARA

South-west of Pokhara lies **Baglung** — approachable only on foot or by dubious road from the Terai—gateway to the **Royal Dhorpotan Hunting Reserve.** Hand-made paper, used for packing and bamboo crafts, is its most famous product. It's the home of the Thakalis, a small group of no more than 20,000 people of Tibetan-Mongoloid stock, speaking a Tibetan-Burmese vernacular, whose faith is a mixture of Buddhism, Hinduism, and Bonpo.

It also earns praise, from the impotent and those on the wane, for the power of a local aphrodisiac — *Silajit.* Locals travel far north to exploit deposits of this tar-like substance that oozes from rocks and fetches high prices in India. Tastefully produced crafts include woolen blankets, vests, rugs, and other sewn or woven handicrafts.

After Baglung you're deep into Nepal's mystical west: closed, barred, and still little known. Yet it once nurtured a great kingdom of the Mallas that reached its height in the fourteenth century. The capital of this ancient kingdom, **Jumla,** set almost 2,400 m (8,000 ft) above sea level, can only be reached by plane — unless you're an untiring trekker prepared to walk for weeks. Consequently, though there's a scheduled Royal Nepal Airlines service to Jumla — subject, of course, to weather and other vagaries — there are few visitors to this region.

Ringed by magnificent peaks, Jumla is truly a natural paradise, a quaint rural town with a bazaar, lined by the flat-roofed houses of the region and boasting no more than 50 shops, a bank, police station, and the inevitable tea houses.

The Mallas kept a winter capital at Dullu, in the south of the Mahabharat Lekh range of hills, and maintained a territory that stretched from the humid Terai to the Taklahar in Western Tibet—over trails that even today few tackle. Yet they left a magnificent legacy in Jumla: sculptured temples, stone pillars, and the still-living folk songs of the region. But this beauty is well-guarded. Few disturb its tranquility and population is sparse. The **Karnali Zone** — one of 14 in Nepal — has a total population of around 300,000: no more than 12 people to every square kilometer.

There's an old highway along the Tila Nadi valley where you measure your pace by the distance between the ancient milestones placed here as long ago as the fifteenth century. Two days hard slog bring reward—a refreshing dip in the hot springs at **Seraduska.** Walk east for three days and you'll reach **Gothichaur,** an alpine valley set more than 2,900 m (9,500 ft) above sea level —flanked by pine forests with a stone shrine and a water spout, a reminder of the Malla dynasty, together with stupendous views of two little-known peaks, Chyakure Lekh and Patrasi Himal. Jumla is also the stepping off point for a long, hard trek to the Shangri-la valley of **Humla.**

Best of all, make the four-day trek over high passes like **Padmara, Bumra,** and the 3,456-m (11,341-ft)-high **Ghurchi pass,** and finally **Pina,** to **Lake Rara,** Nepal's most enchanting National Park. The lake is the

Kingdom of Nepal's largest sheet of water, covering 10 sq km (four sq miles) almost 3,000 m (10,000 ft) above sea level. Snow lingers here as late as May and June but its crystal-blue waters are haven to a treasury of hardy avian visitors, particularly mallards, pochards, grebes, teals, and other species from the north. The park itself covers 104 sq km (41 sq miles). Alpine meadows line the lake shores and fields of millet and wheat are flanked by pine forests.

There are apple orchards and the lake waters are rich with fish. Several villages stand on its shores, their houses, terraced like the land, backed on to steep hillsides. Wildlife includes hordes of impudent monkeys who raid farms and grain stores with seeming impunity. Set like a sapphire in its Himalaya amphitheater, Lake Rara is both a botanical and faunal treasury.

Another national park, **Khaptad** — several days distant, south-west of Rara — stands at much the same elevation, covering 187 sq km (73 sq miles): a floral repository of high-altitude conifers, oak and rhododendron forests, its open meadows reserved for royalty.

West lie more little-known valleys reached only on foot and south, too, the trade caravans — even goats and sheep are used as pack animals — must travel daunting distances over forbidding terrain before reaching the temperate and fertile lands of the Mahabharat and the tropical fields of the Terai.

How to Get There

Permits are needed for travel to these areas. If you obtain one, you can either fly on RNAC's scheduled domestic service or go by foot.

DOLPO

North-east of Jumla, so remote from the nearest road it takes three weeks of tough walking to reach, Dolpo and its monasteries straggle up a pitch of long, tortuous ridges, above an expanse of rumpled, brown and barren mountains. The creed of the Shaman — spirit-possessed holy men — still

rules here, as it has done for 15 centuries. In the rarefied air of these 3,000 to 5,000 m (10,000 to 16,000 ft) heights, perceptions and sensations are acute. Sitting atop a mountain ridge in the dark night in a yak-hair tent, wind howling, rain lashing down, watching the Shaman as he is taken hold of by "Fierce Red Spirit with the gift of the life force of seven black wolves" is enough to convince even the most cynical witness from western civilization of the power of the supernatural.

The population of a few hundred in

Dolpo has been swollen by Tibetan refugees. All make votive offerings, some of tablets of clay and funeral ash delicately carved with a pantheon of Buddhist deities. At a height of more than 4,000 m (13,000 ft), Dolpo's grain fields are among the highest cultivated land in the world. The paths and trails that lead through this tiny principality of old are often no more than fragile, crumbling shale strata sticking out of a sheer cliff face. With a sheer drop centimeters away on one side, as you stoop low under an overhang, it's only for the brave or agile.

This is a land of holy peaks of which the most revered is the valley's sacred Crystal Mountain. According to local legend, a thousand years ago a Tibetan ascetic, Drutob Senge Yeshe, flew to the top of the harsh slab of rock, a massif that rises out of the shale around it, aboard a magic snow lion and challenged the god who lived there. When he defeated him, the rock turned to

Happy Sherpa youngsters reflect the spirit of their mountain homeland.

crystal. Now Dolpo people circle the 16 km (10 mile) circumference of the mountain's base in an annual pilgrimage known as *kora*. Its many strata — layers of rock — also draw pilgrims of a different faith: geologists hunting fossils.

HOW TO GET THERE

On foot with guide and porters.

MUSTANG

Dolpo's neighboring kingdom, where myth and fantasy seem stronger than reality, is Mustang, reached by a long trek through the Kali Gandaki gorge and over the one, desperately high, south-east facing pass into Dolpo. The native name for this lunar land of canyons and ridges is Lo. In the capital, **Mantang,** dominated by fortress walls, the central feature is the massive white-walled **Royal Palace** in which lives the world's least-known monarch. Schools are bringing change. But while the youngsters come home filled with stories of space flights which they've heard on the classroom wireless, their grandparents still believe the world is flat and shaped like a half moon.

Lo Mantang, in fact, is the full name of the 2,000 sq km (772 sq mile) kingdom of His Highness King Jigme Parwal Bista, founded in the fourteenth century by the Tibetan warlord Ama Pal. It lies on a barren valley floor at around 4,800 m (15,000 ft), snug against the Tibetan border on three sides and guarded by formidable 7,300-m (24,000-ft)-high mountains, pierced only by narrow passes. On the Nepal side, massive Dhaulagiri, at 8,167 m (26,795 ft) the world's seventh-highest mountain, provides the defence which has sealed Lo from the outside world through the centuries.

Fabled Mustang, as it's now known on the maps, is only an "honorary" kingdom these days but each night King Jigme, the 25th monarch since the 1480s, orders the only gate of the mud-walled capital shut and barred to keep out invaders or intruders. Twelve dukes, 60 monks, 152 families and eight witches occupy the capital.

King Jigme still owns serfs who plow his stony fields for grain crops. But Lo's treasures are many and priceless: a wealth of Tibetan art, monasteries and forts set in its 23 villages and two other towns. Many of Mustang's monasteries — the name derives from the Tibetan phrase meaning "plain of prayer", *mon thang* — are carved into cliff faces. You climb a ladder to reach them. Other wealth lies in the rocky hills: turquoise, and rich deposits of alluvial gold on the beds of the rivers that course through the land. But Lo's citizens consider the task of panning for this metal beneath their dignity.

The King's subjects — Lopas, who are Laimaist Buddhists — number around 8,000 and speak their own dialect of the Tibetan language. The women practise polyandry

— often marrying two or three brothers. The king keeps his authority as a ruler by virtue of a 160-year-old treaty to King Birendra Shah's dynasty and payment to Nepal of 886 rupees a year and one horse. In return he holds the rank of Colonel in the Nepali Army.

So archaic is the kingdom, matches were unknown until a few years ago and superstitious fears are rampant. The whole land goes to bed in terror of Lo's 416 demons of land, sky, fire, and water, and life is dedicated to warding off the evil spirits which can cause Lo's 1,080 known diseases as well as five forms of violent death. Thus, for three days each year, King Jigme's subjects celebrate New Year by "chasing the demons": with the noise of cymbals, drums, and notes made by playing on human skulls, filling the air.

Not a single tree grows in this arid and withered land. To supplement their monotonous diet of yak milk and sour cheese, they nurture fragile gardens. For trade, the Lopas deal in salt from Tibet. The trail they follow winds for 240 km (150 miles) along the Kali Gandaki gorge between Dhaulagiri and Annapurna.

HOW TO GET THERE

On foot with guide and porters from Pokhara.

Valley in the shadows of Tibet's Cho Oyu, one of the world's highest mountains.

High Altitude Trekking and Treks

THE HIGH MOUNTAIN VALLEYS AND PASSES

All Nepal is geared up to cater for the high-altitude trekker. In summer — between April and October — the major blemish is the number of leeches. These persistent and loathsome creatures infest the muddy trails and infiltrate everything. The best time to trek is late September and early October when the mountain views are incredible (and continue to be so throughout crisp

miss your flight you drop back to the bottom of the list which, on one occasion, meant an extended stay of some three weeks for one unlucky person.

By plane it is only 40 minutes from Kathmandu to Lukla, more than 2,700 m (9,000 ft) above sea level. Its landing strip is on an uphill gradient, one side of which drops precipitously thousands of meters to the floor of the Dudh Kosi valley.

Namche Bazaar is well above Lukla. There is also a 4,000-m (13,000-ft)-high airfield nearby — at **Syangboche** where guests

winter), or in the first quarter of the year when haze tends to cover the peaks.

There are literally hundreds of treks to choose from in the eight major trekking regions of Nepal, Your choice will depend upon the time you have and the time of year.

The major trekking regions are **Kanchenjunga, Makalu, Khumbu Himal, Rolwaling Himal, Langtang Himal–Jugal Himal–Ganesh Himal, Manaslu, Annapurna Himal,** and **Dhaulagiri Himal.**

Khumbu is for the serious, hardy trekker — a 25 to 30 day trip walking between Sherpa villages. Though the scenery is sensational, it's extremely cold. If you fly in and out, expect some delays. **Lukla** flights are inextricably tied to the weather — and if you

of the Everest View Hotel alight. Each bedroom in this hotel is equipped with oxygen.

Almost everybody who visits Nepal dreams of standing at the foot of the world's greatest mountain, but it's an achievement only for the fittest. Most of the trail takes you above 4,000 m (13,000 ft) in thin, freezing, raw air — chest pounding, lungs gasping — to the 6,000-m (20,000-ft)-high Everest base camp, higher than any point in Africa or Europe.

Yet it's not just the mountain and its huddle of neighboring peaks, three of the world's seven highest, which is the sole attraction, for this is also a land of fable and monastery, remote meadows, wildlife, and the home of the hardy Sherpa folk and their colorful culture.

The trail from Lukla climbs up the Dudh Kosi canyon, zigzagging from side to side through stone-walled fields, rustic villages and hardy forests. The Buddhist prayer — *Om mani padme hum*, Hail to the jewel in the lotus — is carved everywhere, on the huge boulders that stand by the side of the trail and on top of long stone walls that look like enormous tables.

These carvings are built to pacify local demons, deities, or the spirit of some dead person and should be circled clockwise, because the earth and the universe revolve in

their prayers of supplication and gratitude are always carried on the breeze to Buddha, the Compassionate One.

Before Namche Bazaar, at the village of Josare, lies the headquarters of **Sagarmatha National Park** where rangers and wardens, used to high-altitude living, relax at 4,000 m (13,000 ft) with games like volleyball. More than 5,000 trekkers a year climb this trail to enter the national park's 1,243 sq km (487 sq miles) of mountain wilderness: the rumpled brown-green buttresses of Everest ascending ever higher as you climb upward.

that direction. If you are walking straight on, keep them on the left as a mark of respect. These are prayers and supplications artistically inscribed with great devotion. Don't take them as souvenirs — it's sacrilege, much as defiling a Christian church, or Muslim mosque is.

Elsewhere, scraps of colored cloth flutter in the breeze, or a bamboo framework is covered with colored threads woven into an intricate design; sometimes you may find dyed wheat-flour dumplings lying on the ground — offerings to malignant demons or deities and not to be touched or disturbed by strangers. These prayer flags may look old and ragged but to the Nepalis, especially the Sherpas, they never fade —

The town, capital of the Sherpa community, is set on a small plateau at the foot of sacred 5,760-m (18,901-ft)-high Khumbila which staunches the long run of the Ngojumba glacier as it slides down from the base of Cho Oyu. It is the focal point of everything that occurs in the Everest region. Every Saturday morning there's a colorful market when hundreds trek in from the surrounding villages and towns to haggle and argue, buying and selling. **Namche**'s streets step up the barren, rocky slopes of Khum-

ABOVE: Sherpa village of Namche Bazaar, main gateway to Everest, nestles in neat rows beneath ice-capped Khumde. OPPOSITE: The glow of Namche Bazaar at night.

bila lined with pleasant white-washed two-story homes with shingle and tin roofs.

Sherpa monasteries, reflecting their Tibetan heritage, are the most striking in Nepal. You'll find them in the towns of **Kunde** and **Khumjung** which stand above Namche Bazaar — and are well worth visiting if you can make the climb — on the slopes of Khumbila. West of Namche, at the foot of the Bhote Kosi valley which is fed by the Jasamba glacier, there's a particularly striking monastery in the village of **Thami.**

You can use Namche to approach **Cho**

Oyu, either west up the Bhote Kosi valley or north of Khumbila up the Dudh Kosi valley. The westward route takes you up the Renjo pass, coming down to **Dudh Pokhari,** a beautiful glacial lake in the Ngojumba glacier. There's a passable chance en route of seeing some of Sagamartha National Park's wildlife: wolf, bear, musk deer, feral goat species, even the brilliantly colored crimson-horned or Impeyan pheasants of this region.

On the trail to Everest, a hard four-hour slog, or a full day's strenuous effort from Namche, you'll come to Khumbu and the most famous of it's monasteries, Thangboche,

Shops and boarding rooms ABOVE in Namche Bazaar, at Solu Khumbu. OPPOSITE: Sherpa porters on market day at Namche Bazaar.

known the world over for its stupendous views of Everest, or maybe Lhotse, or the unmistakable 6,855-m (22,491-ft)-high obelisk of Ama Dablam, in the background.

After his successful ascent of Everest, on 29 May 1953, Sir Edmund Hillary became New Zealand's Ambassador to India and Nepal and devoted much of his diplomatic career and personal life to improving the lot of the Sherpa community that he has come to love. He is a frequent visitor to the monastery and its presiding lama. It was his initiative that led to the establishment of Sagamartha National Park in 1975. The park was run by New Zealand experts until 1981 when Nepal took over its management.Hillary has been back frequently, helping to build schools and community centers.

Civilizing forces, not all for the better, have come apace to the once-isolated Sherpas whose festivals add color and fantasy to life in this otherwise barren but beautiful region. There's also a much more relaxed trek — for those who don't wish to scale great heights — by foot or pony along the old trade route between Kathmandu and Pokhara. Including a visit to Gorkha, this takes between eight and 10 days.

The main trekking area is around **Annapurna Himal** and **Dhaulagiri Himal** from Pokhara with dozens of medium and high altitude walks to choose from, including the "Royal Trek" that follows in the footsteps of the Prince of Wales and gives you three to five days in the Gurung and Gurkha country, east of the Pokhara valley. Highlights of the six- to 10-day Ghandrung to Ghorapani trek are outstanding panoramas of Machhapuchhare, Annapurna, and Dhaulagiri. The 17- to 19-day Kali Gandaki to Muktinah route is in excellent condition in the winter, although some snow is possible at Ghorapani.

Treks around **Dhaulagiri** take you through a veritable wonderland of meadows, forest and villages, and among some of the happiest and most generous people in the world, allowing you to savor the simple lifestyles — and delightful scenery — to the full. The contrast between the stark, ice-white peaks set against the conifer and rhododendron forests, the azure sky above, verdant spring and summer fields below, can draw your breath as much as climbing these heights.

Villages straggle down the hillsides in a series of terraces, just like the paddy and grain fields, and there's always time and reason enough to rest in one of the many Nepali tea houses, simple little cafes where the refreshment helps beat the debilitating dehydration brought about by altitude and exercise. In contrast to the dozens of trekking options around Dhaulagiri and Annapurna, there are few around **Manaslu.** This is all the more delightful perhaps because these still-not-beaten tracks take you to the feet of such giants as 8,158-m (26,766-ft)-high Manaslu and its sister peaks, including sacred 7,406-m (24,298-ft)-high Ganesh Himal I and its seven lesser peaks and forbidding 7,893-m (25,895-ft)-high Himal Chuli.

Take the Trisuli valley through Trisuli Bazaar around the north face of Himal.Chuli and Manaslu and you'll walk through hills clad with evergreen forests, thundering waterfalls, and alpine plants: oaks, alders, firs, and rhododendrons. Villages are built of sturdy gabled, two-storied brick and thatch houses. Among the many large and striking monasteries are some which are surprisingly small — one, with a pagoda-style roof and a circular top, is like a cross between a lighthouse and a Suffolk grain store.

The 14-day trek leaves Ganesh Himal in the east and takes you around the north face of Himal Chuli and Manaslu — almost into China's backyard, through bleak and windswept passes, skirting glaciers and frozen lakes up to a height of more than 4,500 m (15,000 ft).

Close to the border is **Somdu,** Nepal's most remote permanent settlement, a village of 200 souls — about 40 families — whose fields and paddies are covered with snow until late in the year. Nearby, there are also the twin villages of **Li** and **Lo.** All along the way the trails are lined with the inevitable prayer stones, *mani,* of the staunch Buddhists who inhabit the region. Retracing their footsteps to **Trisuli Bazaar,** trekkers turn north-east and climb the trail that winds along the east bank of the Trisuli river to enter one of Nepal's most enchanted regions and another classic trekking region — fabled **Langtang Himal** with its monasteries, stupas, prayer walls and places made sacred by the Hindu scriptures.

When Nepal opened its doors to foreigners in 1950, the first to venture into its hidden mountain sanctuaries were British climbers Eric Shipton and H. W. Tilman who "discovered" the Langtang Himal's many marvels — just 75 km (47 miles) north of Kathmandu — unknown then to many Nepalis. Right at the capital's rear door, no city in the world can claim a more incredible backdrop. Tilman's comment that it is "one of the most beautiful valleys in the world" is still considered an understatement by some. Ancient bo trees, their gnarled limbs like rheumy fingers, spread a thick canopy of shade over Langtang's version of the patio, old stone terraces with seats stepped into the stone work, outside the rustic tea houses which refresh the traveler.

Dominating the valley at its north end is Nepal's 7,245-m (23,769-ft)-high Langtang Lirung, a few kilometers beyond which, on the Tibetan border, rises its sister peak, 7,238-m (23,748-ft)-high Langtang Ri: both overshadowed by Shisha Pangma — sacred 8,013-m (26,291-ft)-high Gosainthan of Hindu mythology — one of the legendary abodes of Shiva. You get sudden and unexpected views of some of these peaks as you take the spectacular trail hacked out of the wall of the gorge above Trisuli Bazaar. On the more level areas, it cuts through thickets of juniper and rhododendron, blue pine and cushion plants.

For centuries it has been a trade route between Kathmandu and Rasuwa Garhi across the border in Tibet. During July and August this rocky track becomes a mass of humanity as devout Hindu pilgrims, worshippers of Shiva, head for Langtang's **Gosainkund** lakeland. These half-a-dozen small lakes sparkle like jewels in the midday sunshine and are said to have been formed when Shiva thrust his trident into the mountainside. From Gosainkund it's possible to walk on over the pass into the remote but eternally beautiful reaches of upper **Helambu,** best in springtime when the rhododendrons bloom. Here, too, the headwaters of Nepal's major river, the **Sun Kosi**, mingle together from scores of tumbling waterfalls, roaring rivers, and laughing streams.

Buddhist prayer stones, *mani*, mark the trails to many sacred mountains in the high Himalayas.

Swiss explorer, geologist, adventurer Tony Hagen shared Tilman's passion for Langtang Himal and ignited the same feelings in another Swiss — a UN farm advisor — who built a Swiss cheese factory close toKyangjin monastery at around 3,840 m (12,500 ft) and which, whatever the quality of the cheese, provides some of the most spectacular mountain views found anywhere.

Langtang's principal purpose is as a wildlife and botanical sanctuary — **Langtang National Park**, a haven for the endangered

snow leopard, leopard, Himalayan black bear, red panda, and wild dog. Outside the 20 or so alpine villages roam 30 different species of wildlife, while more than 150 different kinds of birds have made their home among the region's 1,000 botanical species. It is the most popular of all Nepal's wilderness areas — a wonderland of hardy mountain people, animals, birds, forests, and mountains —much of it preserved as the nation's second largest national park spread across 1,243 sq km (480 sq miles).

In the far west, trekking from **Jumla** always poses problems — simply because it's so difficult to reach this remote region. But the spectacular scenery makes the effort worthwhile. The trekking "high season" is between October and December — the classic time for high-altitude climbing treks when the more popular routes — Khumbu, Pokhara, Ghandrung, Ghorapani, and Annapurna — are congested.

Trekkers rest outside a tea shop ABOVE on the trail to Mount Everest and Sherpa women take to the trail OPPOSITE near Lukla.

KANCHENJUNGA

Astride the Sikkim border with eastern Nepal, **Kanchenjunga** is the world's third-highest mountain, and this 16-day journey depends on absolute fitness and acclimatization, as it takes the trekker from the subtropical lowlands to a height of more than 5,000 m (16,000 ft) above sea level — around the base of some magnificent satellite peaks — to Yalung glacier. You need first-class equipment including rugged tents and Sherpa guides, together with adequate rations as food supplies are not easy to obtain in this region. The bus ride from Kathmandu to Dharan takes between 11 and 13 hours and you should reserve a seat well in advance.

First Day
North from Dharan to **Dhankuta,** through many small wayside hamlets, with teahouses and bazaars, along a wide road that dips down to a riverbed before climbing steeply to **Sangri La pass** at around 1,000 m (3,280 ft), and then down to the first campsite on the banks of the **Leuti Khola** river.

Second Day
The route continues along the left bank of the **Leuti Khola,** a tributary of the Tamar river, then crosses over a toll suspension footbridge to join the road that winds its way up to Dhankuta on the mountain flank on the opposite bank.

When you cross the bridge, report to the **Murughat checkpost,** then walk through the village on to a wide, steep path along a ridge leading to Dhankuta. There's a teahouse on the summit where you can refresh yourself with a cup of sweet Nepali tea before continuing the trek through the twin hamlets of **Teknara** and **Pangure Phedi.**

The next stop after this is **Yuku,** with a well-shaded rest area beneath the lush foliage of its green trees, and then the trail winds along a ridgeback where Dhankuta comes into view.

Roughly four hours after your walk began, you enter the town. Pitched on the hillside, **Dhankuta's** paved main street climbs steeply up to the town center — hospital, hotels, banks and government offices — and then into the bazaar. Beyond this, at the far end of the street, is a military post where the road becomes a mountain trail again. Lined with many houses, it follows the ridge for 1.5 km (one mile) to **Kakati** where there are plenty of teahouses that offer overnight accommodation. It takes roughly 90 minutes to complete this last leg.

Third Day
From Kakati, the trail continues to **Nigare,** after which the wayside houses begin to thin out. A motor road cuts across the trail which then continues through many villages and hamlets, finally arriving at **Hile** which has a market day every Thursday. Tibetan refugees have swollen the town's population. This first leg takes approximately two hours.

From Hile the trail climbs to the right, through the green and peaceful meadows of the Milkia foothills, along a ridge path, to the tiny hamlet of **Mure** which boasts nine timber houses.

A notable feature are the many wooden benches along the road for the weary traveler to rest — an unusual sight in the Himalaya. From Mure the trail climbs to the summit of a mountain ridge and along its crest to the pretty little settlement of Gurashe: just six white-washed houses.

From here to the village of **Jeroboam** it's easy going, all on the level, before the trail winds out of Jhorbhati up the left flank of the next ridge to **Shidua,** at a height of 2,270 m (7,500 ft), where you can refresh yourself at the teahouse before making camp in the nearby meadow. This second leg takes from three-and-a-half to four hours to complete.

Fourth Day
At Shidua you're on the threshold of the Makalu and Kanchenjunga ranges — rearing up like a barrier in front of you. From the village the trail veers left as it winds up the left flank of these increasingly steeper foothills to **Chitre,** and stunning views to the north-west, taking in 8,481-m (27,825-ft)-high Makalu and 7,317-m (24,005-ft)-high Chamlang.

Leave Chitre by a path to the right along the ridgeback through more thick forest to

Basantpur, a village of 25 houses. This leg should take about two-and-a-half hours. From Basantpur follow the path to **Dobhan** which splits into two — one continuing along the ridgeback, the other winding up and down the hillside to the right. Stick to the ridge: it's shorter and the mountain views are spectacular.

An irrigation duct takes water off one of the streams to the nearby fields as the trail climbs a gentle slope through the twin villages of Tsute. Beyond them, through the forest, the path turns right, leaving the ridge

to climb through stands of rhododendrons before emerging in a delightful alpine meadow — ideal for camping but without water.

Re-enter the forest, however, and climb gently upwards for about another 15 minutes to the two houses of **Door Pani,** at a height of 2,780 m (9,000 ft), where there's a beautiful meadow in which to camp with plentiful water. This second leg is also around two-and-a-half hours walk.

Fifth Day
From the meadow you now climb through the forest to another ridge where the trail now begins to switchback — up and down — in true Himalayan fashion. Follow this for approximately half an hour before

descending steeply to the left for about 200 m (650 ft) to the village of Tinjure Phedi with its teahouse.

From here the trail follows a ridgeback through copses of rhododendrons beneath sprawling alpine meadows and is relatively smooth and even, until the hamlet of **Chauki,** with its 11 houses and a teahouse. It's a walk of about three hours.

There's no cultivation around these parts and the meadows are used for summer pastures. As you walk through these from Chauki, the magnificent peak of Makalu dominates the horizon, but not long after this you get your first glimpse—and what a glimpse — of Kanchenjunga. Soon after, the trail reaches the foot of the Mongol Bharari pass.

Lined with *mani* stones, it winds gently up to the saddle, through rhododendron forest, cresting the ridge at the hamlet of Ram Pokhari — two lakes and five small houses.

Now the trail winds along the top of a grassy, undulating ridge before descending to **Gupha Pokhari** and its enchanting lake, at a height of 2,985 m (9,790 ft). This second leg also takes about three hours.

Sixth Day

Take the pass to the right, skirting the ridge directly in front of you, when you leave Gupha Pokhari. You'll get your last glimpse of Makalu and Chamlang before turning north-east into the Kanchenjunga massif.

You enter this range on your right, along a winding switchback trail and after an hour's walking you come to the crests of a 3,025-m (10,000-ft)-high pass that descends to **Dobhan.** Along the downward trail are many bunkhouses for trekkers and porters where it's possible to spend the night if you so wish.

After passing these, the trail climbs the second of two small hills before beginning the real descent, through thick forest, to the bottom of the pass and the rice paddies and grain fields of the hamlet of **Gurja Gaon.** From this trail, there are magnificent views of Jannu and Kanchenjunga.

The path continues its descent from Gurja Gaon, rejoining, on the right, the alternate route from Basantpur, to a campsite near **Nesum,** at 1,650 m (5,400 ft). This second leg takes roughly four hours.

Seventh Day

Trekking in the Himalaya is not for those who seek to climb ever upward. Trails plunge dizzily up and down 3,000 m (10,000 ft) or more, and from Nesum the trail continues its descent through a maze of paddy field paths to **Dobhan** and the valley of the **Tamar river.**

There are many hamlets, villages, and teahouses along the way. After about 90 minutes walk you reach **Dobhan**, a picturesque Newar settlement, with a village store and many houses.

It's here that the trail crosses the **Meiwa Khola,** a tributary of the Tamar, on to a level plain with a small hamlet, after which it reaches the **Tamar.** Cross to the left bank, via the suspension footbridge, where the road divides — one a narrow path to Ghunsa, the other a long, climbing ridgeback trail to **Taplejung.**

Now the track climbs steeply as it zigzags its way to **Deoringe school** before easing back into a more gradual climb through terraced fields and scattered forests, passing by the hamlet of **Taribun.** There are many more houses along this well-traveled route.

Finally, just above a public bathhouse, you reach **Taplejung** at 1,798 m (5,800 ft), the administrative capital of this district with post and telegraph office, hospital, government offices, and a military post. It's a good place to replenish food supplies, but fresh meat and vegetables are only available on the Saturday market day. This last leg takes around three-and-a-half hours to complete.

Eighth Day

You leave Taplejung and its cobblestone streets, past the water reservoir, along the path to the airfield on a really steep climb that will take you roughly two hours.

There's a hotel at the edge of the airfield on a level plateau and there's now a gentle climb through the flower-filled meadowlands to the forest, with the mountains to your right, before descending to **Lali Kharka.**

Across the valley stands **Bhanjyang,** which you reach the next day but for now your descent culminates in the fertile fields around **Tambawa,** at 2,000 m (6,500 ft), where you can camp in the fields or near the school. This second leg takes four hours.

Ninth Day

From Tambawa to **Pa Khola** takes about 90 minutes, first to a ridgeback trail and then circuitously down the mountain to Pa Khola.

At Pa Khola, the trail cuts through terraced rice paddies, then across a suspension footbridge to **Kunjar.** Before you reach this lovely alpine village, surrounded by thick rain forest, it passes through a few hamlets.

The path carries on gently upward out of Kunjar until you are high above **Tambawa.** Soon it reaches **Bhanjyang** with many teahouses and striking views of Kanchenjunga, framed by South peak, Main peak, and Yalung Kang.

It descends again, to the left, on a pleasantly easy slope to the terraced fields of **Khesewa,** at 2,100 m (6,800 ft), where you can camp in the surrounding fields. This second leg takes about three-and-a-half hours.

Tenth Day

From Khesewa, the trail descends through forest to the **Nandeva Khola** on the left and, crossing the river, continues down along its banks before entering the forest to the left to begin the climb up the next range of hills to **Loppoding.**

Now the path switchbacks up and down to the rest area, at the delightfully-named hamlet of **Fun Fun.** After this, follow the ridgeback into the hills on the right bank of the **Kabeli Khola,** before a gradual descent through rice and grain fields to village of **Anpan.** This first leg takes roughly three hours.

From Anpan, the trail follows a ridgeback up an easy slope to **Ponpe Dhara,** which sits on its crest, where you can pause to take in the splendid view of distant Jannu, before continuing the winding descent through hamlets and farm fields, to the Kasshawa Khola which you cross by suspension bridge. On the other side you make the slow climb to the village of **Mamankhe.** This leg takes approximately three hours, also.

Eleventh Day

This starts by taking an easy climb, skirting a formidable ridge, to the village of **Dekadin.** After this, the trail follows the right bank of the **Kabeli Khola,** about 200 to 300 m (600 to 900 ft) above its raging waters, winding around various ridges, cliffs, and streams.

On the whole, this three-and-a-half hour walk is an easy up and down trek with constant views of the river below and the little farmsteads and their fields on the hills opposite.

Finally, you descend some stone steps to the river itself and then on to another that takes you on a gradual climb away from the river through villages and fields.

Eventually, after about two hours hard climbing, it reaches the remote village of **Yamphudin,** at 2,150 m (7,000 ft). Report to the checkpost.

Camp here in fields or house compounds.

You may prefer to engage new porters for the hazards of cold, snow, and altitude ahead, as those from Dharan are not well-suited to the rugged challenge of the Kanchenjunga range.

Twelfth Day

Yamphudin is where the real climbing begins and there are two options for the route to **Lamite Bhanjyang.** The favorite choice is to cross the river and trek through **Dhupi Bhanjyang.**

For those who prefer a tougher challenge, however, the second route involves a climb

Sherpa woman and children ABOVE outside a high country teashop on one of Nepal's many popular trekking trails.

up a mountain path from **Yamphudin,** on the right bank of **Omje Khola,** that crosses a stream early in its course.

It then plunges down through the fields back to the **Omje Khola,** two hours, which you must cross again to reach an extremely steep mountain ridge that, at first, demands care with every step.

But it soon enters the forest and there is little or no sense of height. Gradually the severity of the gradient eases into an easy climb, still through thick forest, until it emerges on a level open saddle. Eventually it reaches the climbing hut at **Chitre** where you can spend the night.

However, in the dry season there's no water and you will have to walk on another 90 minutes to a little tarn beneath **Lamite Bhanjyang.** You can ask if water is available at **Yamphudin** before you set off. This second leg takes approximately three hours.

Thirteenth Day

The ridgeback from Chitre is lined with magnolias and bamboo but when the trail climbs beyond the bamboo belt it reaches **Lamite** and its single shelter — a simple structure consisting of a roof with supporting posts.

The trail then ascends through thick stands of rhododendron, along a ridge to **Lamite Bhanjyang,** at 3,430 m (11,250 ft), with Jannu rising up before you above the ridge in all its magnificence, and behind you panoramic views of the foothills around Dharan.

Climb about 150 m (550 ft) from here on the right before descending, through thick forests of rhododendron, to the **Simbua Khola,** with Kanchenjunga's majestic snowclad peak floating above the trees.

The gentle descent almost takes the trail to the waters of the river and then climbs along the left bank for a short distance before crossing over a wooden bridge to the right bank and the campsite at **Torontan,** at 3,080 m (10,100 ft), where you can sleep in one of the caves. This climb takes from three-and-a-half to four hours.

Fourteenth Day

Follow the path, past the caves, along the right bank of the **Simbua Khola.** The forested walls of the valley are thick with pine and rhododendron.

Eventually, after about two hours walking, it reaches **Whata** with its single hut, where it crosses to the right bank of the stream in front of the hut and continues through the thick forest to the snowline.

You'll see a Sherpa shrine with a huge boulder, shaped like a snake. It's designed to ward off the demons, for the Sherpas believe that if anyone dies after this point, evil spirits will fall upon the mountains.

The path leads down to the river bank and up a difficult trail to **Tseram** where you can see your ultimate destination — the terminal moraine of **Yalung glacier.** Behind it are the 7,353-m (24,120-ft)-high Kabru and 7,349 m (24,112 ft) Talung peak. Camp in one of the caves. This last leg takes from two-and-a-half to three hours.

Fifteenth Day

A steep slope, descending from the left, bars the way out of Tseram and you have to retrace your trail to the bank of the **Simbua Khola,** then around its base, before climbing up through stony, terraced field to **Yalung Bara** where a single stone hut marks the end of the tree line. From here you have to carry enough fuelwood for the rest of the trek.

Just above, past several small stone huts, it comes to the right bank of the entrance to the **Yalung glacier** and **Lapsang,** with Lapsang La valley at the left. This first leg takes about three hours.

Now the trail comes to a tiny pond and skirts a protruding cliff face — when you suddenly see before you a stunning panorama: the peaks of 7,317-m (24,005-ft)-high Kabru S., 6,678-m (21,910-ft)-high Rathong, and 6,147-m (20,168-ft)-high Kokthan. Follow the flat trail to the **Ramze** at 4,560 m (15,000 ft) where there is a hut in which you can sleep. This second leg takes about one hour.

Sixteenth Day

The magnificent Yalung glacier veers left at Ramze and just around the corner next-morning you will get your first close up-views of mighty Kanchenjunga.

Now it climbs the lateral moraine to a **Buddhist stupa** from which it descends steeply to the glacier floor and a trail marked by cairns. Lungs gasp in the rarefied air but eventually, after about four hours of really intense effort, you reach the campsite atop the glacier, at 4,890 m (16,000 ft), with magnificent views of 7,710-m (25,294-ft)-high Jannu.

The vista of the mountains surrounding Yalung glacier opens before you — and at the final camp, **Corner Camp,** at 5,140 m (16,900 ft), on the left bank of the glacier, there is a stupendous mountain panorama — a fitting reward for the effort it takes to reach this point and the 14-day trek back to Dharan.

MAKALU

One of the toughest treks in the world takes you from **Dharan,** through the subtropical floor of the **Arun valley,** and over the 4,000-m (13,000-ft)-high **Shipton pass,** to the slopes of the three great peaks of Makalu, Everest, and Lhotse. You must carry all your supplies and Sherpa guides are absolutely essential. Mountain sickness is an ever real threat and, until the monsoons, Shipton pass is buried in snow. The initial trek from Dharan follows that of the Kanchenjunga trek to **Hile.** If you fly from Kathmandu to **Tumlingtar** you can save at least 10 days.

First Day
Outside Hile, the Makalu route turns left off the one leading to Kanchenjunga, and descends suddenly. A grove of alders, on the right, serves as a military camp.

To reach **Pakeri Bash** and its police station, it travels on the left of the ridge that leads down to the Arun river. The village sits on top of the ridge and from the opposite slope, in the distance below, you can see the Arun river.

The trail continues down a steep, rocky path through terraced fields to a small teahouse, under a bo tree, on top of the narrow ridge. This is **Dikre,** with many houses and a school, and it's here that trail switches to the left side of the ridge and climbs to the crest.

Soon it comes to a thick pine forest and a steep hill where the trail moves again to the right, eventually reaching a rest area, with two large bo trees, that marks the village of **Dihare.**

From Dihare, the path leads down to the **Mangmaya Khola,** a tributary of the Arun

river and a hanging bridge, about one kilometer (two-thirds of a mile) upstream of its confluence with the Amur, where it crosses into the village of **Mongmaya.** Altogether the journey takes about seven hours.

Second Day
From here the path along the right bank of the **Mangmaya Khola** swings around to the left bank of the Arun river which, even during the dry season, is always in spate. It runs through desolate, almost Africa-like savanna with stunted vegetation and little cultivation.

There's a post office and police station at **Legwa,** just above the Legwa Khola, and, slightly upstream of the river's confluence with the Amur, a modern suspension bridge allows you to cross the river safely even during the flood and monsoon melt.

If it's the dry season, you can cut across the wide delta at the confluence by following the paths between the paddy fields to **Beltal** with its unusual two-storied hotel.

The path continues through the rice paddies and crosses the **Kyawa Khola** over some stepping stones, beneath the village of Akibunkabeshi, perched on the mountainside above. Then the trail climbs up from the river to a sandy plateau of cornfields to return to the banks of the river where it is blocked by a cliff thrusting into the water. You have to climb a steep and winding rocky cliff with only a steel handrail for protection.

The trail winds down on the other side of the ridge back to the riverbank and on to

Sherpa father and son ABOVE at Lukla.

Surtibari where you camp for the night. Overall, the trek takes from five to six hours.

Third Day
On the riverbed, beneath the village, a wide, sandy area stretches to the 20-m (65-ft)-wide **Pitwa Khola** which is fordable during the dry season, otherwise there's a suspension bridge upstream.

A small ridge juts out from the left bank of the Arun river and when the trail crosses the col it goes down again to the riverbed, to travel below cornfields, passing the four-house hamlet of **Domkota** beneath a sweltering and merciless sun.

From Domkota, where the Arun river forms a large oxbow bend, the path on the left bank leaves the river level and leads through neat little fields into **Khare** where, among the thatched-roof houses, bo trees provide welcome shade.

Leaving the village, the path turns right and then immediately left through a narrow dry streambed, up a hill of brick-red soil covered with sparse vegetation, and then across some small hills to rest awhile in the shade of the bo trees at Gande Pani, after which you cross the suspension bridge to the plateau of **Tumlingtar.**

It's an hour from the airfield, where there's an hotel. This trek takes a total of six hours.

Fourth Day
From the airfield, climb the hill and walk through level rice paddies and scattered houses and then across a series of terraced hills. To the right you see the waters of the **Shawa Khola.** In the distance stands **Chamlang.** Soon the path becomes a ridgeback with many travelers, teahouses and shaded rest areas.

After passing a bubbling spring it moves to the right flank of the ridge, and after a short climb, you will see more houses and finally arrive at the checkpost at the entrance to **Khandbari,** with its shop-lined main street and large open bazaar. This leg takes about two-and-a-half hours.

It's the administrative capital of the district with a bank, hospital, and school. It's a good place to stock up on food and other essentials. A meadow outside the village makes an excellent campsite.

The ridge trail continues to **Mane Bhanjyang** where it divides—one going left to the ridge route; the other right through the rice paddies. Follow this latter route on the gentle climb to the village of **Panguma.**

There's not too much to see and the walk is somewhat monotonous as you climb to **Bhote Bash,** at about 1,720 m (5,600 ft), where you can camp in one of the fields. The last leg is a brisk three-and-a-half hours.

Fifth Day
When you leave Bhote Bash, you also leave

the farmlands and turn right onto the left of the ridge as it climbs to the pass above. The level path passes through scrub and fields to **Gogune,** and on into forest.

After a walk of about two hours, the switchback trail exits at the Gurung village of **Chichira,** set on top of a ridge, then continues to Kuwapani. At this point you get impressive but far distant views of Makalu.

From the three-house settlement of **Kuwapani,** the path veers to the right of the ridge, arriving at **Samurati**'s lone house, where there are painted *mani* stones and a cave in which you can sleep.

Leaving the village, the path divides into two. Take the left fork into the forest through **Fururu** to the rest area in **Daujia Dhara**

Deorali where the path levels out. Down in the forest on the left, across a small stream and over another ridge, there's an unusual combination of painted *mani* stones.

Eventually, the trail reaches **Mure**, a village at the right of the path, where you can camp in the fields or in one of the house compounds. The last leg takes about three hours.

Sixth Day
Leave the village down a slope facing it and fields of Sedua on the hillside opposite and, beyond them, the walls of the Shipton pass.

spring. The last leg takes from two-and-a-half to three hours.

Seventh Day
From **Sedua**, the trail leaves the Arun river and enters the watershed of the **Kashuwa Khola**. Climb a mountainside dotted with terraced fields and forested areas. After about two hours walk a chorten marks the Sherpa village of **Naba Gaon** with its monastery.

Climb a ridge, lined with *mani* stones on the right, and follow the trail along the right bank of the **Kashuwa Khola** through **Khar-**

Not long after this, the trail cuts down the ridge where it veers left, at a single house, to **Runbaun**. Now the trail becomes extremely steep and rough.

Great care must be exercised — and not only on the trail. The suspension bridge over the Arun river, which takes about three-and-a-half hours to reach, is narrow and precarious with missing footboards. One careless step could be fatal.

After the bridge the trail climbs steeply along a precarious and crumbling incline on the right bank up to the grain fields and hamlet of **Rumruma.**

The trail leaves the hamlet through terraced fields to **Sedua**, set at 1,480 m (4,855 ft), where you can camp at the school near a

shing **Kharka** which has two huts.

The path cuts through thick hill forest where fallen trees can make walking difficult. Eventually, it crosses a small stream and leads into the remote village of **Tashi Gaon,** set at 2,050 m (6,700 ft), with its attractive timber houses covered with bamboo roofing. You can camp in the fields near the village. This second leg takes two-and-a-half to three hours.

Eighth Day
Leave **Tashi Gaon** through forest up a gentle slope, across a rocky area and stream, to the

A precarious log and stone bridge leads across the swollen floodwaters that interrupt a rough mountain trail.

meadows of **Uteshe.** From the top of the next ridge there are striking mountain panoramas where the path veers right.

It continues gradually upwards, across a stream into thick bamboo, with no views. When it leaves the bamboo, the trail enters a rhododendron forest and becomes markedly steeper; passing Dhara Kharka on the crest of the ridge, and then to **Unshisa** on the Ishwa Khola side of the ridge, finally reaching the campsite at **Kauma,** at the top of the ridge, after about five hours walking. Just below the ridge, about 20 m (60 ft) down on the Kashuwa Khola side, there are some caves where you can sleep.

Ninth Day
From Kauma, the trail climbs to the top of a ridge that offers the best mountain landscape of the whole trail — a truly dramatic panorama at the far end of the valley of 7,317-m (24,005-ft)-high Chamlang, 6,739-m (22,110-ft)-high Peak Six, 6,105 m (20,030 ft) Peak Seven, and the long-awaited 8,481-m (27,825-ft)-high Makalu, with the outline of the Kanchenjunga Range to the east.

The trail now begins to climb **Shipton pass.** In fact, there are two passes — **Keke La** and **Tutu La.** Rugged cliffs bar the way and the trail traverses to the left to a small pond, then climbs up to **Keke La,** at 4,127 m (13,500 ft), then down into an ess-shaped valley, past a small tarn, and up to **Tutu La.**

Here the trail descends to a level stretch before veering left, past a waterfall, and across a stream, and on through forest to **Mumbuk,** set at 3,500 m (11,500 ft) amid pines and rhododendron. All in all, this stretch takes from five to six hours to complete.

Tenth Day
The trail leaves the campsite, following the course of a winding stream for about 200 m (650 ft) before turning left and down along the side of another rushing stream, turning left yet again, past a cave, to the **Barun Khola.**

The path takes the right bank with views of Peak Six. Beware of the frequent rockfalls. Soon Makalu comes into view and the trail exits onto a terraced hill and the meadows of **Tematan Kharka.**

It continues along a small range of flat hills to **Yangre Kharka** where there are

some caves and on into rhododendron forest.

Here it leaves the **Barun Khola,** climbing gently up the side of a wide valley and turns right, across a stream, to the single hut of **Nehe Kharka** 2,670 m (8,760 ft) — a total walking time of approximately five hours.

Eleventh Day
Leave the camp site, past a cave, and cross to the left bank of the **Barun Khola** over a wooden bridge set on a large boulder in midstream, into rhododendron forest. The path becomes steep as it zigzags up to the meadowlands on the slopes of **Ripock Kharka.**

Here the path leads away from the Barun Khola, on a modest gradient, through **Jark Kharka** to **Ramara** — offering views along the way, one after the other, of 6,830-m (22,409-ft)-high Pyramid peak, 6,720-m (22,048-ft)-high Peak Four, 6,477-m (21,251-ft)-high Peak Three, 6,404-m (21,101-ft)-high Peak Five, Peak Six, and Chamlang.

At Ramara, approaching the Barun Khola, the trail reaches the snout of **Lower Barun glacier** and continues along the glacier's left bank to the headwaters of the **Barun Khola** and **Mere** where there is a cave for camping. There are no more forests and you must carry enough fuelwood with you from this point for your energy needs.

The trail continues on the right across rocky, glacial terrain to **Shershon,** set at 4,615 m (15,000 ft).

Twelfth Day
The majestic crest of Makalu dominates the horizon at Shershon as the trail skirts the base of its southeast ridge in an easy climb on to lateral moraine. Here, glowering down from its massive height, the mountain seems to fill the sky.

Take the trail down to the riverbed, across the stream, and up a terraced hill to **Makalu base camp,** set in a pastoral meadow at 4,800 m (15,750 ft), where there's a stone hut without a roof.

It's an ideal place from which to explore the area around the foot of this great mountain, including the Barun glacier.

The trail leads down to the riverbed and then along a well-defined path that circles left to a meadow known as **Baruntse base**

camp, with stunning views of Everest and Lhotse at the far end of the valley.

Climb the hill behind for more panoramic views of the world's greatest mountains.

But the best view of all, seen in a 360 degree arc, is from the base of Makalu's south-east ridge which is reached by cutting across the riverbed and climbing for about 90 minutes — when Makalu, Everest, and Lhotse seem to encircle you like a real life cinema.

The return trek to **Thumlingtar** takes about seven days.

visible in the far distance. The trail out of town leads down a wide, gentle gradient through many hamlets to the village of **Dolakha** with its striking three-storied houses.

Turn right in the village square to a steep ridge route that descends to the right bank of the Tamba Kosi and the suspension bridge to the immediate left which crosses over to an easy trail just above the rushing water.

Eventually, it arrives at **Piguti** where the trail crosses the **Gumbu Khola** to a pleasant meadow where you can camp. Altogether, the trek takes from six to seven hours.

ROLWALING HIMAL

Few tourists or trekkers visit Rolwaling Himal, yet it offers some of the finest mountain atmosphere experienced anywhere and trekking trails that are truly delightful. You need full equipment, including durable tents and Sherpa guides. You reach Charikot by bus from Kathmandu to Lamosangu and then by van to **Charikot.**

First Day

From Charikot, Rolwaling Himal is clearly

Second Day

Leave camp, past the suspension bridge over the main stream, and follow the path along the right bank with views of Gaurisankar rising up at the far end of the valley.

Soon the trail reaches **Shigati,** where there is a checkpost and a large tributary of the Bhote Kosi that enters the river from the left.

Once across the suspension bridge over the Shigati Khola, the valley narrows and walls become precipitous cliff faces. The trail leads on to another suspension bridge that takes it back to the left bank and along an undulating path to the village of **Suri Dhoban.**

Leaving this settlement, the trail crosses the **Khare Khola** over another suspension

ABOVE: Three generations of Sherpa women.
OVERLEAF: Winter sunset on Lhotse.

High Altitude Trekking and Treks

bridge and on through the precipitous **Bhote Kosi** valley. The trail is reasonably good, but occasional landslides may mean making a detour down to the riverbed or up over the hills.

Eventually, the trail reaches the terraced hills and cultivated fields of **Manthale,** set at around 1,070 m (3,200 ft), where you can camp. The whole of this trek takes from five-and-a-half to six hours.

Third Day

Leave the village by taking the path through

the fields and over a bridge to the right bank and a moderately sloping, undulating, walled path to Congar where it crosses a stream.

After some distance, the valley narrows and becomes precipitous and the trail traverses an area of tumbled rock and boulders to a waterfall on the opposite bank.

Here there is a crossroads, where you leave the old Silk Road to Tibet, and take the path on the right, down to the bridge and the river below, which then climbs steeply in zigzag fashion through breaks in the valley walls.

At the top it exits onto terraced fields, where the path is lined with many stones and chortens, to **Simgaon,** set at 1,950 m (6,300 ft). No longer visible, but still audible

far below, the the Bhote Kosi cuts deep through the valley gorge, its waters diverted to the fields spread over the hills on either side. Total walking time is about six hours.

Fourth Day

Follow the path from the campsite, through terraced fields, to the crest of the next ridge — with splendid views of 7,146-m (23,438-ft)-high Gaurisankar — and into a dense rhododendron forest that zigzags up the mountain to the crest of another ridge.

The trail follows the crest of the ridge through more rhododendron to emerge in the fields and meadows around **Shakpa** and then up the mountains on the Rolwaling side of the valley into more thick forest.

Leaving this, the path climbs steeply down some dangerous and tricky sections to cross a stream. It then skirts a ridge to reach **Cyalche,** set at 1,760 m (5,570 ft), where you can camp on the grass.

Fifth Day

From the campsite, the path descends steeply and diagonally to the **Rolwaling Chhu** and along the riverbed, before veering to the left bank and through a narrow valley, and over a covered wooden bridge to the right bank.

It continues across a stream by the bridge, and climbing gently, follows an undulating path to **Nyimare,** then **Ramding** and **Gyabrug,** where the roofs of the stone-walled houses are weighed down with stones.

It then crosses another stream before climbing, briefly, to the last permanent village in this region, **Beding,** set at 3,690 m (12,100 ft), which boasts 32 houses and a monastery. You can camp near the river with views of 7,180-m (23,557-ft)-high Menlungtse, Rolwaling Himal's major peak.

From this base you can make a three-day diversion to **Manlung La** by taking the trail, along the mountain flank on the right bank, just after the village.

The first day, it climbs to a 4,900-m (16,000-ft)-high campsite, via Taten Kharka. The second day takes you to Manlung La, set at 5,510 m (18,000 ft), and back. The trail is crevassed and you will need ropes, picks, and ice axes.

Sixth Day

Leave the village, past the **Manlung La** diversion on your left, follow the right bank of the Rolwaling Chhu on a gradual climb through the valley to **Na Gaon,** a village with terraced and walled potato fields.

Leaving the village, the trail crosses a wooden bridge and mountains come into view — 6,698-m (21,976-ft)-high Chobutse and 6,269-m (20,569-ft)-high Chugimago — before the snout of the Ripimo Shar and Tram Bau glaciers push in ahead to block the valley and the view.

five days to return to Charikot from this point.

MANASLU

An inspiring 14-day outward trek, from **Trisuli Bazaar** to the **Burhi Gandaki,** through huge and steep valleys, over snowclad passes and foaming rivers, to the three peaks of Manaslu, known as "the Japanese peaks".

Excellent equipment and Sherpa guides are essential and because of its duration; so are adequate food supplies and physical

The trail crosses a wooden bridge, shortly thereafter leaving the main path and turning left to **Omai Tsho** up a ridge that offers a spectacular vista of 6,735-m (22,097-ft)-high Kang Nachungo and the mountains surrounding Ripimo glacier.

The path to **Tsho Rolpa** skirts the base of the Ripimo glacier and passes between **Ripimo** and **Tram Bau** glaciers on to the right bank of **Tram Bau glacier.** It becomes narrower and narrower as the valley becomes shallower.

Rising up at the far end of the valley are 6,730-m (22,081-ft)-high Pigphera-Go Shar and 6,666-m (21,871-ft)-high Pigphera-Go Nup.

Soon you arrive at the last camp, **Rolpa Chobu,** set at 4,540 m (15,000 ft). It takes

fitness. Plan on extra rest days to help you recover during the course of the trek.

Board a bus at **Sorkhuti** on the northern side of Kathmandu for **Trisuli Bazaar.** Reserve your seat in advance. The journey takes four hours.

First Day

Camp in the meadow in front of the military post, a short climb up from Trisuli Bazaar town. Take the path along the riverbed and up the righthand plateau to Raxun Bazaar.

Dry stone wall OPPOSITE marks the trail into the Himalayan village of Phakdingma. Harvesting potatoes ABOVE in a high country village on the approach to Mount Everest.

High Altitude Trekking and Treks

It's a wide, smooth path that cuts through the paddies to **Gote Thati,** by suspension bridge over the Somrie Khola along its right bank, and on through the villages of **Ghorakki,** Shiraune Bash, and **Kaple Bash.**

Before long, signs of cultivation vanish and the river is dry. Now the path climbs a ridge to **Somrie Bhanjyang,** set at 1,290 m (4,200 ft), over a pass lined with teahouses to the valley floor and the hamlet of **Kinu Chautara** with its many teahouses.

The path continues through farm fields and then crosses to the right bank of the **Thofal Khola,** down a gradual incline to the hamlet of **Jor Chautara.** Soon after this, it reaches **Baran Gurun** where you can camp in the compound of people's homes or in the fields. It's close to six hours walking, all in.

Second Day

Leaving camp, the trail crosses a small stream and then up some steep stone steps to **Baran,** through a small hamlet and along a winding mountain path, to the Tamang village of **Tharpu.**

Shortly afterwards, it reaches **Tharpu Bhanjyang,** with its one general store, then climbs down a pass to Boktani. Not long after reaching here it begins to climb a ridge to **Col Bhanjyang** where it joins the mountain trail along the side of the Thofal Khola.

It's gentle, pastoral countryside — small foothills rolling away to distant horizons, sheltering gentle valleys — and eventually the trail takes you through **Katunche,** which boasts a bank and post office, onto the trail to **Charanki Pauwa** and **Charanki Phedi,** where you can camp in the fields outside the village.

Third Day

Leaving the village, the narrow path crosses a small stream, over Achani Bhanjyang pass, and down to the left bank of the Ankhu Khola where it crosses a suspension bridge to **Kale Sundhara Bazaar.**

At this point, the landscape is sweltering and subtropical all the way to **Gaili Chautara** where, just beyond the village, you leave the main path and take the path to the

left, much of it along the side of the river, through **Hansi Bazaar,** with its teahouses and shops, and between paddy fields in the riverbed.

Where the Ankhu Khola bends to the left, the path veers right to **Arughat Bazaar** through a small, narrow valley, and over a sprawling terraced hill that stands between the Ankhu Khola and Burhi Gandaki.

When it reaches the village of **Soliental,** and the **Burhi Gandaki,** you can see Arughat Bazaar below. Take the path along the left bank of the Burhi Gandaki for **Arughat Bazaar,** a small, bustling town on either side of the river. Its central shopping area, with bank, is on the right side of the river across a suspension bridge.

You can camp in the grove near the school, just outside the town. The entire walk should take from four-and-a-half to five hours.

Fourth Day

Out of Arughat Bazaar the trail follows the right bank of the Burhi Gandaki to its source, along a path through farm fields and **Mordar.**

When you reach **Simre** the dry season trail follows the riverbed to **Arket.** During the monsoon it climbs over the hills. You cross the Arket Khola at **Arket,** through the village and its teahouses, and across more farmland to the **Asma Khola** which you cross to climb up to **Kyoropani.**

From this hamlet, the path is straight and level for a short distance and then descends to the river bank and on through another hamlet to its confluence with the Soti Khola where you can camp in the fields on the right bank. Total walking time is between four-and-a-half to five hours.

Fifth Day

Follow the trail along the riverbed for about 10 minutes and then take the winding path up the forested hill to **Almara, Riden,** and Riden Gaon.

Soon the Burhi Gandaki valley becomes a precipitous gorge until it reaches another valley that cuts into the opposite bank and opens up. Now the trail crosses farmlands to **Lapbesi** and then down to the white riverbed of the **Burhi Gandaki.**

Teahouse and restaurant OPPOSITE TOP in Trisuli Bazaar's main street BOTTOM.

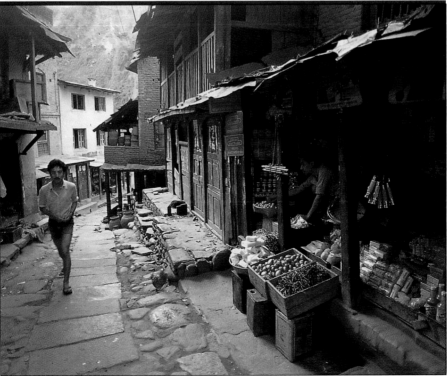

Another path follows the mountain contours, rejoining the trail from the riverbed near the hamlet of **Kani Gaon.**

Continue along an undulating path above the river to **Machha Khola,** with its teahouse, where you can camp in the fields outside the village. It should take no longer than six hours.

Sixth Day

Leave across the Machha Khola and follow the path along the river bank into a precipitous valley and across the abundant flow of

the Tado Khola to **Kholabensi,** a hamlet of eight houses.

The trail now continues along the bank of the **Burhi Gandaki,** between two walls of sheer cliff, to the hot springs of **Tatopani.** Soon after, it crosses a suspension bridge to the left bank into forest and then along a gravel path by the river to **Dobhan** where there is a teahouse.

Here the trail crosses the Dobhan Khola and some rocks, to the point where the Burhi Gandaki bends right into raging rapids. It climbs up the hill above the rapids which suddenly broaden out into a sluggish, meandering stream between white beaches.

Now cross the **Yaru Khola,** climb into the forested hillside to **Lauri** and the suspension

bridge to the right bank, where the trail climbs again—along a winding path that dips down once more to the riverbed and an easy walk through the fields to the checkpost at **Jagat,** set at 1,350 m (4,400 ft). This is the last village with a shop. You can camp in the fields outside the village. Total walking time is between six-and-a-half to seven hours.

Seventh Day

You leave Jagat down some stone steps to the river, crossing the tributary flowing in from the left, and then walk along the right bank before climbing a terraced hill to **Saguleri** where you can suddenly see 7,177-m (23,540-ft)-high Sringi Himal rising up at the end of the valley.

Follow the undulating path along the right bank to **Sirdi Bash** and on to the the next village, **Gata Khola,** where you cross the suspension bridge to the left bank. This is where the trekking trail to Ganesh diverges to the right. You continue along the river bank to Seirishon Gaon.

It's here that the valley walls close in, trapping the Burhi Gandaki between sheer and precipitous cliffs. Not much later, you reach the **Chhulung Khola** tributary, flowing in through the opposite bank, and cross the bridge to the right bank.

The trail climbs for about 100 meters before turning right, along a winding path through a pine forest above the Shar Khola, that flows in from the opposite bank.

The trail follows the river through the center of the valley before crossing over to the left bank. Walk for about another 30 minutes and it returns once more to the right bank.

Soon you come to junction of the **Nyak** trail that climbs up to the left, the main trail continuing along the river's right bank until you have to climb up to traverse its gorge.

Finally, you cross the **Deng Khola** into the tiny hamlet of **Deng,** with four houses. You can camp in the fields outside. The total time for this stretch is between seven and eight hours.

Eighth Day

Leave the village along the high, winding path that soon leads down to the river bank where it crosses a suspension bridge to the left bank and climbs steeply to **Lana.** Then begins a gradual climb through **Unbae,** with its stone gate and *mani* stones, before the trail dips down once more to the river, past a waterfall on the right.

Now it climbs up again across a terraced hill, past the village of **Bih** and across the **Bihjam Khola,** on a twisting path lined by *mani* stones, to a tiny hamlet near the Burhi Gandaki.

Soon it reaches farm fields and a stone gate — entrance to the Tibetan village of **Ghap,** set at 2,095 m (6,800 ft) — where there is a suspension bridge across the Burhi Gandaki. You can camp in the meadow on the left bank, near the entrance to the village. In all, this walk takes about four hours.

Ninth Day

Follow the path along the right bank, past a long *mani* stone wall, into forest and then through **Lumachik,** one lone house, and across the wooden bridge over the **Burhi Gandaki gorge.** The trail climbs upward through forest to a wooden bridge that takes it across to the right bank and on through the forest to the checkpost at **Namru.**

Leave Namru by crossing a stream to a grassy field with a waterfall and stone cliff to the left, over the pastures to **Bengsam** where the trail climbs out of the village through a stone gate and on to **Li.**

Here it crosses the **Hinan Khola,** streaming down from the Lidanda glacier, to climb up to **Sho,** guarded by its stone gate. Soon afterwards, the trail rounds a bend to reveal enchanting views of Naike peak, 7,154-m (23,500-ft)-high Manaslu North, and, finally, 8,158-m (26,766-ft)-high Manaslu.

Climbing gradually, the path passes between houses, farm fields, and a bubbling spring to **Lo,** set at 3,150 m (10,300 ft), and its stonewalled fields. Behind you, at the head of the valley below, stands 7,406-m (24,298-ft)-high Ganesh Himal I. You can camp by the spring at the entrance to the village. Total walking time is around six hours.

Tenth Day

Cut through the village, lined by a long *mani* stone wall, down across the **Damonan Khola,** and then climb along the river. Ahead, the horizon is dominated by the snowcap of

7,835-m (25,690-ft)-high Peak 29, while the Shara Khola flows in from the right.

After a few minutes the trail comes to a left fork — the main path ascends the ridge to **Sama** — that climbs to **Pungen glacier,** via **Honsansho Gompa,** and despite the effort is a worthwhile diversion simply because of the views of Peak 29 and Manaslu.

The narrow path climbs through thick forest to **Honsansho Gompa** and over a gentle ridge, and cuts diagonally across a rocky riverbed to another small ridge. Not long after this it reaches seven stone huts at

Kyubun, then climbs over a small ridge formed by the moraine of Pungen glacier, from which you get a stunning view of the battlements of Peak 29 and graceful Manaslu.

The moraine leads onto **Ramanan Kharka** but to reach Sama climb down the glacier and, from the small ridge, cut across its snout to the rock-strewn riverbed and a chorten.

From this point it's just a short climb down back to the main path and the potato fields and houses of Sama, set at 3,500 m (11,500 ft). Another 20 minutes walk brings you to the meadow at **Sama Gompa** where

Trekkers OPPOSITE cross the foaming waters of the Dudh Kosi in the Everest region. Porters trek ever high ABOVE into the great mountain fastness of Nepal.

you can camp before a panoramic view of Manaslu. The walk takes about six hours.

Eleventh Day
Leave the meadows, skirting a ridge of lateral moraine, to the banks of the **Burhi Gandaki** after crossing a stream born in the icemelt of Manaslu glacier. If you turn left you can make a 60 to 70 minute excursion to a glacial lake.

Meanwhile, the main trail leaves the grasslands down to the riverbed and onto **Kermo Kharka** with stupendous views of Manaslu. From here it passes a long stone

mani wall, at **Kermo Manan,** where the valley begins to close in and the trail climbs above the trickle of the Burhi Gandaki before climbing down to the riverbed.

Cross the river, up a terraced hill on the opposite bank, and through a stone gate to the remote village of **Somdu** where around 40 families share life's alpine travail. There's no more fuelwood after this so take what you will need with you.

The path goes down the mountain from the village, through a stone gate, and across the **Gyala Khola,** before climbing gradually upwards. Below you, to the left, you may see the ruins of Larkya Bazaar.

Larkya glacier soon appears on the opposite side of the valley after the trail

crosses two streams and skirts around **Sarka Khola.** Then it climbs to a strong shelter, at 4,450 m (14,600 ft) where you can spend the night. This leg takes from six to seven hours.

Twelfth Day
From the guesthouse, a short climb takes the trekker up to a glacial valley with views of Cho Dhanda. As the gradual climb continues, the unmistakable image of Larkya peak comes into sight opposite a small glacier on the other side of the valley.

Soon the trail leads into a level glacier

and gradually upwards until a final short, steep climb brings it to **Larkya La,** set at 5,135 m (16,850 ft) — and a breathtaking view to the west of 7,126-m (23,380-ft)-high Himlung Himal, Cheo Himal, Gyaji Kang, 7,010-m (23,000-ft)-high Kang Gulu, and 7,937-m (26,041-ft)-high Annapurna II.

Climbing down the steep, snow-covered west face of the pass, unlike the east face, is a tricky business, so be careful.

Now down to **Larcia,** opposite a hill on the other side, called Pangal, that also offers stupendous mountain views. From Larcia, the trail climbs down some glacial moraine to the roofless stone hut of **Tanbuche,** set at around 3,900 m (12,800 ft). All in, this part of trek runs to around six hours.

Thirteenth Day

Leaving Tanbuche, as you head for **Bimtang,** you can study the west face of Manaslu and 6,398-m (20,100-ft)-high Phungi. From the ghost town of **Bimtang,** with its *mani* stones and deserted houses, the trail climbs a lateral moraine and then down to a river-bed where it enters the Burdin Khola to **Manaslu** base camp.

If you climb a 4160-m (13,600-ft)-high ridge hereabouts you'll be rewarded by fine views of the west face of 7,154-m (23,500-ft)-high Manaslu North peak, Annapurna ll,

right, to the farm fields of **Karche,** set at 2,785 m (9,130 ft), on the opposite bank. Total time is from four-and-a-half to five hours.

Fourteenth Day

The trail leads up to the paddy fields on top of the terraced hill, and over **Karche La pass,** then down through the fields to **Goa,** and along the right bank of the Dudh Khola to **Tilije.**

Here the trail crosses a wooden bridge to continue down along the left bank to the Marsyangdi Khola where it returns, across

and 6,893-m (22,609-ft)-high Lamjung Himal.

Now follow the riverbed, over the wooden bridge above the headwaters of the Dudh Khola, and up a lateral moraine, before descending through a magnificent rhododendron forest to **Hampuk.**

Finally, before entering the forest again, draw breath for your last look at the west face of Manaslu, then continue through the forest along the right bank of the **Dudh Khola** to **Sangure Kharka** and its single hut.

Manaslu North peak and Larkya peak are now behind as the trail continues down the right bank of the narrow valley, crossing the **Surki Khola** where it enters from the

a wooden bridge, to the right bank and the checkpost at **Thonje.**

Leave the village and follow the trail on the left bank of the **Marsyangdi Khola,** returning to the right bank across a covered wooden bridge. Now there's a short climb and the trail joins the trekking trail around Annapurna.

From here the path leads gradually down to the checkpost at **Darapani,** and, on to **Bhotehura** and **Dumre** where you can take a bus to Kathmandu.

Sixteen thousand feet up in the Himalaya, a smooth, glassy lake ABOVE and rough, scattered moraine OPPOSITE are contrasting elements of a glacial landscape.

ANNAPURNA

A 12-day trek along the **Marsyangdi Khola,** into the **Manang basin,** over **Thorung pass** and down into the **Kali Gandaki gorge** — the world's deepest — gives the trekker a roundabout tour of the Annapurna massif. It is also one of the most varied and comfortable. There are many hotels and teahouses en route so you do not have to carry camping equipment. You can take the bus, or a scheduled flight, from Kathmandu to **Pokhara.**

First Day

Take the bus from Pokhara to **Sisuwa** where you begin the trek. The trail leads up from the bus stop through the neighboring villages to a wide mountain path that climbs a ridge path where there are excellent views of the Manaslu and Annapurna ranges above and the blue waters of Begnas Tal to the left below.

The ridge trail leads right to **Rupa Tal** where it dips down into the valley on the right. It travels upstream, through paddy fields, to **Tarbensi** with its teahouse. Here the trail enters a small valley and travels upstream between two rivers that eventually dry up, just before **Sakkara Bhanjyang,** a village with many teahouses, set at the top of a pass.

When you go down into the valley the trail veers left to **Achari Bhanjyang,** with three teahouses, and continues into the valley where it becomes rocky and difficult.

Soon the valley broadens out into fertile grain fields and rice paddies and when it reaches the ridge on which Bagwa Bazaar

stands you will see the snowcap of 7,937-m (26,041-ft)-high Annapurna II.

Walk through the paddy fields and take the right bank of the **Madi Khola** until the trail reaches a suspension bridge across the river to **Karputar** where there are shops, teahouses, and health clinic. You can camp in the meadows on the left bank of the Madi Khola or stay at one of the teahouses. Total walking time is from five to six hours.

Second Day

The trail leads along the right bank of the Madi Khola, some distance from the river, across the paddy fields and along a mountain path to **Laxmi Bazaar.**

After this it follows an irrigation canal through the fields, moving nearer and nearer the river as the valley narrows, and finally reaches **Shyauli Bazaar** which boasts several teahouses. But there is little shade.

Now the trail becomes undulating, climbing up the hills from the riverbed into a well-shaded area, through a hamlet, and across a suspension bridge to a teahouse on the left bank.

In the dry season, from here the trail follows the riverbed but in the monsoon it winds up the hills to a final steep climb to the top where it levels off. Turn right into the hills, through terraced fields to **Nalma,** atop a ridge where Manaslu's three peaks, and the Annapurna Range, come into view.

Nalma is a Gurung village with several scattered settlements. You can camp in the central village, the one with a school. Total time is between four-and-a-half to five hours.

Third Day

A stone path leads out of Nalma up an undulating ridge with excellent views from its summit of 8,156-m (26,766-ft)-high Manaslu to the right and Annapurna to the left — standing up incredibly high, their snows glittering in the morning sun.

The trail passes through a rest area into a forest on the left, and then down and up past a spring to **Baglunpani,** set at 1,620 m (5,300 ft). The two great mountain massifs are still visible, Manaslu in particular filling the horizon with its majestic pinnacles.

Now the trail climbs down through forest to a rest area where the valley broadens and cuts through terraced fields to **Samrong.** Turn left, and down toward the Bhoran Khola and Lama Gaon, across a suspension bridge and down to the riverbed.

As you approach the Marsyangdi valley, the trail leaves the riverbed and crosses farm fields, at the left of the valley, to **Sera** which is on the right bank of the Marsyangdi Khola.

Leave the village along the river bank about 100 m (320 ft) above the foaming

The path begins to climb but in the dry season you can follow the riverbed and then up a gradual incline to the Manang village of **Ngatti,** lined with hotels and teahouses.

The trail out of the village crosses a stream to the left bank of Ngatti Khola, a tributary that has its source in the snows of 7,893-m (25,895-ft)-high Himal Chuli, and across a long suspension bridge to the right bank.

Soon it leaves the bank and climbs up to the crest of the ridge that divides the Marsyangdi and Ngatti. By the teahouse at the summit is a well-shaded rest area.

waters, past a hamlet, where the valley bends to the right. Now Manaslu and Peak 29 rear up above the far end of the valley as the trail reaches **Khudi,** at the base of a suspension bridge across the Khudi Khola.

You can camp in the meadows on the left bank or stay at one of the village's two hotels. Total time for this walk is between five-and-a-half to six hours.

Fourth day
Walk through the village, past a school on the lower right, to the path on the right bank. Just after the school it crosses a stream and then travels through two hamlets, across a suspension bridge to the left bank, to **Bhul Bhule** which has hotels and teahouses.

The path from here follows the left bank of the **Marsyangdi,** climbing gradually all the way, through the village of **Ranpata,** to the **Bahundhara pass** at 1,270 m (4,100 ft) where there is a checkpost. There's a village on the hill overlooking the pass with teahouses, shops, and hotels. You can stay overnight in one of the hotels or camp in the fields around the pass. It takes roughly four hours to complete this leg.

Fifth Day
Follow a small ridge, branching out from the

ABOVE: Rain sheds its blessings over the terrace paddies of Chane valley on the trekking trail around the mighty Annapurna massif.
OPPOSITE: The Annapurna massif.

High Altitude Trekking and Treks

pass, down to flat and fertile farm fields, then through a forest, across a stream, and up again to a teahouse, on to a stone path that takes about 10 minutes to traverse before it crosses the rice paddies and grain fields into **Kani Gaon.**

Ahead, the Marsyangdi valley begins to narrow into a steep and precipitous valley, along a winding mountain path. On the opposite bank of the river a waterfall heralds the approach to **Sange**, over a suspension bridge to the right bank, past hotels, teahouses, and houses, and down to the riverbed where the trail almost at once begins to climb upwards, past a single house, to a flat plateau.

Not long after this, the rocky trail dips down some 200 to 300 m (650 to 1,000 ft), past a spring, to the riverbed and then into **Jagat,** set at 1,290 m (4,200 ft), where there are hotels and teahouses. Or you can camp in the fields near the village. Total walking time is just three-and-a-half hours.

Sixth Day

From Jagat, the path leads down almost to the river bed and then climbs an extremely precipitous trail opposite a sheer cliff. When the climb ends, the trail levels out all the way to **Chyamche**, which is notable for the splendid waterfall on the opposite bank.

Soon after it dips down to cross a suspension bridge to a hair-raising trail on the left bank — precarious and narrow along the edge of the gorge's sheer wall. One slip could be fatal. It's not for the vertiginous.

Now the path undulates until it reaches a tributary that flows in from the other bank. The main river is littered with massive boulders, some as big as office blocks, and in the dry season it's hard to see the river water at all.

Not long after this, the trail leaves the river bank and takes a zigzag course to the top of a hill overlooking the Tal river, enclosed by precipitous walls of rock. But the path is level, extremely soothing after the perilous journey that preceded it. It goes down to the river bank and into **Tal,** which has hotels and teahouses.

OPPOSITE: A footbridge spanning an alpine gorge makes a challenging passage for trekkers and porters on the trail.

Soon after this village, the valley narrows and the riverbed becomes much narrower, while the trail cuts through rock walls high above, before descending to **Karte.**

Take the stone steps behind the village, past **Naje**, to climb to **Kurumche Kharka** with a splendid view of the south-west face of Manaslu. This diversion takes a day and a half.

From Karte, the path continues down to the river bank and across a suspension bridge to the right bank, close to **Darapani** and its checkpost, set at 1,860 m (6,000 ft).

You can sleep in one of many hotels or camp in the fields behind the checkpost. This leg takes five hours walking, possibly longer if you exercise extreme care on the dangerous sections.

Seventh Day

Follow the trail through a narrow field when you leave the village and come to the confluence with the **Dudh Khola,** spawned in the icemelt of Manaslu's south face, on the opposite bank.

Below, to the right as you climb the path through pine forest, you will be able to make out the roofs and streets of the village of **Thonje.** Now the Marsyangdi bends left, and when you see Annapurna II ahead, you are at the entrance to the Bhote village of **Bagarchap,** prayer flags fluttering in the breeze.

The path continues its climb, past the teahouses at **Dhanagyu,** across a stream and by a cascading waterfall on the left, to where the Marsyangdi Khola valley becomes a gorge traversed by steep stone steps.

Look back here for splendid views of Manaslu and Phungi, then continue the lung-sapping climb to a level path through a colorful rhododendron forest and two houses at **Ratamron,** then on up and across a stream to the lone house at **Tanzo Phedi.**

Here the trail cuts through pine forest, over an area of crumbling rocks, to the checkpost of **Kodo,** dominated by the mighty mass of Annapurna II and Peak 29 towering, it seems, almost directly over the hamlet.

The trail cuts through the village and up through more pine forest to **Chame,** set at 2,670 m (8,750 ft), with government offices, shops, and hotels. It's a good place to replenish

your food rations. You can stay in one of the hotels or camp near the school — or by the hot springs across the bridge on the left bank. Total walking time is roughly six hours.

Eighth Day

Cross a wooden bridge as you leave the village to the left bank and, with wonderful views of the shimmering snows of 6,893-m (22,609-ft)-high Lamjung Himal, pass through **Chame.**

As the trail climbs up the valley, past **Kreku,** the mountain is hidden by the foothills and then the trail cuts deep into pine forest and up a winding rocky face. On the other side, the valley wall is a sheer cliff, evidence of the change of terrain.

The valley is extremely steep and the path leaps back and forth across the river, following the easiest route available until it crosses a wooden bridge to the former military fortress of Buradhan on the right bank. Now only the ruins remain.

From here, the trail climbs a rocky path to first one wooden bridge, and then up again to another timber bridge leading into thick forest on the right bank.

Where the forest ends the valley broadens out into more gentle terrain and the east peak of Annapurna II dominates the horizon as the track leads gradually down, past a *mani* stone, to a level field with a pond. It leads to another timber bridge over the river and through a terraced field with scattered clumps of trees. There are good views of the north face of Annapurna II.

Finally, it skirts the lower level of the village of **Upper Pisang** and crosses the Marsyangdi to **Lower Pisang,** set at 3,200 m (10,500 ft). You can stay in one of the village's two hotels or camp in the meadow next to the spring. Total walking time is five hours.

Ninth Day

Take the timber bridge across the **Tseram Tsang Changu,** past a *mani* stone and chortens, to the right bank and through thick forest up to the mountain pass marked by a chorten. From here you can see Manang airfield dead ahead.

The trail dips down to a level section, past **Ongre** where the north-east face of Annapurna III is visible, to the airstrip at **Omdu,**

and then across flat broad plain and across the Sabje Khola. Here the massive peak of 7,525-m (24,688-ft)-high Annapurna IV appears on the horizon.

The trail then crosses another bridge, over the trickle of the newborn Marsyangdi Khola, to the left bank and **Mungji,** encircled by verdant farm fields. To the right, beneath a small mountain, stands **Braga** with its magnificent monastery.

There are many large chortens and *mani* stones and soon you come to **Manang,** set at 3,520 m (11,500 ft) beneath a panoramic vista surely made in heaven — from a terraced hill above the town spread out before you are Annapurna II, Annapurna IV, Annapurna III, 7,555-m (24,787-ft)-high Gangapurna and, behind, 7,134-m (23,406-ft)-high Tilitso peak.

Manang's streets and houses are lined with many fluttering prayer flags and there are five hotels. You can stay in one of these or camp on their rooftops. Total walking time to Manang is about four hours.

Tenth Day

Now begins the toughest part of the trek, through Manang and up to the village of **Tinke.** All along this route you will see Annapurna Himani on the horizon with Peak 29 and Himalchuli in the distance behind it.

Tinke is the last permanent settlement in the Marsyangdi Khola valley but the path winds up through the summer village of **Kutsuan** and, soon after a deserted village, the trail levels out and crosses a bridge over the Gundon Khola. In the mountains ahead you can see the walls of the Thorung pass — your destination.

The trail now becomes a gentle switchback before crossing a delta with many yak meadows and then across the Kenzan Khola to **Churi Latter** with its lone hotel. From here the trail climbs a gradual incline to the snout of a ridge.

Then it dips down to cross the bridge over the Marsyangdi Khola and up the mountain path on the right bank, then down a rocky section to the riverbed which it follows for between 10 and 15 minutes walk.

Finally, it climbs a rocky path to the plateau and **Thorung Phedi,** set at 4,500 m (14,750 ft), which has one combined hotel-teahouse, serving very basic Tibetan fare.

You can bed down on its earth floor or camp nearby. Total walking time is from six to seven hours.

Eleventh Day
Leave early, prepared for extreme cold and severe gale-force winds as you climb the most testing section of this trek — **Thorung pass.** Climb the zigzag trail up the steep hill in front of the hotel, through a rocky area to the top of the ridge. Here it crosses a frozen stream, then some lateral moraine, and continues over a frozen lake to the glacier above.

which flows in from the left, to the lunar landscape of the Jhong Khola valley which you descend with magnificent views of 8,167-m (26,795-ft)-high Dhaulagiri I and 6,920-m (22,704-ft)-high Tukuche peak.

Once through the valley you are close the the checkpost at **Muktinah,** set at 3,798 m (12,500 ft), where there are three hotels. Total walking and climbing time for this section is from seven to nine hours.

Twelfth Day
With Dhaulagiri I, Tukuche Peak, and Dhau-

It then traverses to the left, between small hill-like ridges above 5,000 m (16,500 ft), and soon Annapurna II, in the rear, passes out of sight. Now the angle eases as you begin the ascent to Thorung pass at 5,416 m (17,770 ft), its crest marked only by cairns and no shelter at all from the cruel wind.

This is one of the entrances to the eight-kilometer (five-mile)-deep **Kali Gandaki gorge** and ahead, as you enter an old lateral moraine for the precipitous descent, Dhaulagiri II, III, and Tashi Kang, rise up over the valley. The final leg is down an extremely steep cliff. Finally, you reach **Chabarbu** and its one hotel.

From hereon, the path levels out through the valley and across the **Khatung Kang**

lagiri II and III, still in view, the trail leads down from Muktinah to **Jharkot** where there are the ruins of an ancient fortress.

Now the path passes through two stone walls to a gradual climb down the mountains and along a wide level trail to **Khingar,** after which it dips gradually to a crossroads. The right turning leads to Kagbeni, famous for the ruins of its medieval castle.

The path on the left leads down the mountain flank to the left bank of the Kali Gandaki river and **Akkara Bhatti** and then on to **Jhomsumba** in the afternoon.

Two youngsters at Dhampus ABOVE in the shadows of mighty Annapurna.

The path follows the river bank to a wooden bridge that takes it onto the right bank which it follows briefly before returning to the riverbed. Continue thereafter along the river path, with Dhaulagiri I in view. The trek from Jhomsumba to Pokhara takes from five to six days.

DHAULAGIRI

Starting in **Pokhara**, this takes you through some of the finest pastoral and mountain landscapes in Nepal — providing the savor of simple lifestyles in and around the **Myagdi Khola basin.** You need full camping equipment, rations, and Sherpa guides.

First Day
Trek from Pokhara to **Naudhara** along the Jhomsumba route, turning to the left when leaving Naudhara, down a gradual slope through forest, past **Pandor,** and across a stream to **Daudari Dhara.**

Leaving the village, take the left fork past the school, and follow the trail down the mountain through **Bane Kharka** to **Sallyan.** Here you climb over a ridge and through forest to **Thamarjung** — a walk of about six hours. You can camp in the compounds of some of the houses.

Second Day
Leave the village, down a gradual decline to **Tihar,** and a level trail to **Gijan,** with splendid views of the sacred peak of 6,993-m (22,940-ft)-high Machhapuchhare, Gangapurna, and **Annapurna South.** From the ridge take the steep trail down to the confluence of the **Dobila Khola** and **Modi Khola.**

Here, the trail crosses a suspension bridge and climbs the mountain on the right bank of the Modi Khola to **Chuwa,** winding its way over several small ridges and through farm fields, to the shops and teahouses of **Kusma.**

From here, cut through forest and down a steep hill from **Chamurkang** to the **Kali Gandaki** river, where the trail follows the left bank, past **Marmati** with its teahouse, to **Nayapur.** This walk takes about six to six-and-a-half hours. You can camp near the village.

Third Day
Continue along the left bank, past the suspension bridge, through **Saus Dhara** with its row of teahouses, where, soon after, from the high path, you get splendid views of Dhaulagiri I, before the trail dips down to the riverbed.

Soon it climbs back to the left bank path and into **Khanyagar** with hotels and teahouses. The trail leaves the village up a gradual incline, past the suspension bridge to **Baglung** on the opposite bank, and continues to **Pharse,** where there are more teahouses and hotels.

Still on the left bank, the path crosses a stream into **Diranbhora**, then up a gentle incline to **Beni,** on the opposite bank of the **Myagdi Khola,** where there is a checkpost.

It's a bustling town and administrative center and you can camp in fields outside the village. The walk takes anything from five-and-a-half to six hours.

Fourth Day

The trail from Beni cuts through **Beni Mangalghat**'s single street of shops and into desolate mountain country, past the lone teahouse at **Jyanmara,** and on a wide, level path to **Singa,** with many shops and teahouses.

Beyond this village, the trail follows the left bank of the **Myagdi Khola** above the riverbed, past a hot spring to the left below, and through the farm fields that herald the approach to **Tatopani.**

Soon after leaving this village, it crosses a suspension bridge to the right bank, through the hamlet of **Bholamza,** more fields, before swinging back to the left bank via another suspension bridge, to **Simarchor.** Some distance beyond this village there's a suspension bridge across the Newale Khola which flows in from the right.

The trail continues along the left bank of the **Myagdi Khola,** past the villages of **Shiman** and **Talkot,** and then climbs up to shops and teahouses of **Babichor.** You can camp on the grass next to the village granary. The walk takes approximately five hours.

The peaks of regal Annapurna, with a crown of fresh snow.

Fifth Day

From Babichor, the high, winding trail crosses the mountainside into a broad and fertile valley, across paddy and grain fields, and through the cobblestone street of **Shahasharadhara** where you cross the Duk Khola. Continue through the paddy fields to the hamlet of **Ratorunga** where the valley ends.

Now the undulating trail follows the river bank on the left, past **Bodeni** to **Chachare.** The valley narrows at the town of **Darbang,** its main street lined with many shops.

Here the trail crosses to the right bank, via a suspension bridge, past the Ritum Khola tributary at left, and through the hamlet of **Darbang.**

The trail then skirts a gaunt cliff face to **Phedi,** set at 1,100 m (3,500 ft), where there are two teahouses. It's not a pretty place but it's the only camping site for several miles around. The walk takes about four hours.

Sixth Day

When you leave Phedi you face a long climb to **Phalai Gaon** and should make an early start. Soon after leaving the village the trail crosses the **Dang Khola,** where it flows in from the left, and climbs a ridge on the opposite bank in a series of hairpins, above the Myagdi Khola.

Soon the gradual climb leads into **Dharapani,** and steeply out again, before descending to the farm fields beyond **Takum.**

After **Sibang,** it cuts through forest, past **Mattim,** to the crest of a ridge which provides a magnificent view of Dhaulagiri Himal, dipping down to the Gatti Khola, to skirt the base of the ridge and enter **Phalai Gaon,** set at 1,810 m (6,000 ft). You can camp in the school grounds outside the village. The walk takes between six and seven hours.

Seventh Day

For **Mur,** follow the stonewalled path from Phalai Gaon over the terraced fields to the right, and cross the suspension bridge over the Dhara Khola. During the dry season the trail goes down the valley next to the school, across to the opposite bank, and up a steep hill.

But the main path from the suspension bridge climbs up the mountain, above the village of Dhara, and through a hamlet to an undulating walk that joins up with the short-cut. After skirting a ridge it emerges once more on the right bank of the Myagdi Khola.

Now it climbs again, in a series of hairpins, and then skirts another ridge, to reveal stupendous views of Dhaulagiri I and 7,193-m (23,600-ft)-high Gurja Himal. Soon it reaches the Magar village of **Muri** which you leave down a gentle slope, across a rocky stream.

Continue down to the farm fields along the Dhara Khola, cross the river and then climb up the mountain on the right to **Ghorban Dhara pass** with its superb views — including your first glimpse of 6,465-m (21,211-ft)-high Ghustung South.

From the pass, the trail leads down to the right bank of the **Myagdi Khola,** and a lone house where you can camp in the surrounding fields — beneath the village of **Jugapani,** perched on the mountainside above. Total walking time is around five hours.

Eighth Day

Leave along the right bank, past **Naura,** and climb the mountain for a short while to a path that traverses a steep, grass-covered hill. Where the traverse ends, the Myagdi Khola valley becomes a precipitous gorge. Even though the path along the steep, grassy edge of the gorge is well-constructed with many stone steps, take care.

At the top of the climb, the trail traverses right — and you need to exercise great care to avoid falling into the gorge. Eventually, the trail dips down through forest, across a ridge, and some terraced fields to **Boghara,** set at 2,080 m (6,800 ft).

You can camp in the compounds of the houses or the terraced fields. It takes around four-and-a-half to five hours to complete this stretch.

Ninth Day

Leave the village as the trail descends through the fields, crossing a small ridge to the left, and on through thin forest to **Jyardan,** the region's most remote village.

From the village the trail is high and winding, then it cuts across a boulder-strewn landscape to a grass-covered traverse, before dropping down some steep stone steps to the river bank.

It follows upstream some distance, then starts climbing again, crossing a stream beneath a beautiful high waterfall, where it eases into a gradual incline to **Lipshe.**

Now the trail continues its undulating course through the forest-lined walls of the steep **Myagdi Khola gorge** before emerging at a little glade, **Lapche Kharka,** where you camp overnight. All in all this leg takes no more than five hours.

the end of the valley and then you cross a stream, to the plateau at **Chartare,** set at 2,820 m (9,250 ft).

There's a a crystal clear stream flowing through the middle of the meadow, making it excellent for camping. Total walking time is no more than five hours.

Eleventh Day

From Chartare, return to the forest trail until it passes two small caves. Here it leaves the forest and cuts across some rocks up the mountainside, across a small stream, to the

Tenth Day

When you leave camp, the trail continues to climb through forest to a level area at **Dobang.** Soon after this, it crosses a timber bridge over the Konabon Khola, flowing down from the Konabon glacier.

Here the trail continues through thick forest with occasional glimpses, through breaks in the trees, of the west face of majestic Dhaulagiri I. Some distance beyond, the trail dips down and the Myagdi Khola comes into view. You cross to the left bank by a wooden bridge with a handrail.

Once again the path cuts through forest as it climbs the course of the **Pakite Khola,** never too far from the river. The crest of 6,062-m (19,889-ft)-high Jirbang dominates

Choriban Khola which it skirts for some distance, before finally crossing it to climb the bank on the other side.

Look behind at this point and you will get a splendid view of the ice-white silhouette of 6,380-m (20,932-ft)-high Manapati. Soon after climbing the steep hill, the path narrows into a gentle gradient, through the forest, to a small grassy clearing at **Puchhar.**

It now crosses a small glacier down to another glacier born on the west face of Dhaulagiri, and then climbs the opposite wall to another grassy area, **Pakabon,** set at 3,585 m (11,750 ft), where you can camp.

Woman carries firewood up a precipitous stone walkway overlooking lush, terraced hillsides.

Ahead stand the massive western ramparts of Dhaulagiri I. To the right is Manapati — and behind, the granite walls of Tsaurabong peak shadow the sky as if about to fall over the camp. Total time is around five hours.

Twelfth Day

From Pakabon, follow a lateral moraine to a rocky ridge which you descend to the right, and into a valley deep in snow and glacial detritus. Approaching the headwaters of the Myagdi Khola, you are closed in by daunting and forbidding rock walls.

The precipitous path follows its course high above the right bank before descending to the valley floor and on, by an intermittent footpath through the gorge, to the terminal moraine of **Chhonbarban glacier.** It enters the glacier area from the right bank, crossing the undulating glacial surface where the valley bends right through a large gorge.

At this point, 6,837-m (22,432-ft)-high Tukuche Peak West stands brooding over the far end of the glacier.

Soon the trail levels out into easy walking up the gradual gradient of this section, then the glacier veers left and the trail moves onto the right bank.

It terminates at **Dhaulagiri base camp,** set at 4,750 m (15,500 ft), with a stunning perspective of Dhaulagiri I's north and, to the west, 7,751-m (25,429-ft)-high Dhaulagiri II, 7,703-m (25,271-ft)-high Dhaulagiri III, and 7,660-m (25,133-ft)-high Dhaulagiri IV — a sheer ice fall streaming from the northeast col. Walking time is between six and seven hours.

Thirteenth Day

At this stage, there's a sound risk of mountain sickness as the trail climbs out of the camp up the right bank of the glacier, and then up another mountainside to where it cuts across the flank to cross the moraine on the side of 6,611-m (21,690-ft)-high Sita Chuchura, to an easy snow covered incline on the right that leads to **French pass,** at 5,360 m (17,600 ft).

Early morning sun lights up a frosty trekkers' camp at 5,500 m (18,000 ft).

From here you can see Sita Chuchura, the mountains of Mukut Himal, and the 6,386-m (21,000-ft)-high Tashi Kang. To the right is Tukuche Peak West and to the rear stands Dhaulagiri I. It takes 11 to 12 days to return to Pokhara.

LANGTANG HIMAL–JUGAL HIMAL–GANESH HIMAL

Regarded as the most perfect alpine landscape in the world, the **Langtang Himal massif** — clearly visible from Kathmandu

some water pipes to the foot of the iron bridge that carries them across the Trisuli river.

When you cross the bridge take the road left. You can travel along this by jeep, past the village of **Bainshi,** and along the **Trisuli river** with its picturesque hamlets, to **Betrawati** with many inns and hotels. The journey by foot takes about two-and-a-half hours.

Second Day
Cross the **Phalongu Khola,** passing the

— is right on the city's back door and this nine to 10 day trek allows you to enjoy it in full. With many hotels and eating places it's also one for the casual and not-so-hardy trekker.

First Day
Take the bus from **Sorkhuti** on the northern side of Kathmandu to **Trisuli Bazaar** reserving your seat in advance. The journey takes four hours. When it reaches **Kakani hill** there's a fantastic panorama consisting of the Manaslu massif, Ganesh, Langtang, and Jugal Himal.

Leave the bazaar and climb the terraced hills, past the reservoir on the left where the road ends and a level path follows

checkpost through the village to an old path that climbs left to Bhotal where you can follow the path to **Banwa** with its teahouse-restaurant.

Now cross some terraced fields to a mountain path which leads to the crest of a ridge with views of Mani Gaon ahead. Follow the gradual decline to the stream on the right, before climbing up to **Mani Gaon.**

The trail runs through fields and houses for some distance and then up a gentle slope across another ridge, where it circles a stream on the right, before a steep hairpin climb to Handebre. Here it eases into a more gradual incline to **Ramche,** set at 1,820 m (6,000 ft), with one hotel and some restaurants.

You can stay at the hotel or camp in the garden of the restaurant. Pay your park fees at the national park office at the entrance to the village. This walk takes about five hours.

Third Day

The road leads out of Ramche, around to a subsidiary ridge, along a level path high above the Trisuli river, to the stonewalled, broad roofed houses of **Garang.** From the top of the ridge out of Garang you get your first glimpse of snowcapped 7,245-m (23,769-ft)-high Langtang Lirung.

Fourth Day

The road leaves Dunche across some fields, down the forested banks of the **Trisuli Khola,** across a suspension bridge, and up a steep hill along a small stream.

Some 20 minutes distance, the trail leaves the stream and travels up the hillside on the left to a teahouse atop a ridge. There's a fork in the trail here — straight on to Gosainkund and left to Syabru, a rather narrow path past the teahouse.

It skirts the ridge, with Dunche in view on the opposite bank, and carries along the

Now the path undulates along the hillside to **Thare,** across a stream and rockstrewn area, skirting a ridge, to **Bokajundo** with excellent views of Langtang Lirung.

Take the road through the village, marked by chortens and into mountain forest that leads into a gorge where you cross two streams, and the path becomes a gravel road. Now it passes a rock path leading into a side valley before reaching the checkpost at the right of the entrance to **Dunche,** set at 2,040 m (6,700 ft), focal point of the district with hotels, shops, and government offices.

Here, you can enter the valley of the Trisuli river to travel to **Gosainkund,** the sacred Shiva lake. The journey to Dunche takes around six hours.

mountainside on the left bank of the Trisuli river to some fields where the path to **Syabrubensi** branches left, near **Bharkhu.**

From Bharkhu, cross the fields and climb the steep mountain pass, an exercise rewarded, to your rear where the path levels out and leads left through forest, by a view of Ganesh Himal. Then it passes another village, to the left below, and through more forest to a rest area at the crest of a ridge.

Young women of Pokhara OPPOSITE reap an additional harvest of small fish from the muddy waters of their rice paddies. Other youngsters use a traditional fish trap ABOVE LEFT in the rushing waters of the Trisuli river to catch their supper while a conical net RIGHT hauls in a writhing catch for another team fishing the same waters.

From here it dips down gradually to **Syabru,** set at 2,230 m (7,300 ft), where you can camp in the monastery grounds or hotel garden. This leg takes approximately five-and-a-half to six hours.

Fifth Day

Walk down the ridge, between the houses, turn right past some fields, then through forest, across a stream and a flat mountain trail on the left that leads to the crest of a ridge.

The other side leads down a steep slope through thick forest to the **Langtang Khola**

where it follows the left bank. Soon it crosses a stream and continues the climb up the valley to a wooden bridge across the Langtang Khola which takes it to the right bank.

Here the path climbs high, leaving the river far below, and then down around the flank of the mountain, to join the path from Syarpa Gaon.

Not far from this junction the trail veers back to the river bank and later, climbs up to the **Lama Hotel,** surrounded by other teahouses and hotels. When it cuts into forest, through breaks in the tree cover you will see majestic Langtang Lirung in the distance.

The path climbs steadily past **Gumnachok,** and its lone hotel, to a short steep hill where it leaves the river bank and the valley broadens. Not long after this it reaches the checkpost at **Ghora Tabela,** set at 3,010 m (9,900 ft). Time taken is around six hours.

Sixth Day

The trail leaves Ghora Tabela through the farm fields that stud the valley floor and after a short distance crosses over a steep

hill. Here the forest ends and it becomes a gentle path, through colorful shrubs and meadows.

Now Langtang appears, against the backdrop of 6,387-m (21,000-ft)-high Ganchempo. The trail climbs gradually up a grassy knoll, above a monastery below, to **Langtang,** where gardens are enclosed by stone walls. Some little distance from the village there is a chorten followed by one of the longest *mani* walls in Nepal.

The trail leads along the top of green and lovely hillsides, past two villages, after which the valley broadens out and the path enters a level, dry riverbed. Where it crosses the flow from **Lirung glacier,** 6,745-m (21,250-ft)-high Kimshun, and 6,543-m (21,467-ft)-high Yansa Tsenji can be seen to the left.

Now the trail cuts across moraine covered with loose stones to **Kyangjin Gompa,** set at 3,840 m (12,500 ft) where there's a cheese factory.

To the north of the village, on a 4,000-m (13,000-ft)-high crest there are magnificent views of Langtang Lirung's north face and the surrounding mountains.

You can stay in the town hotel or camp in one of the stonewalled fields. Beyond this point you will need tents and supplies and beware of mountain sickness. The walking time is between five and six hours.

Seventh Day

The trail from Kyangjin Gompa crosses a wide alluvial delta, across a stream, to an airstrip with stupendous vistas of Langtang Lirung's full profile.

From the airstrip, the trail follows the river and 6,300-m (20,600-ft)-high Langshisa Ri comes into view at the far end of the narrow valley, with Ganchempo visible on the opposite side.

Up from the river, the trail goes through the rocky hills, to the seven stone huts of **Jatang.** Just beyond, it descends once more to the dry riverbed, then up some more hills with views of Shalbachum glacier pushing its snout into the valley. Nearby the glacier is **Nubamatang,** with five stone huts.

Now the trail cuts across the grassy fields and climbs the glacial moraine with perspectives of the far end of the valley, dominated by 6,830-m (22,400-ft)-high Pemthang Karpo Ri, Triangle, and 6,842-m (22,490-ft)-high Pemthang Ri; to the right is Langshisa Ri.

Now the trail descends to **Langshisa Kharka,** at 4,125 m (13,500 ft) for views of 6,078-m (20,000-ft)-high Kanshurum and 6,151-m (20,200-ft)-high Urkinmang at the far end of the Langshisa glacier. The journey time is around four hours.

You can camp in the stone huts at **Langshisa Kharka** or in the grassy fields. The return to **Trisuli Bazaar** from this point takes five days.

the valley ends, it begins to climb to the glacier. This is the extreme for most trekkers, with an excellent camp and outstanding views. Total time is around five hours.

It is possible to visit Langshisa glacier, following the trail upstream from **Langshisa Kharka** for a short distance to a log bridge. It sometimes gets hurled away by landslides so check before you start if it is there.

Then the trail climbs through scrub before descending to one of the streams running off the glacier which you enter at the snout. Then it slowly climbs until 6,966-m

Eighth Day

To trek from Langshisa Kharka to **Langtang glacier** and **Langshisa glacier** you have to be exceptionally fit and well equipped.

The trail from Langshisa follows the top of a level hill and down a winding path to the riverbed. Here it begins to climb, past a small stone hut and through thorny scrub, to a second hut. The trail now becomes vague and difficult as the trek is not often used.

Some distance after this a valley leads to the **Morimoto peak base camp** on a wide plain with views of 6,874-m (22,550-ft)-high Gur Karpo Ri and 6,750-m (22,150-ft)-high Morimoto peak.

The trail crosses the plain and enters the valley again. Around the corner, where

(22,855-ft)-high Dorje Lakpa comes into view — magnificent from Kathmandu, unbelievable when so close.

The glacier veers right and when you round the corner you get a breathtaking view of 7,083-m (23,240-ft)-high Lenpo Gang, the highest of the Jugal Himal's peaks.

You can camp at a site set at 4,800 m (15,750 ft) often used as a base camp by climbing expeditions. The climb takes about five hours.

Protected against glaring snow and high-altitude ultraviolet rays a climber OPPOSITE reaches 4,500 m (15,000 ft) during his attempt on one of the major peaks of the Himalayas. ABOVE: The 7,245 m (23,769 ft) Langtang Lirung near the Tibetan border at the head of Trisuli Valley.

Travelers' Tips

ARRIVING IN NEPAL

INTERNATIONAL FLIGHTS

Most international visitors — more than 90 percent — fly to Nepal's Tribhuvan International Airport, eight kilometers (five miles) from Kathmandu.

If the skies are clear there is no more exciting flight in the world. Left-seated passengers on eastbound flights to Kathmandu will see in succession Gurja Himal, 7,193 m (23,600 ft); Dhaulagiri I, 8,167 m (26,795 ft); the dark, deep gorge of the Kali Gandaki river leading north to Mustang; the six peaks of the Annapurna Range; Manaslu, 8,158 m (26,766 ft); and the three lumps of Ganesh Himal, 7,406 m (24,298 ft), that dominate the Kathmandu Valley.

Right-seated passengers on westbound flights will see, in succession, Kanchenjunga, 8,598 m (28,208 ft) on the border with Sikkim; Makalu, 8,481 m (27,825 ft); Everest, 8,848 m (29,028 ft); Cho Oyu, 8,153 m (26,750 ft); Gaurisankar, 7,144 m (23,438 ft); Dorje Lhakpa, 6,966 m (22,855 ft); and, finally, standing above the Kathmandu valley, Langtang Lirung, 7,245 m (23,769 ft).

International airlines operating scheduled services to Nepal include the national flag carrier, Royal Nepal Airline Corporation (RNAC); Bangladesh Biman; Burma Airways Corporation (BAC); Indian Airlines; Thai International Airlines; and Pakistan International Airlines.

There are two daily services to Delhi, and one to Varanasi (Benares); 10 weekly services to Dhaka; nine to Calcutta and Bangkok; four to Rangoon and Hong Kong; three to Karachi; two to Colombo, Singapore, and Patna; and one to Dubai.

Between Nepal and India, Nepali and Indian nationals fly at reduced rates.

All those departing Nepal on international flights pay 100 rupees airport tax at check-in.

The major international airlines with offices in Kathmandu are:

Aeroflot Soviet Airlines, Kanti Path (212397.
Air France, Durbar Marg (213339.
Air India, Kanti Path (212335.
Air Lanka, Kanti Path (212831.

Bangladesh Biman, Durbar Marg (212544.
British Airways, Durbar Marg (212266
Burma Airways Corporation, Durbar Marg (214839.
Cathay Pacific, Kanti Path (214705.
Indian Airlines, Durbar Marg (211198.
Japan Air Lines, Durbar Marg (412138.
K.L.M. Royal Dutch Airlines, Durbar Marg (214896.
Lufthansa, Durbar Marg (213052.
Northwest Airlines, Kanti Path (215855.
Pakistan International, Durbar Marg (212102.
Pan American World Airways, Durbar Marg (411824, 410584.
Royal Nepal Airlines, Kanti Path (214511.
Swissair, Durbar Marg (412455.
Thai International, Durbar Marg (213565.
Trans World Airlines, Kanti Path (214704.

OVERLAND INTO NEPAL

ENTRY POINTS

Land travelers have a vast choice of routes and means of transport by which to enter Nepal. In addition to Tribhuvan Airport, there are 11 other official entry points:
Kakar Bhitta (Mechi zone), with connections to Darjeeling and Siliguri, India;
Rani Sikijha (Kosi zone), just south of Biratnagar;
Jaleshwar (Janakpur zone); Birganj (Narayani zone), near Raxaul, India, the most common point of entry for overland travelers;
Kodari (Bagmati zone), on the Chinese Tibetan border; and
Sonauli (Lumbini zone), near Bhairawa on the road to Pokhara.

Other entry points, on foot only, are at **Kakarhawa** (Lumbini zone); **Nepalgunj** (Bheri zone); **Koilabas** (Rapti zone); **Dhangadi** (Seti zone); and **Mahendranagar** (Mahakali zone), all unsuitable for motor vehicles.

By Rail

India runs frequent rail passenger services throughout India including trains to the Nepal border. But there are only two lines in

OPPOSITE: Moonrise over the distinctive peak of Ama Dablam on the trail to Everest base camp.

Nepal. The 47-km (30-mile) line between Raxaul, India, and Amlekhganj, built in 1925, is no longer used. The only line still working in Nepal, for freight only, built in 1940, runs for a brief 27 km (17 miles) through Janakpur.

By Road and Rail

The combined rail-road route to Nepal from Delhi offers two real options — the others being far too time-consuming, boring, and too much of a hassle. The quickest route is via **Gorakhpur,** while the other allows an interesting stopover in **Varanasi.** From either city, buses make their way to Kathmandu or Pokhara via **Sunauli.** Taking this route allows one to visit **Lumbini,** Buddha's birthplace, which is close to Sunauli.

If traveling on to **Kathmandu,** it means you can also stop over at **Narayanghat** and visit **Royal Chitwan National Park,** just two hours away by local transport.

Similarly, the combined rail-road route to Nepal from **Calcutta** offers two interesting alternatives — via **Muzaffapur** or **Patna** — with bus connections to Kathmandu via **Birganj.** The journey takes about 36 hours. By ferry from Muzaffapur, across the Ganges to Patna, takes approximately 90 minutes.

Any other suggested routes to the Nepali border from India simply isn't worth the effort or aggravation.

But if you wish for this, then from **Darjeeling** there's a train to **Siliguri,** followed by a 60-minute taxi drive to **Kakar Bhitta** where you can catch a bus to **Kathmandu.** The two advantages to be gained from taking this route are the ride on the miniature Darjeeling railway followed by traveling through almost 400 km (250 miles) of the Terai, including panoramic views of the Siwalik Hills.

You need a special permit to enter Darjeeling (required for all, including Commonwealth passport holders). And on your return from Nepal remember that you'll need an Indian visa to enter India through a border post. If you intend to travel more than once between Nepal and India, a multiple-entry Indian visa is useful.

Driving into Nepal

Those who drive to Nepal by private car should allow at least two hours to clear the Indian border and make sure that they carry a *carnet de passage en douanes* (for cars and motorcycles) which gives a three-month exemption from customs duty.

Motor vehicles in Nepal are driven on the left side of the road. Drivers must hold a valid national or international driver's license.

VISAS

All visitors require a visa and must carry a valid passport and proof of inoculation against cholera and yellow fever. A single-entry visa to Nepal costs US$10 for 30 days. Indian and Bhutanese citizens require no visas.

Visas, valid for 30 days in the Kathmandu valley, Pokhara, and other parts of Nepal linked by highway, are issued by Royal Nepali embassies. Any visitor travelling outside the main highway areas (see OFF THE BEATEN TRACK page 131) must carry a trekking permit.

Visitors arriving at Kathmandu's Tribhuvan airport can obtain a seven-day visa for US$10 which can then be extended to the full 30-day period at no additional cost.

Visas can also be extended for up to three months, at a rate of 75 rupees a week for the second month, and 150 rupees a week for the third month. Longer stays require approval by the Home Ministry.

Extensions are issued at the Central Immigration Office in Maiti Devi, Kathmandu, (412337 (10 am to 4 pm except Saturdays and government holidays; carry your passport and two passport-size photos).

Visitors with trekking permits — 65 rupees a week — can extend their visa at no additional cost.

Visitors wishing to cross the border at the Friendship Bridge to the Tibetan town of Khasa need to get a visa — a fairly easy process — at the Chinese Embassy (see EMBASSIES, page 200), in Kathmandu.

CUSTOMS

Duty Free Travelers are allowed to carry 200 cigarettes, 20 cigars, one bottle of spirits, and two bottles or 12 cans of beer free of duty. Personal effects exempt from duty include binoculars, cameras, film stock, record player, tape recorder, transistor radio, and fishing rod and accessories.

Forbidden imports Firearms and ammunition (unless you hold an import license obtained in advance), radio transmitters, walkie-talkies, and drugs.

Video and 8 mm and 16 mm movie cameras require special permits.

Souvenirs On departure, souvenirs can be exported freely but antiques and art objects need special clearance (see below).

Antiques and art objects need special clearance from the Department of Archaeology, National Archives Building, Ram Shah Path, Kathmandu, which takes at least two days. Nepal is concerned to preserve its priceless art treasures and it is forbidden to export any object more than 100 years old. If in doubt, consult the Department of Archaeology.

Forbidden exports Precious stones, gold, silver, weapons, drugs, animal hides, trophies, wild animals.

Pets such as Tibetan dogs, may be exported.

CURRENCY AND EXCHANGE

Non-Indian visitors are not allowed to import or export Nepali or Indian currency.

All other travelers must fill in a currency form giving their name, nationality, and passport number but not the amount of currency imported. All your foreign exchange transactions are recorded on this form and stamped by the bank or other authorized dealer.

The official exchange rate is published daily in *The Rising Nepal* newspaper and broadcast by Radio Nepal in the Nepali language. At press date the exchange rate was 30.30 rupees to the US$.

Excess Nepali rupees can be converted back into hard currency as long as they do not exceed 10 percent of the total amount changed.

There is an exchange counter at Tribhuvan Airport open throughout the day, every day. The New Road Gate exchange counter of Rastriya Banijya Bank is open daily from 8 am to 8 pm. The Nepal Bank on New Road is open from 10 am to 3 pm, Sunday to Thursday, and from 10 am to noon on Fridays.

The official rate of exchange fluctuates against all currencies. Dollars are in high demand, but black market dealings are illegal.

There are 100 paisa to one Nepali Rupee. Banknotes are in denominations of 1,000, 500, 100, 50, 20, 10, 5, 2 and 1 rupee. Coins are in denominations of 1.00 Rupee and 50, 25, 10 and 5 paisa. Half a rupee (50 paisa) is called a *mohar*, while 25 paisa is referred to as a *sukaa*.

TRAVELING IN NEPAL

INTERNAL FLIGHTS

Flying is the quickest way of traveling to different regions. The national flag carrier, **Royal Nepal Airlines** has a monopoly on domestic flights and runs an extensive network with a fleet of 44-seat Avro 748s, 19-seat Twin Otters, and five-seat Pilatus Porters.

From **Kathmandu** there are scheduled services to **Dang, Dhangadi, Jumla, Mahendranagar, Nepalgunj, Rukumkot, Safi Bazaar, Siliguri Doti, Surkhet,** in the west; to **Baglung** and **Bhairawa** in the midlands; and to **Bhadrapur, Biratnagar, Janakpur, Lukla, Lamidanda, Rajbiraj, Rumjatar Taplejung, Tumlingtar** in the east.

Fares are reasonable, but lower still for Nepali and Indian nationals. And Royal Nepal grants a 25 percent discount on both domestic and international flights to card-holding students under 25 years.

There is also a daily 60-minute "Mountain Flight" that leaves Kathmandu early in the morning and flies along the Himalaya for a view of Mount Everest. In turn, the captain invites each passenger forward to take photographs from the cockpit. The fare is extremely reasonable.

On many domestic flights there is a 25-rupee airport tax and in contrast to Royal Nepal's splendid international service the inflight service is minimal: sweets — and, sometimes, tea.

Book well ahead, especially to destinations only served by the smaller aircraft. If you cancel 24 hours in advance, you pay a 10 percent cancellation fee; 33 percent if less than 24 hours in advance, and 100 percent if you fail to show up. If the flight is canceled the fare is refunded.

Occasionally, it's possible to charter one of the airline's small planes.

If you are flying to a restricted area you will need to produce your trekking permit before you depart from Tribhuvan Airport. And always carry your passport. Police frequently set up checkpoints on all roads, without warning.

AIRPORT TRANSFERS

Royal Nepal and Indian Airlines provide a bus service from Tribhuvan Airport to

Kathmandu. Travelers on the other airlines must use a taxi which accommodates three passengers. The driver often has an "interpreter". Travelers from Kathmandu to the airport can board the bus that leaves the RNAC building, New Road.

HIRE CARS

Hire cars are available from most travel agencies. The hire fee is high, but the cars are comfortable and less likely to break down. A car holds three or four people; metered taxis usually no more than two.

Yeti Travels, near the Annapurna Hotel, run the **Avis** agency and Gorkha Travels, also on Durbar Marg, run the **Hertz** franchise.

ROADS IN NEPAL

Until the '50s Nepal was virtually roadless. The only links between different communities were village trails and mountain paths. Trading was a laborious affair, conducted over weeks and months. But, since then, there has been a major highway construction program supported in the main by Nepal's big power neighbors, India and China.

There are six main roads: the **Tribhuvan Raj Path**, linking Kathmandu with Raxaul at the Indian border, 200 km (124 miles) away, opened in 1956 and built with Indian help.

The **"Chinese Road"** or **Araniko Highway,** 110 km (68 mile) long, to the Tibetan border at Kodari, opened in the mid-'60s and built by China.

Chinese engineers also helped build the 200 km (124 mile) long **Prithvi Raj Marg** between Kathmandu and Pokhara, opened in 1973. There have been two extensions: Dumre to Gorkha and Mugling to Narayanghat and in 1970, Indian engineers completed the 188 km (117 mile) extension from Pokhara to Sanauli on the Indian Border, the **Siddhartha Rajmarg**.

But Nepal's most ambitious road project came about as a co-operative effort between the Soviet Union, United States, Britain, and India. The 1,000 km (621 mile) east-west **Mahendra Raj Marg** through the southern lowlands is part of the planned Pan-Asian Highway, linking the Bosphorus with the Far East.

The newest 110-km (69-mile)-long highway, from **Lamosangu** to **Jiri** east of Kathmandu, built with Swiss help was opened in September 1985.

During the rainy season, whole portions of existing roads are damaged and must be repaired. Inquire locally before setting off on a long-distance road trip.

BUS SERVICES

Bus operators run services on all the highways roads, with express coaches on the main routes. Most services connect with Kathmandu. For details of bus departures from Kathmandu, see BUS SERVICES, page 72. **Minibuses,** less crowded, faster, and more costly, also operate on the same routes. Book one day ahead.

ON FOOT

Above all, Nepal is a land best explored on foot. The most beautiful and the most interesting places can only be reached by walking. No Nepali counts distance by kilometers or miles, but by time. And a leisurely stroll through the rice and mustard fields, across villages, up, down, and around, is certainly the best way to "absorb" Kath-

Health and Precautions

Health experts recommend inoculations against tetanus, polio, cholera, typhoid, and paratyphoid. A gamma globulin injection provides some protection against hepatitis, an endemic infection in Nepal.

A risk that the trekker shares with the climber is that of altitude sickness: a combination of nausea, sleeplessness, headaches, and potentially lethal edemas, both cerebral and pulmonary. Sudden ascents to heights of 3,650 m (12,000 ft) and more, without acclimatization, can lead to an accumulation

mandu valley and the other regions, the people, and their culture.

TREKKING

Every trekker — or traveler for that matter — needs a permit to visit areas outside those included in your Nepali visa. These are issued for one destination at a time on a set route. The charges are based on weekly rates and the permits can be obtained in Kathmandu and Pokhara.

Any reasonably fit person can trek, but the fitter you are, the more you will enjoy it. Do as much walking and exercise as possible to prepare yourself for Nepal's mountain trails.

of water, either on the lungs or brain. Swift descent for prompt medical treatment is the only answer (See ALTITUDE SICKNESS, below, page 188).

Trekking Gear

Trekking along these rough, rocky trails demands that you wear strong, comfortable boots with good soles. At low altitude, tennis shoes or running shoes provide adequate cushioning for the feet .

But good boots are essential at higher elevations, and in snow, large enough to

Trekkers resting OPPOSITE on the Everest trail while umbrellas guard rickshaw drivers against sun and rain ABOVE in Kathmandu valley's benign climate.

allow one or two layers of heavy woolen or cotton — never nylon — socks, of which you will need plenty. Wearing light casuals or sneakers after the day's work will help relax your feet.

For women, wrap-around skirts are preferable to slacks. Shorts offend many mountain communities. Men should wear loose fitting trousers or hiking shorts. For clothing, two light layers are better than a single thick one. If you get too hot, you can peel the top layer off. At really high altitudes wear thermal underwear. It's best to carry too many clothes than not enough. Drip-dry fabrics are best.

Your pack should be as small as possible, light, and easy to open.

The following gear is recommended:

Two pairs of woolen or corduroy trousers or skirts; two warm sweaters; three drip-dry shirts or T-shirts; ski or thermal underwear (especially from November to February); at least half-a-dozen pairs of woolen socks; one pair of walking shoes; one extra pair of sandals; light casual shoes or sneakers; woolen hat; gloves or mittens; strong, warm sleeping bag with hood; a thin sheet of foam rubber for a mattress; padded anorak or parka; plastic raincoat; sunglasses and sun lotion; toilet gear; towels; medical kit; water bottle; and a light day pack.

Your medical kit should include pain killers (for high-altitude headaches); mild sleeping pills (for high-altitude insomnia); streptomagna (for diarrhea); septram (for bacilliary dysentery); tinidozole (for amoebic dysentery); throat lozenges and cough drops; ophthalmic ointment or drops; one broad spectrum antibiotic; alcohol (for massaging feet to prevent blisters); blister pads; bandages and elastic plasters; antiseptic and cotton; a good sun block; and a transparent lip salve.

In addition to these, you should carry a torch, candles, lighter, pocket knife, scissors, spare shoelaces, string, safety pins, toilet paper, and plastic bags to protect food, wrap up wet or dirty clothes, and carry your litter, plus food, tents, and photographic equipment. Much of this can be bought in Kathmandu.

Cooking and eating utensils are normally provided by the trekking agency and carried by the porters.

Always carry your trekking permit in a plastic bag where you can get to it easily. Lock your bag against theft or accidental loss. Make sure you have plenty of small currency for minor expenses along the way.

Carry a good supply of high-energy food like chocolate, dried fruits, nuts, and whisky, brandy, or vodka for a warming nightcap.

Water is contaminated so do not drink from streams no matter how clear or sparkling they look. Chlorine is not effective against amoebic cysts. All water should be well boiled or treated with iodine: four drops a liter and left for 20 minutes before drinking.

But note that at high altitude water boils at temperatures below 100 °C (212 °F) — not warm enough to kill bacteria. A pressure cooker solves the problem and also cooks food quicker!

Normally the day starts with early morning tea at around six o'clock. Break camp and pack, followed by a breakfast of hot porridge and biscuits, ready to be on the trail by around seven o'clock.

Lunch is taken around noon, the cook having gone ahead to select the site and prepare the meal. By late afternoon, the day's trek is ended and camp pitched, followed by dinner. At these high altitudes, after a hard day's walking, there's little dallying over the camp fire. Though sleep is fitful and shallow, most are ready to hit the sack by 8 pm.

Speed is not of the essence. Pause frequently to enjoy the beauty of a particular spot, talk to the passing locals, photograph, or sip tea in one of the rustic wayside tea shops.

Walk at your own pace. Drink as much liquid as posible to combat high altitude and heat dehydration. Never wait for blisters to develop but pamper tender feet with an alcohol massage.

ALTITUDE SICKNESS

There are three main types. Early mountain sickness is the first, and acts as a warning. It

---

OPPOSITE: A Newar priest dressed in sacred crimson-red, Kathmandu.

can develop into pulmonary edema (water-logged lungs) or cerebral edema (water-logged brain). The symptoms are headache, nausea, loss of appetite, sleeplessness, fluid retention, and swelling of the body.

Altitude sickness develops slowly, manifesting itself two or three days after reaching high altitude. The cure is to climb no higher until the symptoms have disappeared.

Pulmonary edema is characterized, even when resting, by breathlessness and a persistent cough, accompanied by congestion

(more than 3,000 ft) higher than the summit of the Matterhorn. Above 3,000 m (10,000 ft) the air becomes noticably thinner.

Youth, strength, and fitness make no difference. Those who climb too high, too fast, expose themselves to the risk of Acute Altitude Sickness. At 4,300 m (14,108 ft), for example, the body requires three to four liters of liquid a day. At low altitude try to drink at least a liter a day.

You should plan frequent rest days between the 3,700- and 4,300-m (12,000- and 14,000-ft) contours, sleeping at the same alti-

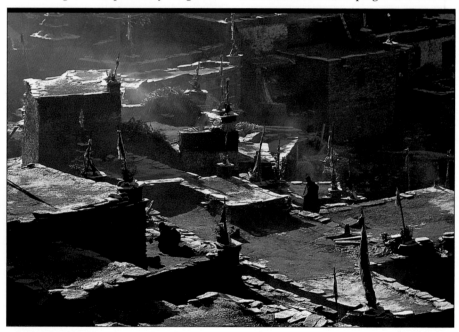

of the chest. If these symptoms appear, descend at once.

Cerebral edema is less common. Its symptoms are extreme tiredness, vomiting, severe headache, staggering when walking, abnormal speech and behavior, drowsiness, even coma. Victims must return at once to a lower altitude and abandon all thoughts of their trek.

If left untreated mountain sickness can lead to death. It's endemic in the high Himalaya where even experienced mountaineers sometimes forget that the mountains begin where other mountain ranges end. For instance, the Everest base camp is some 1,000 m

Fields under snow OPPOSITE and weathered roofs ABOVE at Nar village.

tude for at least two nights. Climb higher during the day but always descend to the same level to sleep.

Never pitch camp more than 450 m (1,500 ft) higher in any one day, even if you feel fit enough for a climb twice that height.

If you begin to suffer early altitude sickness, go no higher until the symptoms have disappeared. If more serious symptoms appear, descend immediately to a lower elevation. Mild symptoms should clear within between one and two days.

If the victim is unable to walk he should be carried down on a porter's back or by yak. No matter what the reason, never delay, even at night.

Some victims are incapable of making correct decisions and you may have to force them to go down against their will. The victim must be accompanied.

Treatment is no substitute for descent. If a doctor is available, he can treat the victim but the patient must descend.

Because of a lack of radio communications and helicopters, emergency evacuations are difficult to organize. Such a rescue operation takes time and costs a great deal of money.

Some agencies may be able to arrange

helicopter rescues for its trekkers but individuals stand no chance.

COMMUNICATIONS

The Central Post Office in Kathmandu has three sections, located close to one another at the junction of Kanti Path and Kicha-Pokhara Road.

The **Foreign Post Office** (℡ 211760) handles parcels sent or received from abroad but the best advice is to avoid sending or receiving any during your stay as it will just cause you one enormous headache. If you do want to send a parcel, take advantage of the packaging and parcel service offered by many shopkeepers.

Letters can be sent Poste Restante to the **General Post Office** (℡ 211073. 10 am to 5 pm, daily except Saturdays and holidays; closing time 4 pm between November and February). Check that stamps are franked in front of your eyes. Major hotels will also handle your mail which is a lot easier.

The **Telecommunication Office** at Tripureshwar deals with telephone calls, cables, and telexes. The telex at the Central Telegraph Office works only during government hours.

Incoming cables are sometimes inexplicably delayed. But since the installation of the British earth satellite station, international telephone connections are excellent.

TIPPING

As a rule, for good and exceptional service, a gratuity of about five percent will be well received. For exceptional service by taxis, a tip of 10 percent of the fare is in order. This is also now customary in restaurants that cater for tourists and travelers.

CLIMATE

Nepal enjoys an extreme variety of climates. Altitude and exposure to sun and rain are the most influential factors.

Kathmandu valley knows three seasons. The winter — from October to March — is the best time to visit Nepal. Night time temperatures drop close to freezing point, but by day these climb from 10°C to 25°C (50°F to 77°F) and the skies are generally clear.

Mornings and evenings are invigorating. There is often an early-morning mist. October and February are particularly pleasant.

In Pokhara valley, where temperatures rise to 30°C (86°F) at midday in the lower altitude, it is much warmer.

From April to early June the weather becomes hot and stuffy, with occasional

FOLLOWING PAGES: Warden's house nestles beneath the high peaks of Sagarmatha National Park.

evening thunderstorms. The land is frequently shrouded in heat mist.

Temperatures in Kathmandu vary between 11 ℃ and 28 ℃ (52 °F and 83 °F) in April to between 19 ℃ and 30 ℃ (66 °F and 86 °F) in June, with maximum temperatures of 36 ℃ (97 °F).

Pre-monsoon rains normally start in May and the monsoon, which normally arrives at the end of June, lasts three months.

For most of this time the Himalaya remain hidden. The torrential downpours cause much flooding but it is still possible to tour Kathmandu valley.

With the rains come the leeches (*jugas*), however, and trekking stops and the lowlands are cut off by swollen rivers and landslides.

When the monsoon ends, around mid-September, the skies clear, the nights become cooler, and the landscape is a symphony of fall colors, brown and gold.

CLOTHING

Comfortable, casual clothing is recommended unless you are on business meetings with businessmen and government officials are planned.

During winter days in the Kathmandu Valley you'll be warm enough with light clothing but carry a warm sweater, padded anorak, or jacket for the evenings.

Jeans, cord trousers, or long skirts, are fine and casual shoes essential, even if you don't

intend to walk much. Forget fashion. During the rainy season you can buy umbrellas for protection from both rain and sun locally.

Trekking gear, in standard sizes, can be bought or rented in Kathmandu and Pokhara together with sweaters, ponchos, caps and other woolen or down clothing.

During the hot season, between April and September, all you need is light summer clothing, preferably cotton. This is true for most of the year in the Terai except in December and January when you need a sweater or jacket for evening wear.

HEALTH

Travelers are advised to take inoculations and immunization against typhoid, hepatitis, cholera, and tetanus.

Never drink unboiled and unfiltered water. Avoid ice cubes and raw vegetables. Always peel fruit and clean your hands often. Never walk barefoot. Stomach upsets are known locally as the "Kathmandu Quickstep".

If trouble persists, it can develop into something more serious like amoebic or bacillary dysentery or giardiasis so get a stool test and seek medical help.

Malaria is on the increase, but most of Kathmandu is too high to support the malaria-carrying species of mosquitoes. For visits to the south, however, take a recognized prophylactic two weeks before you arrive in the Terai and continue to take this for six weeks after you leave. You should also carry a mosquito repellent during the warm months.

Pharmacies in Kathmandu, mainly along New Road, offer a wide range of Western drugs at low prices, and some traditional Indian ayurvedic remedies.

Most international hotels have a consultant doctor on call and the following hospitals in Kathmandu have English-speaking staff:

Bir Hospital, Kanti Path, Kathmandu, (211119;

Patan Hospital, Patan, (521034, 521048, 521634, 522266; and

Tribhuvan University Teaching Hospital, Maharajgung, (412303, 412404, 412505.

Kathmandu's Freak Street ABOVE where the hippies of the 1950s and 1960s finally found their pot if not gold.

POWER

Major towns in Nepal are on the 220-volt AC system, though this sometimes fluctuates. Hindus adore light and, during festivals, towns and villages are ablaze with light. Some of the international hotels maintain standby generators that cut in during the frequent power cuts.

PHOTOGRAPHY

Film stock is only available in Kathmandu and is extremely costly. Shops in New Road process black-and-white and color film. Telephoto lenses are useful for wildlife and landscape photography.

TIME

Nepal is 15 minutes ahead of Indian Standard Time and five hours 45 minutes ahead of Greenwich Mean Time.

Government hours are from Sunday to Friday between 10 am and 5 pm. They close one hour earlier during the three winter months. Only embassies and international organizations enjoy a two-day weekend. Shops, some of which remain open on - Saturdays and holidays, seldom open before 10 am but do not usually close until 7 to 8 pm.

Remember that in this deeply religious country there are many holidays devoted to various deities, mythological events, astrological signs, traditional festivals, in addition to several secular holidays marking phases of Nepal's modern history.

ACCOMMODATION

Travelers to Kathmandu have a wide range of choices—from five-star international hotels to basic board and lodging with shared toilets and bathrooms.

But apart from the five-star game lodges in Royal Chitwan National Park the choice outside Kathmandu valley is more homey and less expensive.

During the high seasons — spring and fall — Kathmandu's international hotels near 100 percent occupancy and it's advisable to book well in advance. At the lower end of the price scale there are plenty of comfortable hotels. Most offer a choice of bed and breakfast; half board (breakfast and one other meal); or full board.

There are also a number of basic lodges with minimal amenities. Rates vary depending on facilities. Toilets and showers are generally communal, heating extra. Most are in old Kathmandu, around Durbar Square or in Thamel district.

Tariffs are subject to a 12 to 15 percent government tax.

MOUNTAIN LODGES

In the mountains there are many basic lodges, usually near airstrips, as well as the many traditional Nepali teahouses found in every village on the trekking routes. The most comfortable accommodation available in the high Himalaya is at **Lukla** (see page 138, **Phaphlu**, and **Jumla** see page 132).

NATIONAL PARKS AND WILDLIFE DIRECTORY

CHITWAN NATIONAL PARK. 932 sq km (360 sq miles). Wildlife include elephants, tigers, leopards, rhinoceros, wild boar, deer, monkeys, and a multitude of birds. (See page 118)
GODAVARI ROYAL BOTANICAL GARDENS. 66 different species of fern, 115 orchids, 77 cacti and succulents, and about 200 trees and shrubs. (See page 79)
KHAPTAD NATIONAL PARK. 187 sq km (73 sq miles). A floral repository of high-altitude conifers, oak and rhododendron forests. (See page 133)
KOSI TAPPU WILDLIFE RESERVE. Wild buffaloes and thousands of migratory birds. (See page 117)
LAKE RARA NATIONAL PARK. 104 sq km (41 sq miles). Floral repository of high-altitude conifers, oak and rhododendron forests. (See page 132)
LANTANG NATIONAL PARK; 1,243 sq km (480 sq miles), haven for the endangered snow leopard, leopard, Himalayan black bear, red panda, and wild dog. (See page 144)

PARSA WILDLIFE RESERVE (1,200 sq km (470 sq miles). Elephants, tigers, leopards, rhinoceros, wild boar, deer, monkeys, and a multitude of birds. (See page 118)

ROYAL BARDIA RESERVE A sanctuary for the endangered swamp deer. (See page 123)

SAGARMATHA NATIONAL PARK (1,243 sq km (487 sq miles). Wolf, bear, musk deer, feral goat species, even the brilliantly colored crimson-horned or Impeyan pheasants. (See page 139)

SHEY-PHOKSONDO NATIONAL PARK. (See page 113)

SHUKLA PHANTA WILDLIFE RESERVE. Endangered Blackbuck. (See page 123)

JAWAKAKHEL ZOO, Patan. A selection of exotic south Asian animals, especially Himalayan species. (See page 91)

MEDIA

English language news bulletins are broadcast twice daily by Radio Nepal at 8 am and 8:30 pm, with a special 45-minute "tourist program" at 8:15 pm. Nepal Television has two hours of broadcasting between 7 and 9 pm.

Several English language newspapers are published in Kathmandu, as well as many in Nepali.

Of the English press, *The Rising Nepal* gives wider coverage of foreign news than the more parochial *Motherland*. Both devote much of their front page to the activities of the royal family.

The *International Herald Tribune*, one day old, is on sale at newsstands and in hotels, as are *Time, Newsweek, The Far Eastern Economic Review, Asiaweek*, and *India Today*, but very little else except for the Indian newspapers that arrive on the daily morning flights.

ENTERTAINMENT

By 10 pm, Kathmandu is nearly asleep. The only life centers around some temples, restaurants, and tourists hotels.

The few movie houses screen heavy Indian melodramas and sloppy romances. Westerners may draw more from audience reaction than the screen. The European and American cultural centers have a program of Western films.

There are few discos, no nightclubs, and no massage parlors, but you can dance at the **Soaltee Oberoi, Yak and Yeti,** and **Everest Sheraton** hotels.

The **Copper Floor** disco at Hotel Lali Guras in Lazimpat is open Fridays and Saturdays. The only late evening action is at the **Up and Down Bar** or **Pumpkins** in the Everest Sheraton.

Nepal's only **casino** — Nepalis not allowed — is at the Soaltee Oberoi Hotel, where mostly Indian visitors to one of the few international casinos between Malaysia and the Suez, stake small fortunes on the turn of a card at baccarat, chemin de fer, and the turn of the roulette wheel. The chips are valued in Indian rupees or foreign exchange.

Some hotels stage **folk dances** and **musical shows.** The best is at the **Everest Cultural Society,** Lal Durbar. Folk dances, accompanied by an authentic Nepali dinner, are presented daily at 7 pm.

Another group, the **New Himalchuli Cultural Group,** stage classical and folk dances, together with songs and music, daily from 6:30 to 7:30 pm (November to February), and 7 to 8 pm (March to October). For more information, write to P.O. Box 3409, Lazimpat, Kathmandu, Nepal. (411825.

Go to the **Ghar e Kebab** restaurant, Annapurna Hotel, Durbar Marg, for the best in Indian classical music.

The finest show of all, however, is **Bhaktapur's** *son et lumière:* spectacular local dancing, and a Nepali dinner in the ancient square, lit by countless oil lamps. For groups only, this has to be arranged in advance.

LANGUAGE

Nepali is an atonal and phonetic language. No matter how long the word, the accent is always placed on the first or second syllable. Words are pronounced exactly as they are spelled.

Apart from a few peculiarities, consonants are pronounced as in English: *ch* is pronounced *tch* as in bench

chh is pronounced *tch-h* as in **pitch here**
th is pronounced *t-h* as in **hot head**
kh is pronounced *k-h* as in **dark hole**
ph is pronounced *p-h* as in **top hat**
j is pronounced *d-j* as in **Jesus**
dh is pronounced *d-h* as in **adhere**

The *t, d, th,* and *dh,* with a dot beneath them are pronounced by rolling the tongue back and putting it in the center of the roof of the mouth, so that the sound produced is like *"rt"* in "cart" or *"rd"* in **card.**

Vowels are pronounced either long or short:

e is always *e (ay)* as in **cafe**
u is pronounced *oo* as in **moon** (never *yu* as in *mute)*
y is pronounced *yi* as in **yield** (never *ai* as in *my)*
i is pronounced *oh* as in **toe.**

SHOPPING TIPS

Shopping is best done in Kathmandu, Patan and Bhaktapur, although craft items such as pottery and carpets may be found in Thimi (see page 95) and Jawalkhel respectively. See PATAN section SHOPPING page 89 for recommendations. Remember that genuine prayer wheels hold a roll of parchment or paper bearing a mantra (prayer formula).

An authentic Gurkha knife, the *khukuri,* has a small notch at the base of the blade to carry blood away from the handle, and there should be two small knives in the back of the scabbard for skinning and sharpening.

A tooth mark will make a small indentation in real gold.

Consider "antiques" to have been made the week before and, unless otherwise certified by specialists, pay accordingly.

TOURIST INFORMATION

There are tourist information centers at:
Main office (English-language): Ganga Path, Basantpur, (215818 (in front of Hanuman Dhoka Palace; open 10 am to 4 pm Sunday to Friday).
Tribhuvan Airport Exchange, (211933 (other offices in airports at **Pokhara, Bhairawa, Birganj,** and **Kaka Bhitta**).
Department of Tourism, (211293, 214519.
Telephone enquiry, Tripureshwar, (197.

RELIGION

Minority faiths practise freely in the Hindu Kingdom of Nepal. The major places of worship are:

Roman Catholic
Jesuit St. Xavier College, Jawalkhel (521050.
Annapurna Hotel (Sunday Mass) (211711.

Protestant
Church of Christ, Nepal, Ram Shah Path.

Blue Room, USIS, Rabi Bhawan (213966.

Muslim
Main Mosque, Durbar Marg.

Jewish
Israeli Embassy (211251.

TRAVEL AND TREKKING AGENCIES

Adventure Travel Nepal, Durbar Marg (215307.

Traditional Nepali dance ABOVE honors Bhairav, Shiva's demoniac incarnation.

Annapurna Mountaineering and Trekking, Durbar Marg (212736.
Annapurna Travel and Tours, Durbar Marg (213940.
Everest Travel Service, Ganga Path (211216.
Express Trekking, Naxal (213017.
Gauri Shanker Trekking, Lazimpat (212112.
Gorkha Travels, Durbar Marg (214895.
Great Himalayan Adventure, Kanti Path (216144.
Himal Trek, Maharajgung (211561.
Himalayan Adventures, Thamel (212496.
Himalayan Journeys, Kanti Path (215855.
Himalayan Rover Trek, Naxal (412667.
Himalayan Travels, Durbar Marg (213803.
International Trekkers, Durbar Marg (215594.
Kathmandu Travels and Tours, Ganga Path (212985.
Lama Excursions, Durbar Marg (410786
Malla Travels, Malla Hotel, Lekhnath Marg (410635.
Manaslu Trekking, Durbar Marg (212422.
Mountain Travel, Durbar Marg (412455.
Mountain Travel, Naxal (414508, 411562.
Natraj Tours and Travels, Durbar Marg (212014.
Natraj Trekking, Kanti Path (216644.
Nepal Travel Agency, Ram Shah Path (213106.
Nepal Trekking and Natural History Expeditions, New Road (212985.
Nepal Trekking, Thamel (214681.
Orchid Express Travels, Thamel (215775.
Shanker Travel and Tours, Shanker Hotel, Lazimpat (213494.
Sherpa Cooperative Trekking, Kamal Pokhara (215887.
Sherpa Trekking Service, Kamaladi (212489.
Tiger Tops, Durbar Marg (212706.
Trans Himalayan Tours, Durbar Marg (213854.
Trans Himalayan Trekking, Durbar Marg (213854.
Universal Travel and Tours, Kanti Path (214192.
World Travels, Durbar Marg (212810.
Yeti Travel, Durbar Marg (211234.

OPPOSITE: Kathmandu Valley's Swayambhunath Temple and stupa.

NEPAL EMBASSIES AND CONSULATES ABROAD

Australia: Consulate, 870 Military Road, Suite 1 Strand Centre, Mosman, NSW 2088, Sydney. ((02) 9603565; 6/204, The Avenue, Parkville 3052, Melbourne; House of Kathmandu, 66 High Street, Toowong 4066, Brisbane, ((07) 3714228; 16 Robinson Street, Nedlands, Perth.
Austria: Consulate, A-1190 Vienna, Karpfenenwaldgasse 11.
Bangladesh: Embassy, Lake Road, No.2, Baridhara Diplomatic Enclave, Baridhara, Dhaka, (601790, 601890.
Belgium: Consulate, Nepal House, 149 Lamorinierstraat, B-2018 Antwerp, (03-2308800.
Burma: Embassy, 16 Natmauk Yeiktha (Park Avenue), P.O. Box 84, Tamwe, Rangoon, (50633.
Canada: Consulate, 310 Dupont Street, Toronto, Ontario, ((416) 9687252.
China: Embassy, No. 1 Sanlitun Xilujie, Beijing, (521795. Consulate, Norbulingka Road 13, Lhasa, (22880.
Denmark: Consulate, 36 Kronprinsessagade, DK 1006, Copenhagen K., (01 143175.
Egypt: Embassy, 9 Tiba Street, Dokki, Cairo, (704447, 704541.
Finland: Consulate, Parkgatan 9, Helsingfors 14, (90-626789.
France: Embassy, 7 Rue de Washington, 75008 Paris, (43592861, 43593123. Consulate, 10 Rue Claude Gonin, 31400 Toulouse, (348413.
Germany: Embassy, Im-Hag 15, D-5300 Bonn, Bad Godesberg 2, ((0228) 343097. Consulates, Flinschstrasse 63, D-6000, Frankfurt am Main 60, (069-40871; Landsbergerstrasse 191, D-8000 Munich 21, (089-5704406; Busako Luyken GmbH, Postfach 080206, Handwerkstrasse 5-7, D-7000 Stuttgart, 80 (Vaihingen), (5-28933255.
Hong Kong: Liaison office, HQ Brigade of Gurkhas, Prince of Wales Building, British Forces Post Office, (893 3255.
India: Embassy, Barakhamba Road, New Delhi-110001, (381484, 388191, 387361, 386592, 387594. Consulate 19 Woodlands, Sterndale Road, Alipore, Calcutta-700027, (452024, 459027.
Italy: Consulate, Piazza Medaglie d'Oro 20, 00136 Rome, ((06) 3451642, 348176, 341055.

Japan: Embassy, 16-23 Higashi-Gotanda, 3-chome, Shingawa-ku, Tokyo 141, (444-7303, 444-7305.

Lebanon: Consulate, Rue Spears, Beirut, (386690.

Mexico: Consulate, Avellanos, No. 24 Jardines de Sam Mateo, Naucalpan, Estado de Mexico.

Netherlands: Consulate, Lange Voorhut 16, NL-2514 EE Den Haa, (070 458882; Prinsengracht 687, Gelderland Bldg, NL-1017 JV Amsterdam, (020-25-0388, 020-24-1530.

Norway: Consulate, Haakon VIIs gt.-5 P.O. Box 1384 Vika, 0116 Oslo, ((2) 414743.

Pakistan: Embassy, House 506, 84th Street, Attaturk Avenue, Ramna G-6/4, Islamabad, (823642, 823754. Consulate, 1st Floor Union Bank Building, Merewether Tower, Chundrigar Road, Karachi-2, (234458, 228947.

Philippines: Consulate, 1136-1138 United Nations Avenue, Paco 2803, Manila, (589393, 588855.

Saudi Arabia: Embassy, P.O. Box 94384, Al-Morabba, Nasir Bin Saud Bin Farhan Street, Behind Capital Marriage Palace, Riyadh, (11693.

South Korea: Consulate, 541 Namdaemoon-ro, Jung-Gu, Seoul-100. (22-9992, 771-91.

Spain: Consulate, Finca Ca'n Martin, Son Sardinia, Carretera Vaudemossa, Palma de Mallorca, ((71) 202604; Gran Vai de Les Corts, Catalanes, 1075-7e La, Barcelona-20.

Sri Lanka: Consulate, 290 R.A. de Mel Mawatha, Colombo-7.

Sweden: Consulate, Karlavagen, 97 S - 115 22, Stockholm.

Switzerland: Consulate, Schanzengasse 22, P.O. Box CH-8024, Zurich, (01475993.

Thailand: Embassy, 189 Soi - 71, Sukhamvit Road, Bangkok-10110, (391 7240, 390-2280.

Turkey: Consulate, Ramtas A.S., Y.K.B. Ishani Valikonagi Cad. 4/4 Nisantas, Istanbul.

UK: Embassy, 12A Kensington Palace Gardens, London W8 4QU. (229-1594, 229-6231.

United Nations: Permanent Mission 820 Second Avenue, Suite 1200, New York, NY 10017. ((212) 370-4188. (212) 370-4189; Rue Frederic Amiel, 1203, Geneva, ((022) 44-44-41.

USA: Embassy, 2131 Leroy Place N.W., Washington D.C.-20008, ((202) 667 4550. Consulates, 473 Jackson Street, San Francisco, CA-94111 ((415) 434-1111; 16250

Dallas Parkway, Suite 110, Dallas TX-75248, ((214) 931-1212; 212, 15th Street N.E., Atlanta Georgia-30309, ((404) 892-8152.

USSR: Embassy, 2nd Neopolimovsky Pere Look 14/7, Moscow, (2447356, (2419311.

EMBASSIES

Australia, Bhat Bhateni (411578
Bangladesh, Naxal (410012
Burma, Pulchok (521788
China, Baluwatar (412589
Egypt, Pulchok (521844
France, Lazimpat (412332
Germany, Kanti Path (211730
India, Lainchaur (410900
Israel, Lazimpat (411811
Italy, Baluwatar (412743
Japan, Pani Pokhari (414083
North Korea, Patan (521084
Pakistan, Pani Pokhari (411421
South Korea, Tahachal (211172
Thailand, Thapathali (213910
USSR, Baluwatar (412155
UK, Lainchaur (410583
USA, Pani Pokhari (411601

CULTURAL CENTERS

British Council, Kanti Path (211305.
French Cultural Center, Bag Bazar (214326.
Indian Cultural Center and Library, RNAC Building (211497.
USSR Cultural Center, Ram Shah Path (216248.
Goethe Institute, Sundhara (215528.
United States Information Service, New Road (211250.

Further Reading

AMIN, WILLETTS, TETLEY. *Journey through Nepal.* London: The Bodley Head.

BERNSTEIN, JEREMY. *The Wildest Dreams of Kew: A Profile of Nepal.* New York: Simon and Schuster, 1970.

FLEMING, ROBERT AND LINDA. *Kathmandu Valley.* Tokyo: Kodansha International, 1978.

FRANK, KEITMAR, *Dreamland Nepal.* New Delhi: S. Chand, 1978. Photographic book.

GURUNG, HARKA. *Vignettes of Nepal.* Kathmandu: Sajha Prakashan, 1980.

HASS, ERNST. *Himalayan Pilgrimage.* New York: Viking Press, 1978. Nice photographic book.

HAGEN, TONI. *Nepal: The Kingdom in the Himalayas.* Berne: Kummerly and Frey, 1961.(Second edition, 1971).

His Majesty's Government Of Nepal. Nepal Kathmandu: Ministry of Industry and Commerce, Department of Tourism, 1974.

HOAG, KATHERINE. *Exploring Mysterious Kathmandu.* Avalok, 1978.

MATTHIESSEN, PETER. *The Snow Leopard.* London: Chatto and Windus, 1979.

MURPHY. DERVLA. *The Waiting Land: A spell in Nepal.* London: John Murray, 1967.

PEISSEL, MICHEL. *Tiger for Breakfast.* London: Hodder, 1966.

RAGAM, V.R. *Pilgrim's Travel Guide: The Himalayan Region.* Gunter: 1963.

SHAH, RISHIKESH. *An Introduction to Nepal.* Kathmandu: Ratna Pustak Bhandar, 1976.

SUYIN, HAN. *The Mountain Is Young.* London: Jonathan Cape, 1958.

Historical

FISHER, MARGARET W. *The Political History of Nepal.* Berkeley: University of California, Institute of International Studies, 1960.

HAMILTON, FRANCIS. *An Account of the Kingdom of Nepal and of the Territories Annexed to This Dominion by House of Gurkha.* Edinburgh: Archibold Constable and Co., 1819.

HODGSON, BRIAN H. *Essays on the Languages, Literature, and Religion of Nepal and Tibet; Together with Further Papers on the Geography, Ethnology, and Commerce of Those Countries.* London: Trubner and Co.,1974. Reprinted by Bibliotheca Himalayica, New Delhi.

HOOKER, SIR JOSEPH DALTON. *Himalayan Journals.* London: Ward, Lock, Bowden and Co., 1891.

KIRKPATRICK, COL. F. *An Account of the Kingdom of Nepaul.* London: 1800. Reprinted by Bibliotheca Himalayica, New Delhi, 1969.

LANDON, PERCIVAQL. *Nepal.* Two volumes. London: Constable, 1928. Reprinted by Bibliotheca Himalayica, New Delhi.

OLDFIELD, HENRY AMBROSE. *Sketches from Nipal. Historical and Descriptive, with Anecdotes of the Court Life and Wild Sports of the Country in the Time of Maharaja Jang Bahadur, G.C.B., to Which Is Added an Essay on Nepali Buddhism, and Illustrations of Religious Monuments, Architecture, and Scenery from the Author's Own Drawings.* Two volumes. London: W.H. Allen, 1880. Reprinted by Bibliotheca Himalayica, New Delhi.

RANA, PUDMA JUNG BAHADUR, *Life of Maharaja Sir Jung Bahadur of Nepal.* Allahabad, India: Pioneer Press, 1909.

REGMI, D.R. *Ancient Nepal.* Third Edition. Calcutta: Firma K.L. Mukhopadhyaya, 1969.

REGMI, D.R. *Medieval Nepal.* Three volumes. Calcutta: Firma K.L. Mukhopadhyaya, 1965.

REGMI, D.R. *Modern Nepal: Rise and Growth in the Eighteenth Century.* Calcutta: Firma K.L. Mukhopadhyaya, 1961.

STILLER, LUDWIG F. *The Rise of the House of Gorkha.* New Delhi: Manjusri, 1973.

WRIGHT, DANIEL, Editor. *Vamsavali: History of Nepal, with an Introductory Sketch of the Country and People of Nepal.* Translated from the Parbatiya by Munshi Shew Shunker Singh and Pandit Shri Gunanand. Cambridge: University Press 1877. Second edition, Calcutta: Susil Gupta, 1958.

Peoples, Art and Culture

ANDERSON, MARY M. *Festivals of Nepal.* London: George Allen and Unwin, 1971.

BAIDYA, KARUNAKAR. *Teach Yourself Nepali.* Kathmandu: Ratna Pustak Bhandar,1982.

BROWN, PERCY. *Picturesque Nepal.* London: Adam and Charles Black, 1912.

DEEP, DHRUBA KRISHNA. *The Nepal Festivals.* Kathmandu: Ratna Pustak Bhandar, 1982.

FURER-HAIMENDORF, CHRISTOPH VON. *The Interrelation of Caste and Ethnic Groups in Nepal.* London: University of London, 1957.

FURER-HAIMENDORF, CHRISTOPH VON. *The Sherpas of Nepal: Buddhist Highlanders.* Berkeley and Los Angeles: University of California Press, 1964.

HAALAND, ANE. *BHAKTAPUR: A Town Changing.* Bhaktapur Development Project, 1982.

HOSKEN, FRAN P. *The Kathmandu Valley Towns: A Record of Life and Change in Nepal*. New York: Weatherhill, 1974.

INDRA. *Joys of Nepali Cooking*. New Delhi: 1982.

JERSTAD, LUTHER G. MANI-RIMDU: *Sherpa Dance Drama*. Calcutta: International Book House, 1969.

JEST, CORNEILLE. *Monuments of Northern Nepal*. Paris: UNESCO, 1981.

KANSAKAR, N.H. *Nepali Kitchens*. Kathmandu: 1978.

KORN, WOLFGANG. *The Traditional Architecture of the Kathmandu Valley*. Kathmandu: Ratna Pustak Bhandar, 1977. Limited edition with many diagrams.

KRAMRISCH, STELLA. *The Art of Nepal*. New York: 1964.

LALL, KESAR. *Lore and Legend of Nepal*. Kathmandu: Ratna Pustak Bhandar, 1976.

LALL, KESAR. *Nepali Customs and Manners*. Kathmandu: Ratna Pustak Bhandar, 1976.

MACDONALD, A.W., AND ANNE VERGATI STAHL. *Newar Art*. New Delhi: Vikas, 1979.

MCDOUGAL, CHARLES. *The Kulunge Rai: A Study in Kinship and Marriage Exchange*. Kathmandu: Ratna Pustak Bhandar, 1979.

NEPALI, GOPAL SINGH. *The Newars*. Bombay: United Asia Publications, 1965. Subtitled: *An Ethno-Sociological Study of a Himalayan Community*.

PAL, PRATAPADITYA. *Nepal: Where the Gods are Young*. Asia House Exhibition: 1975.

PRUSCHA, CARL. *Kathmandu Valley: The Preservation of Physical Environment and Cultural Heritage, A Protective Inventory*. Two volumes. Vienna: Anton Schroll, 1975. Prepared by His Majesty's Government of Nepal in collaboration with UNESCO and the United Nations.

RUBEL, MARY. *The Gods of Nepal*. Kathmandu: Bhimratna Harsharatna, 1971.

SANDAY, JOHN. *The Hanuman Dhoka Royal Palace, Kathmandu:* Building Conservation and Local Traditional Crafts. London: AARP, 1974.

SINGH, MADANJEET. *Himalayan Arts*. London: UNESCO, 1968.

SNELLGROVE, DAVID L. *Buddhist Himalaya*. Oxford: Bruno Cassirer, 1957.

VAIDYA, KARUNAKAR. *Folk Tales of Nepal*. Kathmandu: Ratna Pustak Bhandar, 1980.

Natural History

FLEMING, R.L. SR., R.L. FLEMING JR. AND L.S. BANGDEL. *Birds of Nepal*. Kathmandu: Avalok, 1979.

MANANDHAR, N.P. *Medicinal Plants of Nepal Himalaya*. Kathmandu: Ratna Pustak Bhandar, 1980.

MCDOUGAL, CHARLES. *The Face of the Tiger*. London: Rivington Books and Andre Deutsch, 1977.

MIEROW, D., AND H. MISHRA. *Wild Animals of Nepal*. Kathmandu: 1974.

MIEROW. D., AND T.B. SHRESTHA. *Himalayan Flowers and Trees*. Kathmandu: Sahayogi Prakashan, 1978.

STAINTON, J.D.A. *Forests of Nepal*. London: Murray, 1972.

Mountains

BERZRUSCHKA, STEPHEN. *A Guide to Trekking in Nepal*. Seattle: The Mountaineers, 1981.

BONINGTON, CHRIS. *Annapurna South Face*, London: Cassell, 1971.

BONINGTON, CHRIS. *Everest South West Face*, London: Hodder and Stoughton, 1973.

BONINGTON, CHRIS. *Everest the Hard Way*. London. Hodder and Stoughton, 1976.

FANTIN, MARIO. *Mani Rimdu Nepal*. Singapore: Toppon, 1976.

FANTIN, MARIO. *Sherpa Himalaya Nepal*. Bologne, Italy: Arti Grafiche, 1978.

HACKETT, PETER. *Mountain Sickness*. American Alpine Club.

HERZOG, MAURICE. *Annapurna: First Conquest of an 8,000-Meter Peak (26,493 Feet)*. New York: E.P. Dutton, 1955.

HILLARY, EDMUND. *High Adventure*. New York E.P. Dutton, 1953.

HILLARY, EDMUND. *Schoolhouse in the Clouds*. Garden City, N.Y: Doubleday, 1964.

HILLARY, EDMUND AND DESMOND DOIG. *High in the Thin Cold Air: The Story of the Himalayan Expedition Led by Sir Edmund Hillary*. Garden City, N.Y: Doubleday, 1962.

HILLARY, EDMUND, AND GEORGE LOWE. *East of Everest: An Account of the New Zealand Alpine Club Himalayan Expedition to the Barun Valley in 1954*. New York: E.P. Dutton, 1956.

HORNBEIN, THOMAS F. *Everest, the West Ridge*. San Francisco: Sierra Club, 1965.

HOUSTON, CHARLES S. *Going High: The Story of Man and Altitude*. American Alpine Club: 1980.

HUNT, JOHN. *The Ascent of Everest*. London: Hodder and Stoughton, 1953. Also *The Conquest of Everest*. New York: E.P. Dutton, 1954.

HUNT, JOHN. *The Conquest of Himalayas*. New York: E.P. Dutton, 1954.

HUNT, JOHN. *Our Everest Adventure: The Pictorial History from Kathmandu to the Summit.* New York: E.P. Dutton, 1954.

IOZAWA, TOMOYA. *Trekking in the Himalayas.* Tokyo: Yama-Kei, 1980.

IZZARD, RALPH. *The Abominiable Snowman Adventure.* London: Hodder and Stoughton, 1955. Also Garden City, N.Y.: Doubleday, 1955.

IZZARD, RALPH. *An Innocent on Everest.* New York: E.P. Dutton, 1954. Also London: Hodder and Stoughton, 1955.

JONES, MIKE. *Canoeing Down Everest.* New Delhi: Vikas, 1979.

KAZAMI, TAKEHIDE. *The Himalayas.* Tokyo: Kodansha International, 1973.

MCCALLUM, JOHN D. *Everest Diary, Based on the Personal Diary of Lute Jerstad, One of the First Five Americans to Conquer Mount Everest.* New York: Fallet, 1966.

MESSNER, REINHOLD. *Everest: Expedition to the Ultimate.* London: Kaye and Ward, 1979.

NAKANO, TOURI. *Trekking In Nepal.* New Delhi: Allied Publishers.

NICHOLSON, NIGEL. *The Himalayas.* New York: Time-Life Books, 1978. Part of the "World's Wild Places" series.

PEISSEL, MICHEL. *Mustang, the Forbidden Kingdom: Exploring a Lost Himalayan Land.* New York: E.P. Dutton, 1967.

ROWELL, GALEN. *Many People Come, Looking, Looking.* Seattle: The Mountaineers, 1980.

SCHALLER, GEORGE B. *Stones of Silence.* London: Andre Deutsch, 1980.

SHIRAKAWA, YOSHIKAZU. *Himalayas.* Tokyo: Shogakukan, 1976. Also New York: Harry N. Abrams, 1977.

TENZING NORGAY AND JAMES RAMSEY ULLMAN. *Man of Everest: The Autobiography of Tenzing.* London: George G. Harrap, 1955. Also *Tiger of the Snows.* New York: G.P. Putnam's Sons, 1955.

TILMAN, W. *Nepal Himalaya.* Cambridge: Cambridge University Press, 1952.

TUCCI, GIUSEPPE. *Journey to Mustang.* Translated from Italian by Diana Fussell. Kathmandu: Ratna Pustak Bhandar, 1982.

ULLMAN, JAMES RAMSEY. *Americans on Everest: The Official Account Led by Norman G. Dyhrenfurth.* New York: J.B. Lippincott, 1964.

UNSWORTH, WALT. *Everest.* London: Allen Lane, 1981.

WADDELL, L.A. *Among the Himalayas.* Westminister, England: Archibold Constable and Co., 1899.

Photo Credits

Quick Reference A–Z Guide
to Places and Topics of Interest with
Listed Accommodation, Restaurants and
Useful Telephone Numbers